D1278927

DOUBLE

Your Retirement Income

DOUBLE

Your
Retirement
Income

Three Strategies

for a

Successful Retirement

PETER MAZONAS

WILEY

John Wiley & Sons, Inc.

Published by John Wiley & Sons, Inc., Hoboken, New Jersey.
Published simultaneously in Canada.

For general information on our other products and services or for technical support, please contact our Customer Care Department within the United States at (800) 762-2974, outside the United States at (317) 572-3993 or fax (317) 572-4002.

Designations used by companies to distinguish their products are often claimed by trademarks. In all instances where the author or publisher is aware of a claim, the product names appear in Initial Capital letters. Readers, however, should contact the appropriate companies for more complete information regarding trademarks and registration.

Wiley also publishes its books in a variety of electronic formats. Some content that appears in print may not be available in electronic books. For more information about Wiley products, visit our web site at www.wiley.com.

Library of Congress Cataloging-in-Publication Data:
Mazonas, Peter, 1943-
    Double your retirement income : three strategies for a successful
retirement / Peter Mazonas.
        p.   cm.
    Includes bibliographical references.
    ISBN-13 978-0-471-71401-9 (cloth)
    ISBN-10 0-471-71401-1 (cloth)
    1. Retirement income—United States—Planning.   2. Investments.   I. Title.
    HG179.M365 2005
    332.024'014—dc22   2005004376

Printed in the United States of America.

10 9 8 7 6 5 4 3 2 1

ACKNOWLEDGMENTS

The example of past mentors and the generosity of fellow professionals have inspired my pursuit of a fundamental understanding of the topics in this book. Tom Clausen and Sam Armacost at Bank of America taught me to expect and deal with the unexpected. The clarity of vision exhibited by Dr. Thomas Paine in shaping Citibank in the 1960s and NASA during the Apollo years was awe-inspiring and inspirational. Tony Frank helped me understand what it takes, in his words, "to get a customer to walk past the other guy's branch and choose your bank." And Barry Abbott's keen understanding of financial service markets helped me design products to make a better retirement possible for many Americans.

My search of unbiased investment results was facilitated by the Vanguard Group, Morgan Stanley Capital International, and Russell/Mellon Analytics, who provided access to and interpretation of historic data. Other specialists shared ideas and reviewed chapters. Special thanks go to Rick Darvis, Marc Freedman, Bob Rosenberg, Mark Clark, Paul Solli, John Cheplick, and Guy Lampard.

Deepest gratitude goes to my wife Marcia, my sounding board, for tireless editing to make complicated subjects easier to understand. Early editing by Caroline Pincus and the support of my agent, Amy Rennert, were invaluable.

P. M.

CONTENTS

INTRODUCTION

The concept of doubling your retirement income was not part of my early goal of helping make retirement possible for more American workers by showing how to save more for retirement and how to avoid losing your savings through bad investments. Previously I had not challenged the conventional wisdom that you could not withdraw more than 4 to 5 percent annually from your retirement savings and still have enough money. But when I examined how index investing consistently outperforms 80 percent of individual investors, I realized that you could withdraw 8 percent per year, cost of living adjusted, and still have enough money to retire. Index funds' low management fees and lack of sales commissions turn an 8 percent average annual return into 12 percent. Making the right asset allocation decisions and not trading in and out of funds allow the miracle of compound interest to double your income. Brokerage firms and mutual fund companies spend $5 billion annually to advertise their hottest funds' performances, while index funds' lower fees do not allow for mass advertising costs. I share the goal of people like John Bogle, who started the Vanguard Group, to convert investors to this better way of growing retirement assets.

Three key strategies are important to reach your goal of a financially successful retirement. Each is simple to write and say, but requires continuous discipline to accomplish. Hardest of all is taking the step to begin each of these three strategies.

1. Live by a budget that has built-in categories for routine saving. Never miss the opportunity to benefit from an employer match in a retirement plan.
2. Invest in index-tracking mutual funds to benefit from the lower cost and consistently higher performance.
3. At age 50, take stock of your chances for a financially secure retirement. If the odds do not look good, consider modifying your career to permit a part work/part leisure retirement.

First we must develop a saving strategy to make this possible without dramatically altering your life.

Much of the 1980s and early 1990s and certainly 2000 through 2002 have been humbling times for middle-class baby boomers as their confidence in being able to save enough for retirement has eroded. Eighty percent of Americans have pensions requiring them to contribute annually in order to receive any benefits at retirement. Current maximum contribution levels plus often meager employer matching mean that a single-income household that delays saving until age 40 will probably not be able to put enough away to retire comfortably at age 65. You will find in this book the tools you need to be better prepared for your future.

I show you how to save for the future and give you strategies to maximize financial opportunities as they predictably arise. Once you know how much you must save to attain your goals, but more importantly, once you start a savings program to meet those goals, you are on your way to achieving financial independence. Take heart if you are a baby boomer; there are strategies to allow you to retire and still meet your other obligations during the frantic 15 to 25 catch-up years before you retire.

After 30 years as a wealth manager I spent a year gathering ideas at numerous seminars and classes presented by nationally recognized attorneys, fellow certified public accountants (CPAs) and financial planners, psychologists, investment gurus, and others who are experts in their respective fields of retirement planning, pensions, educational funding, investments, and estate planning. Many articles and computer software programs have been written that contain worthy nuggets, but they often don't relate to real life in a way that enables people to utilize them. This book contains comparative examples that allow you to evaluate alternative paths. For example, you will see how various types of home loans qualify you for more house at the same monthly payments. You will learn to maximize college financial aid at any income level and to shift your retirement funding strategy beginning at age 42 to better deal with your underfunded retirement.

Double Your Retirement Income is directed toward employees who participate in or should be contributing to the self-directed contributory pension plan provided by their employer. For private companies these are 401(k) plans, for teachers these are 403(b) plans, and for government workers they are 457 plans. All were created by Congress and are administered by the Internal Revenue Service and the U.S. Department of Labor. For most people, their pension plan is their retirement savings vehicle. As you will see, a winning strategy has housing, cars, and the kids' education playing important but supporting roles. Strategies are not limited to the 47 million people in 401(k) plans, because as employees change jobs or become self-employed, there are other types of tax-advantaged pension plans available. If you get downsized and leave an employer's defined benefit pension plan, you need to be aware that if you don't contribute you get nothing—neither matching monies now nor a retirement later.

There are three stages to *Double Your Retirement Income*:

1. *Getting started.* We start the financial planning process at any age by designing a budget, understanding why and how to follow it, and developing a savings program by squeezing every possible dollar out of what I assume is a relatively fixed income.

2. *Accumulation phase.* The choices you make during the accumulation phase of life dramatically affect your retirement, whenever it may occur. Along the way you will buy one or more homes, own cars, possibly change jobs, and provide for your children's education. How to wring out more value in house and car purchases are key strategies in this section. We explore little-known methods for maximum utilization of college grants and aid at any income level. While saving, you must learn how to invest your pension dollars in index-tracking products so you can sleep at night. Investors with taxable investment accounts should apply the same principles, but with strategies to reduce the negative effects of taxation.

3. *Getting prepared for retirement.* The cold reality is that if you are 50 years old and have not saved $250,000 to $500,000 for retirement you may be unable to retire in the classic sense. Semiannual reevaluation of your retirement plan will keep you on track. Depending on the size of your employer or whether you are self-employed, various unconventional retirement plans exist along with age-specific strategies. Once your lack of retirement savings is realized, the focus shifts to Plan B—Retirement Redefined.

The book helps you define your future needs and engineer a plan for retirement savings, but does not address the choice of individual stocks and mutual funds. As you seek portfolio tuning advice among the many qualified professionals available to you, I hope to make you a smarter shopper by giving you the basic investment principles for management of your own retirement portfolio. Start out with the right investment mix of index-tracking funds and then *leave it alone*. I suggest how to allocate your assets to balance your investment risk for the long term based on your risk tolerance and on your stage in life.

Empowered with this knowledge, you must then make the decisions about how to invest, given the array of options available. Recently providers of 401(k), 403(b), and 457 self-directed pension plans have begun to reduce the number of investment choices to a less bewildering list, including index fund options. If these are highly rated low-fee index-type mutual funds, you or an adviser can tune this to an appropriate asset allocation. Equally good alternatives are self-directed plan administrators such as Vanguard Group, Fidelity Investments, and Charles Schwab, which offer you a broad array of index funds, plus individual stocks, bonds, and exchange-traded funds. This may be a more challenging choice, but also more rewarding as you learn and become more confident making investment choices.

Unless you are already wealthy, your exposure to financial advisers is probably limited to an annual group meeting with a pension plan administrator and maybe a tax preparer. If you have taxable investment accounts outside of your tax-advantaged pension funds, I show you how the same basic strategies still apply. Any participation of your other advisers in this process is encouraged.

If you have a spouse/partner, that person should be equally involved with the education and planning process, recognizing up front that mistakes may have been made in the past and that compromise may be necessary in the future for the whole family. This may be your retirement lifeline, so do not let go.

Facing Reality: What's It Going to Take to Be Able to Retire?

Seventy million American workers and their families are dependent on their individual ability to save enough during their work years to fund their own retirement. The average 60-year-old worker with 30 years of continuous service has only $146,000 of retirement savings,[1] enough to add only $400 per month of income on top of Social Security. This has occurred because the average worker changed jobs 9.6 times in the 1980s and 1990s, often forfeiting eligibility for retirement programs.[2] The problem is multigenerational, but the baby boomers (born between 1946 and 1964) will be the first to be confronted with this harsh reality. The oldest of the 80 million baby boomers will begin to reach age 65 in 2011, but more than half of them will not be financially able to retire.

Let's examine the root of these problems, the probable outcome of these cumulative misdeeds, and the winning strategies you can initiate now to avoid becoming a poor retiree.

The One-Way Tide of Change

Ever since the early 1980s, the financial ground rules for retirement have been changing. Employers have quietly been shifting the responsibility for retirement savings from the corporation to the individual worker. This self-serving shift created a short-term boost to corporate earnings and share price and filled budget gaps in government spending, but was not accompanied by a sufficient caution to workers that if they did not force themselves to save, their retirement income would be limited to Social Security and the proceeds from selling their homes. Employers and policy makers who have had the most to gain from shifting this funding responsibility to employees have done so silently and without intervention by regulators. The time for silence is over.

Today 80 percent of American workers must rely on self-directed contributory pension plans to fund their retirement.[3] In addition to the plans commonly known by the Internal Revenue Code sections that established them—401(k), 403(b), 457—there are individual retirement accounts (IRAs) and other contributory pension plans. Simply put, if you do not contribute to these plans out of current income, you do not develop any retirement savings. If you are over age 30 (and don't stand to inherit a substantial sum of money), you must make retirement saving a central issue or you may never be able to retire. It's that simple.

Balancing home expenses, children's education, and retirement savings necessitates a plan. In this chapter we look at the economic realities facing you while developing a strategy to help you reach your goals. Once you decide on a strategy, your job is to be consistent in how you save and how you invest.

Most of us hope for:

- Our own house.
- A comfortable lifestyle.
- Well-educated children.
- Good health care.
- Retirement years to pursue favorite or new activities.

Achieving all or most of this is a tall order requiring discipline and planning.

Some common myths often prevent people from achieving these goals. Each myth will be examined, and either dispelled or put in perspective:

- I can't save any money.
- I will never be able to afford my own house.
- I earn too much to qualify for college financial aid.
- Scholarships are for only the best students.
- I can't afford to send my child to an expensive private college.
- When I start, I will be able to save enough to retire.
- Strong future economic growth will bail out my mutual fund portfolio.
- I will postpone retirement until age 70 when I will be more financially able to retire.

Baby boomers came of age in an era of abundant housing, access to new model cars and merchandise for every need. Their freewheeling consumption transformed our nation and the rest of the developed world into a consumer-driven economy. The economic run-up to the bursting of the tech bubble in March 2000, combined with events since then, has changed this country to our, and most likely our children's, detriment. Seven key elements affecting our changing economic climate are:

1. Executives and the stock prices of their companies get punished if quarter-over-quarter earnings don't beat analysts' expectations.

   Result: Companies cut costs (jobs) and don't add them back until there is shareholder perception that the economy has turned positive.

2. Much of the tech boom was fueled by companies investing in automation that promised near-term positive impact. But the positive impact took years longer than anticipated to be successfully realized by these companies.

   Result: Many of the 2.7 million worker layoffs[4] in the past three years may well be permanent, resulting from technology allowing people to work more efficiently and moving jobs offshore as the so-called positive impact trickles down in companies. Of the nine million out of work, 20 percent are managers and specialty workers.[5]

3. As a nation we are on a track to annually spend 4 percent of gross domestic product (GDP)—the sum of all the goods and services we produce—while collecting only 3 percent in taxes and other revenue to cover our costs,[6] meanwhile just selling more bonds to other nations.

   Result: Escalating debt and the loss of confidence in our economy by other nations may push interest rates up, affecting housing prices and the cost of corporate debt for continued expansion and adding more volatility to the stock markets.

4. In 1980, 58 percent of American workers' pensions were provided by company-funded pension plans. Today only 13 percent of American workers' retirement depends solely on these vanishing defined benefit company-funded pension plans.[7] Eighty percent of American workers today rely on their own contributions and some employer matching to provide for their retirement income.[8]

   Result: Seventy million American workers and their families are dependent for retirement on their individual ability to save, plus modest matching contributions from employers. Although they should be better informed, many of these workers have no idea how much money they must save in order to retire.

5. In the mid-1990s, Larry Kotlikoff, a professor of economics at Boston University, predicted that baby boomers would inherit $10 trillion from their parents in the greatest wealth transfer in the history of the world.[9]

Reality: The stock market plunge and the continued reduction of corporate and government spending on programs for today's middle-class seniors have brought new meaning to the bumper sticker: "I Am Spending My Children's Inheritance." Today only 15 percent of boomers surveyed by AARP expect to receive an inheritance.[10] The average baby boomer stands to inherit $90,000, with the median at $30,000—not a meaningful supplement to retirement savings.[11]

6. It is estimated that large employers will pay only 10 percent of retirees' medical costs by 2031,[12] as opposed to 68 percent coverage in 1988 and 38 percent medical cost coverage for retirees in 2003.[13] Over the same period the cost of Medicare Part B health insurance will escalate from 6 percent of Social Security payments to 10 percent—a 70 percent increase.[14]

   Result: The Employee Benefit Research Institute (EBRI) estimates that a 65-year-old who retires today and lives to age 80 will pay well over $100,000 for health care. A retiree living to age 100 can expect over his or her retired lifetime to pay $700,000 for health care.[15]

7. Eighty million baby boomers, the oldest of whom are age 59 and will start retiring in six years, expect to start collecting Social Security and participating in Medicare.[16]

   Reality: During the baby boom era, six workers paid into Social Security to fund the benefits for each worker who had retired. By 2011 there will be only 2.8 workers funding the benefits anticipated by each retiring worker.[17] The Bush administration is waging war against the AARP and its 32 million members over the future of Social Security.

   Shocker: A study prepared in 2002 for Treasury Secretary Paul O'Neill, but never released by the government, predicts a $44 trillion budget shortfall in Medicare and Social Security (now $51 trillion because of the new Medicare drug benefit), based on current government revenue and spending.[18] Put in perspective, this is the equivalent of one entire year's world GDP, or, closer to home, the equivalent of all the money that would be collected from a fire sale of all stocks, bonds, and residential real estate in the nation.[19] As Larry Kotlikoff points out, this gap can be closed only by major tax increases and/or spending cuts. Martin Feldstein of Harvard University adds to this list "or change the way we finance the system."[20] The latter method means contributing more for benefits you already paid for, plus a dramatic reduction in future benefits.

   Bigger Shocker: Today, the portion of our official cumulative national debt amassed through good and bad times since Benjamin Franklin's times in 1776 is about $14,000 for each man, woman, and child in the country. Add the future impact of Medicare and Social Security and it explodes to $159,000 if paid today—more than the

$146,000 the average 60-year-old has saved for retirement. Wait 15 years to pay it and the amount swells to $76 trillion with interest (more about the positive effects of compound interest later).

Changing also is the composition of the average household. While married couples account for 50 percent of households, breadwinner dads and stay-at-home moms now account for only 1 in 10 households.[21] Sixty-two percent of two-income households have children between the ages of 1 and 6.[22] They believe they can start saving for retirement after they satisfy their near-term home and family needs. Unless they change their saving habits by age 35 and certainly by age 40 when they have their first home and two kids, they won't be able to put enough away in their 401(k) type accounts to retire at age 65. This is where the two-income household has a distinct advantage if it contributes to two retirement plans. Unfortunately, much of this extra money goes to support a lifestyle. Being able to just pay the bills leaves very little to save for anything, let alone retirement—a concept way out in your distant future.

Saving is difficult when at every turn another need is tugging on your wallet. You do this by learning what you will need financially to attain each goal and alternative ways to pay for it. By balancing reality with both your short-term goals and the desire to put something away for the long term, my aim is to keep you focused on your biggest, most often overlooked long-term need: retirement savings.

Imagine the Year 2025

Fast-forward to the year 2025 when the oldest of the nation's 80 million baby boomers begin to turn 80.

For many middle-class baby boomers this is the year they never expected to see. After all, the actuarial tables all say one-half will be dead before age 80, so most continued to live as if they expected to be in that half. In more than 70 percent of married couples, however, at least one spouse will survive to age 85. No matter that 50 percent more women than men will be alive. Generally, men managed the family money and spent it with only a subliminal fear of the future.

Baby boomers have always been an optimistic generation full of denial about their long-term future. Too late to make a difference, most baby boomers either began to save too little for retirement or threw their hands in the air and continued to rely on the system to protect them. They didn't notice the muted cries to save, nor did they pay much attention to the sleight-of-hand actions in Washington shrinking the social safety net by privatizing programs long thought to be entitlements. These collective misdeeds have coalesced to create a new breed of once middle-class seniors facing poverty without a safety net, but with 10 plus years left to live.

A succession of bad bets by both past administrations in Washington and many ordinary Americans will have made our country a vastly different place by the year 2025. China, India, Europe, and Japan have reacted harshly to the debt our government has taken on by forcing interest rates to an all-time high. These prolonged high interest rates have put a damper on business output and new housing while driving the stock market to uncustomary volatility. All of this world economic turmoil has caused a de facto devaluation of the dollar. The dollar has lost one-half of its value relative to the yuan (China), the rupee (India), and the euro since 2004.

As many people had predicted back in the 1980s, Social Security has failed. The program still exists, but the payout has shrunk to almost nothing relative to the current cost of living. Although in 2005 a married couple could receive $18,000 annually from Social Security, government policies to reduce cost-of-living increases have eroded Social Security's spending power. Legislation passed in 2010 has fully privatized Medicare. But without effective cost controls and with no limits on co-payments, seniors can no longer afford coverage, or have been dropped by insurance companies that are abandoning markets and discontinuing coverage. Meanwhile, medical science is keeping us alive longer, further focusing attention on health care management issues (living with Alzheimer's, arthritis, etc.).

As the illusion of a social safety net disappears, individuals must rely on their own savings.

Seniors with formerly parallel lifestyles now regard each other from opposite sides of a great divide separating the haves from the have-nots. The haves, the minority, either had retirement provided by a big employer or were disciplined savers and took advantage of corporate matching in their 401(k) type pension plans. The other group, the have-nots, to differing degrees, did not put enough money away, nor did they have enough to put away in the first place. Worse, they did not learn how to manage what they did have. They continued to buy mutual funds with high management fees that underperformed the markets and further eroded their savings. They have spent or lost much of their retirement savings.

A new generation of 15-year fixed-term reverse mortgages has come to the rescue, allowing seniors at age 65 to spend the equity in their homes; however, at age 80 the monthly payments to them are stopping before they are ready to move out. Seniors who sought to improve their lifestyle by jumping on this bandwagon early are about to lose this lifeline. Their loans are coming due, and the banks are going to take possession of their homes.

Seniors in this predicament are threatened by a radical change in their living arrangements. With their savings mostly depleted, their possessions sold, and their house gone, these seniors will be forced to rent in a more communal living situation. Widows are especially threatened by unfortunate compromises to their comfort and privacy.

Unprepared for this new form of retirement, seniors are forced to compete for minimum-wage jobs. The same employers who switched to contributory-type pension plans as a way to shift the retirement funding liability to workers now exploit these seniors as part-time workers without providing benefits. As always, the savvy get richer and the legions of poor keep growing.

Fiction? Yes, but unless procrastinators over the age of 30 can be shaken into abandoning denial about the need for retirement savings, the future will be grim. Taken to heart, savings strategies in this book will make their retirement years better for many Americans. Forward-thinking, and I believe inevitable, new concepts in this book will lead to a new social contract between corporate employers and their would-be retirees: in exchange for their much-needed skills that are in short supply, corporations will agree to provide both health care benefits and continue matching pension contributions. This reversal of the tide by progressive corporate managers will be encouraged by the government, which is incapable of solving the problem by itself. However, I cannot guarantee there will not be years of pain before this compromise is reached.

Why Saving Is Difficult

There was a time when you could expect to be rewarded for years of loyal job performance with a relatively comfortable retirement. Sadly, that has become a myth, whether you are a union worker or a professional. If you don't use every trick you can to put money aside for a house, the kids' education, and your retirement, it won't be there.

Chances are, your costs are growing faster than your income. Employers try to keep wage increases equal to inflation. Inflation and thus wage increases tend to be about 2.5 to 4.0 percent, but increases in payroll taxes and health insurance co-payments probably take half or more of that before you even see it. So, except for the occasional bonus, you are ahead 1 percent to 2 percent annually in a world where college costs go up annually by 7 percent to 14 percent[23] and inflation often increases housing prices by 4 percent. No wonder you think you can't save for the future.

Most policy makers and economists assume that retirement is such an important issue that everyone will automatically plan and save for it. Therefore, government and employers need not intervene. In 2000,

Matthew Rabin, a University of California at Berkeley professor of a new discipline known as "psychological economics," used the latest mathematical formulas and a healthy dose of common sense to theorize that instant gratification is far more powerful than saving now for future rewards (such as a comfortable retirement). Rabin argues that most individuals will postpone anything that involves immediate costs and/or delayed gratification. And the higher the costs in terms of time and effort and the greater the price of failure, the more they will procrastinate. That's why so many people put off retirement planning for so long.[24]

"The real killer," Rabin says, "is our overoptimism about our discipline in the future." Rabin, a self-proclaimed procrastinator, makes the compelling point that "people who admit they're slugs are better off than those who don't."

Planning for retirement is a multistep process with constant challenges in overcoming procrastination and denial. Procrastination occurs because we can always find something more pressing to spend money on than saving and investing for retirement, at least until retirement stares us in the face. Denial exists because we try to convince ourselves that what we have saved somehow will be enough if we just change our lifestyle when retirement does come.

Matthew Rabin's later work is more encouraging. He observes that saving is like any other thrill: once you start, it becomes habit-forming. He argues that even if you start small, the discipline of accumulating savings will become addictive.[25] If you will give savings a chance, even modestly at first, this book and its tools will help you identify and attain your goals. None of the book's savings examples taken alone will buy you a house or let you retire, but the cumulative effect will be significant. For example:

The Miracle of Compound Interest

Supposedly, Albert Einstein once said that the most powerful force in the universe was compound interest.[26]

Instead of buying a new car, buy a two-year-old "nearly new" "preowned" car that has just come off a dealer lease. You have seen the TV commercials. What the dealers are not advertising is that this two- or three-year-old car is one-third to one-half the price of a new one. It has a dealer/factory-approved warranty and can be financed at an interest rate just slightly higher than if it were new. This single trick alone over two years can save you $6,000 per year toward your 401(k) contribution. With 50 percent employer matching, that equals $9,000 in each of two years toward retirement if you put it in your 401(k) and don't spend it. Bear in mind the miracle of compound interest: the earlier you save, the more dramatically it grows toward retirement. Table 1.1 shows how at an 8

TABLE 1.1   Results of Compounding $18,000, Assuming 8 Percent Annual Return

Age When Invested	Retirement at 65	Retirement at 70
Invested at 30	$283,000	$422,000
Invested at 40	$127,000	$190,000
Invested at 50	$ 57,000	$ 86,000

percent annual investment rate of return that $18,000 compounds tax-free until retirement at age 65 or age 70, when you start to gradually take it out.

> **Observation:** Thanks to the miracle of compound interest, the earlier you start saving, the more annual interest is added to principal. This compounding more than doubles the balance available for a 30-year-old ($283,000) as opposed to someone who starts saving at age 40 ($127,000), both retiring at the same time.

Unfortunately, the amounts in Table 1.1 are future dollars without shrinkage for inflation. Inflation destroys the purchasing power of your wealth. If we assume 3 percent annual inflation and keep the math simple, then your average annual rate of return drops to 5 percent. The initial two-year $18,000 investment with returns compounded monthly at an annual 5 percent rate is shown at various points in Table 1.2. This would mean that the 30-year-old who wants to retire at age 65 would have $101,000 in today's equivalent dollars from that single investment. Likewise, the 40-year-old retiring at 65 would have only $61,000.

And that is just one year's contribution. If our 30-year-old does this every four years when the old car loan is paid off and the cycle is repeated, by age 65 he will have put away $464,000[27] in today's dollars, with an annual 4 percent draw of $18,500 starting at age 65. Considering

TABLE 1.2   Results of Compounding $18,000, Assuming 5 Percent Inflation-Adjusted Annual Return

Age When Invested	Retirement at 65	Retirement at 70
Invested at 30	$101,000	$129,000
Invested at 40	$ 61,000	$ 78,000
Invested at 50	$ 37,000	$ 47,000

Observation: When the investment yield drops from 8 percent to 5 percent, your investment return drops 60 percent. Further, at a 5 percent rate of return, each 10 years you wait to start saving costs you another 60 percent on what your balances could have been— again, the miracle of compound interest at work. Chapter 7 looks at the reality of sustaining an 8 percent, preinflation investment rate of return, especially in postretirement years.

a 30- or 40-year-old who retires at age 65 can expect to live 20 to 35 years in retirement, we can quickly observe how retirement savings must become an annual routine to be started as early as possible.

Observation: This trick of buying a pre-owned car will reward you $18,500 per year in retirement, which is the same as or more than you can expect to get per year from Social Security. Add the two together and you are up to $36,000 per year, cost of living adjusted, in retirement. Not great, but it is a meaningful start.

Key Tip: Now for the real incentive! When you combine the practice of buying a *nearly* new instead of brand-new car every four years with the miracle of compound interest and the low-cost index investment philosophy in Chapter 7, the diligent 30-year-old can grow the $464,000 from this single savings strategy into $1,250,000 in today's dollars at age 65. As you will learn later, this single trick can provide you $100,000 of retirement income per year, in today's dollars (purchasing power) cost of living adjusted.

Congress passed the Employee Retirement Income Security Act (ERISA) in 1974 to further protect participants' rights in pension plans. Traditionally, most large employers offered plans in which the contributions were made by the employer and the participant's benefits were defined by some combination of years of service, final retirement age, and final pay. The focus on pension benefits forced smaller employers to offer pension plans to compete for skilled workers. These smaller employers turned to a new contributory type of plan where the ultimate retirement benefit was determined by the amount the employee put away toward retirement, plus some tax-free employer matching contribution. Congress made the contributions by the employee tax-deductible, and the earnings compound tax-free until amounts are withdrawn at retirement. By the 1980s, large corporations, eager to contain costs, seized upon this new form of pension plan. In 1980, 58 percent of American workers had defined benefit pension plans as part of their pay packages. Today that percentage has shrunk to 13 percent of workers.[28]

As many baby boomers began shifting away from careers in large corporations, they for the most part forfeited their benefits under the older defined benefit plans, and now they themselves had to create any retirement savings. The transition of this mobile workforce from the old to the new paralleled that of the economy. Between 1980 and 2000, the average worker changed jobs 9.6 times.[29] At each job change, the typical corporation made the new worker wait from one to three years before becoming eligible to participate in the company's 401(k) plan, often never becoming eligible to participate because of their short stay with each employer. Today, although 80 percent of workers are eligible to participate in company-sponsored 401(k) plans, only 51 percent of white-collar workers and 38 percent of workers in blue-collar occupations participate in their employers' 401(k) plans.[30]

No wonder 75 percent of American households are underfunded for retirement! Let's look at the most common self-directed plans: the 401(k) for private employers, the 403(b) plan for teachers, and the 457 plan for government employees. We will use the 401(k) for an example.

If you started making maximum annual $14,000 401(k) contributions at age 30 and continued them annually until retirement at age 65, these contributions plus compounding would total $1,700,000 in today's dollars, using 25 percent employer matching and discounting for inflation. Let's assume at retirement you draw down 4 percent of the balance each year for 35 years, but add 3 percent each year to your draw for inflation to maintain your spending power. In today's dollars, your annual draw starting at age 65 would be $68,000 and you would run out of money at age 99 when your inflation-adjusted annual draw is $145,000, the equivalent of the $68,000 the year you retired. If you delayed retirement until age 70, your first draw, again inflation-adjusted, would be $91,000 and you would run out of money at age 103. Thanks to modern medicine, 30-year-olds today have a strong chance of living to be 90 and even 100. (See Chapter 6 on pension plans for more detail.)

If your employer is typical today, it matches 50 percent on your first 7 percent of wages.[31] If you contributed only at this $9,000 level ($6,000 your money and $3,000 employer's) this would yield $35,000 for your first year in retirement if you started at age 30 in the example. For a two-income household in which both parties contribute to these employer-sponsored tax-deferred-type pension plans, these amounts would be double if both continued to work.

As a point of reference, assume in the first column in Table 1.3 that you put away only $6,000 each year with a 50 percent employer matching contribution starting at ages 30 and 40. In the second column, you increased your contribution to $14,000 per year. This is the maximum

TABLE 1.3   Funds at Retirement, Assuming 5 Percent Inflation-Adjusted Annual Return

Starting Age	$6,000 with 50% Match	$14,000 with 25% Match
Age 30	$875,000	$1,700,000
Yields	$ 35,000 per year	$ 68,000 per year
Age 40	$459,000	$ 890,000
Yields	$ 18,000 per year	$ 35,600 per year

allowable for a tax deduction in 2005 ($15,000 in 2006). Even though you get only $3,000 in matching money (a 25 percent match up to typical employer matching limits) the difference is dramatic: the miracle of compound interest.

Now the shocker (see Table 1.4): You are age 50, and waited to start saving until after you have educated the kids and they're self-sufficient. The fewer years of saving and compounding make a material difference. We'll assume you put away $6,000 per year with 50 percent employer match in the first column. In the second column we push the annual contribution to $14,000 with a 25 percent in matching money from your employer. Look at the difference if you retire at age 65 and age 70.

Establish Your Nest Egg Goal

Given where you are today financially and where you want to be at retirement, establish a pretax annual retirement income goal in today's dollars. This goal is really two numbers: first, how little money you would be *willing* to live on if you restructured your cost of living, and second, how much you would *like* to have to live on. Your first challenge is to get somewhere in this range. In today's dollars and at the 8 percent average annual return from mutual funds, for each $40,000 of retirement income you want you will need to have $1,000,000 in your investment account at age 65 steadily earning 5 percent after inflation. To accomplish this income level in the earlier example, our 50-year-old would have had to

TABLE 1.4   Funds at Retirement, Assuming 5 Percent Inflation-Adjusted Annual Return (Starting Age 50)

Retirement Age	$6,000 with 50% Match	$14,000 with 25% Match
Retirement at 65	$206,000	$400,000
Yields	$ 8,200 per year	$ 16,000 per year
Retirement at 70	$316,000	$615,000
Yields	$ 12,600 per year	$ 24,600 per year

start out with $250,000 at age 50 and contribute the maximum deferral, including additional catch-up contributions allowed by law ($14,000 plus $4,000 for 2005 and $15,000 plus $5,000 for 2006) to get to the initial $40,000 starting annual benefit level from the 401(k). For each additional $40,000 of annual retirement income, you would need to have had an additional $450,000 in your account at age 50. Short of a big inheritance or your ship coming in, this is where you would stand in this example.

If our 50-year-old had started saving at age 40, when his first child entered high school, done sufficient planning, and developed a good college funding strategy, the retirement savings would look much different, as shown in Table 1.5 (miracle of compound interest plus using even more of the government's money).

These examples demonstrate the importance of saving early for retirement.

Double Your Retirement Income

I am going to jump ahead because the improved retirement income results possible from applying a better investment strategy are too important to not contrast at this time. You will learn in Chapter 7 the compelling reasons to change your investment approach and start buying and holding no-load, low-fee index-tracking investment products. This hands-off approach will increase the typical average annual investment yield from 8 percent to 12 percent (from 5 percent to approximately 9 percent after inflation). Had this added annual investment yield been applied in the earlier 401(k) type example, the amounts in Table 1.6 would be the pretax outcome. As you will see later, applying this winning investment strategy will allow you to substantially increase your retirement nest egg and *double your retirement income.* If you apply the indexing investment strategy to the last 28 years (1978–2005) of balanced index data, you can not only double your first retirement year income draw from $40,000 to $80,000 per one million dollars of retirement portfolio, but continue to draw down double the 4 percent inflation-adjusted

TABLE 1.5   Funds at Retirement, Assuming 5 Percent Inflation-Adjusted Annual Return and Good Planning (Starting Age 40)

Retirement Age	$6,000 with 50% Match	$14,000 with 25% Match
Retirement at 65	$460,000	$ 890,000
Yields	$ 18,400 per year	$ 35,600 per year
Retirement at 70	$641,000	$1,240,000
Yields	$ 29,000 per year	$ 49,600 per year

TABLE 1.6   Funds at Retirement, Assuming 9 Percent Inflation-Adjusted Annual Return (Starting Age 40)

Retirement Age	$6,000 with 50% Match	$14,000 with 25% Match
Retirement at 65	$ 882,400	$1,715,000
Yields	$ 77,000 per year	$ 137,000 per year
Retirement at 70	$1,441,000	$2,800,000
Yields	$ 115,000 per year	$ 224,000 per year

portfolio income amount while having substantial growth in your retirement portfolio. This is not voodoo; again, it's the combination of increasing your annual returns using the indexing strategy, combined with 28 years of compounding returns. The same cyclical investment returns that have occurred over the past 28 years can be expected over the long-term future.

Table 1.6 shows what happens when the same 40-year-old starts putting money away in a 401(k) type plan, but this time following the improved investment strategy.

You have been introduced you to the "nearly new" car idea. Chapter 5 shows you how the government's money can finance your children's education. (Did you know that most of the $105 billion in annual gift aid, money grants, scholarships, and loans to students and their parents comes from the federal government?[32]) No improved investment strategy in the world is going to help if you do not add to your retirement savings. Our challenge together is to see how all these pieces can fit together and have them work for you.

Although the 401(k) annual contribution limits will go up over time, the discussion is kept in today's dollars to help orient you. Whether by contributing at the higher 401(k) annual limits or by supplementing your retirement savings, you are probably going to have to do something more to put enough away. At today's benefit levels, Social Security will add up to another $18,000 per year, but that benefit cannot be counted upon.

The historic rule of thumb is that you will need 80 percent of your pay in your final working years in retirement. That 80 percent number is low! Today's consuming baby boomers will lead a different and more active retirement than their parents. Plan on spending at least 100 percent of final salary in your first five years in retirement on travel and all the things you wanted to do when you were working.

Why five years? Retirees today are healthy and throw themselves into activities and travel. By the end of five years many have reduced their wish list of things to do. This pattern adds to your costs in those early years, so plan for it.

What Is Expected of You and What You Will Get in Return

The process of evaluating where you are, identifying your goals, and deciding on action steps that can help you meet those goals is a process with a path. Once you commit to a set of action steps that are right for you, the process continues as you reevaluate your status a couple of times yearly. Just one in six investors with self-directed pension plans made changes of any kind to their investments in the past year.[33] Almost half did not adjust their investment mix over the last four years. They bought go-go mutual funds in 1999 and stared at the headlights as their nest egg disappeared. It is time to get an investment education and take an active part in your retirement destiny. The key is getting started and making a commitment to stick with it.

Three things are being asked of you in this process:

1. Honesty, no matter how painful.
2. If you have a spouse or partner, their equally honest involvement in the process.
3. Timely completion of the budgeting, self-assessment, goal setting, and action step processes.

My job as coach is easier than yours: I will provide you with the education and tools to start you on this path. I will help you be a smarter shopper when looking for financial advice. While I will offer you time-tested solutions that will work in most instances, I am no substitute for your good judgment.

If you are honest and stick with the process, you can expect to accomplish the following:

- Quantify your present situation with a valid (snapshot) budget.
- Quantify your retirement needs in today's dollars.
- Compile a thoughtful set of near-term and long-term goals.
- Balance short-term expectations with the realization that some goals will take longer and may involve sacrifice.
- Get a jump on planning to use other people's money to fund your children's education.
- If you admit you are too busy and do not want to take an active part in investing your retirement assets, I propose a hands-off, low-cost investment strategy that will allow you to outperform 80 percent of actively managed mutual funds.[34] Buying and holding a balance of low-cost index-tracking mutual funds or stocks will help you to weather a market downturn and maintain your target rate of return in the long term. More importantly, this investment strategy will potentially increase your average return from 8 percent to 12 percent. This can double both the size of your retirement portfolio and your income in retirement.

- Create a written plan for how to fund your future obligations and how to invest your retirement and other savings.
- If you are self-employed, consider types of pension options that allow you to put away lots more money tax free.
- Take your new knowledge and challenge yourself twice a year to reevaluate your performance and goals.
- Explore alternative strategies to hedge the need to supplement your investment income during your part-work, part-leisure later years. Many people may even change jobs to prepare for a rewarding career in a new job that experts say will be in demand during the next 25 years.
- Keep your checklists and references available for updating via my web site, www.RetireYes.com.

I hope you think this is a good trade and worth your effort.

Don't Overlook Plan B

Admitting to yourself where you are financially and being realistic is the subject of Chapter 9, but let's look at the salient facts. By age 50 you should be able to project whether or not you will have enough money to retire. The typical employee in a 401(k) type contributory pension plan will not have put away enough money to completely retire at age 65 and probably not at age 70 (unless they want to sell their home and live off the proceeds). The practical rules of retirement are going to be rewritten to include part-time work and part-time retirement.

You are your own best earning asset. With my help, you will assess your skills and figure out what you can improve upon or add to those skills to make you more marketable as a full-time or part-time worker later in life. Think about what you could do as a part-time skilled worker in your own business in a combined retirement/work-sharing future. Studies predict that employers will need to retain many older workers to fill required jobs.[35] Positioning yourself and figuring this out may be the key to enjoying life on your own terms. In the meantime, don't stop saving in every way you can today. If you sit on your hands and do nothing, your so-called second career may be flipping hamburgers.

Working on This Together

It is important that couples work through this book together. Until there is common agreement that they need to make a change, couples are often locked in a power struggle. Behind power and control is the fear of losing control. This often translates into hiding true feelings.

How you were taught to think about money as a child has a lot to do with your perceptions about money and thus your spending as an adult. As a child, if you got your allowance even when you wiggled out of your assigned chores, and worse, if you got extra money every time you asked for it, then you learned (were taught) to expect to get what you want. You also are a mirror of either your mother's or father's spending habits. These long-seated habits are why you and your partner need to talk about money issues to understand and overcome these blocks.[36]

If you have credit card debt, start by agreeing on a timetable to pay it off. This often brings other issues to the surface that will need to be talked through. In working through this credit card payoff strategy it is important to set the goals far enough out to be attainable. Paying off credit card debt out of current income is a challenge that requires sacrifice. You both will have to sacrifice during nine months to a year or longer to accomplish this goal. Remember that what happened in the past is past. Look toward the future.

Numerous studies and books have shown that men and women have fundamentally different views on risk tolerance, dependent children, and estate planning. A key tension between parents occurs when one wants to spend money on vacations and cars, and the other wants to save for college. Women tend to be more conservative and focus on issues that affect the family (for example, educating the kids and family security).

It is important to get each party to step into the other person's shoes, looking at money and its related concerns from the other's standpoint. College funding is often a tool to accomplish this because everyone is concerned about how to fund their children's college education. Clarifying the boundaries of what you think you can afford is important. Key is opening up a dialogue and reaching even tentative agreement.

2

Budgeting: Finding New Money to Save for Retirement

Knowing where you spend your money and gaining control over that spending is key to your financial success. Preparing a budget is easier than living within a budget. When asked how much you make annually, you say $60,000, $90,000, or $200,000—whatever you or your employer says is your salary, and maybe bonus. This is before the governments get their share—which is probably 25 percent or more. If you're single, $60,000 is really $45,000, $90,000 is really $60,000, and $200,000 is really more like $120,000. Those are big differences. This is where budgeting begins—being honest with yourself and setting limits.

Your earnings minus spending and taxes equal your disposable income. You don't control earnings unless you are self-employed and want to work longer, harder, and smarter. We want to look at all of your costs, but expenditures you can control are of primary interest. Our goal is to find ways to increase disposable income to pay down credit card debt or add to savings. This requires immense self-discipline based on a plan and on understanding how your mistakes compound and work against you.

For example, if you charge $3,000 on your credit card and pay the $50 monthly minimum with a 19.8 percent finance charge, it will take 24 years to pay off the balance. In the meantime you will have paid more than $11,000 in interest charges. If you decide to pay off the balance in 24 months, you will have to make monthly payments of $150. That same

$3,000 put into an individual retirement account (IRA) at an 8 percent annual return would be worth $20,000 in 24 years.

The first step is to prepare a preliminary budget. You need an overview of expenses to help you decide where to squeeze out extra money. If you decide you can live without certain activities or things, at first you may miss some of them. Several months down the road you probably won't mind as much. Many people know with surprising accuracy what their expenses are from numbers they pull out of their heads. You know what you spend in individual categories; you just don't link it all together. This budget will do that for you.

Preliminary Budget

A budget is a summary of how the money in your household comes in (cash inflow) and where it goes (cash outflow). Income (cash inflow) is usually wages, or, for the self-employed, what you draw out of your business to live on. Your cash outflow is the combination of what is deducted from your paycheck, what you spend, and what you save. You have four kinds of cash outflow:

1. Deductions from your paycheck.
2. Fixed expenses that recur every month:
   - House payments or rent.
   - Car payments.
   - Monthly payments on things you borrowed money to buy, other than credit card debt.
   - Insurance other than what may be included with your mortgage payment or deducted from your paycheck.
   - Property taxes if not included in your mortgage payment.
   - Utilities (electricity, gas, water, phone, etc.).
   - Minimum payment amount on credit card debt, if applicable.
   - Alimony and child support.
3. Variable expenses and discretionary expenses:
   - Commuting expense.
   - Work-related lunches, morning coffee/tea, and so on.
   - Food at home.
   - Clothes.
   - Amount in excess of minimum payments on credit card debt.
   - Meals out.
   - Entertainment.
   - Health club dues.
   - Vacations.
   - Home repair expenses and things for the house.
   - Extras.

4. Savings and monies you set aside:
   - Retirement contributions deducted from your paycheck.
   - Investment savings.
   - Savings for kids' education.
   - Vacation fund.
   - Rainy-day fund.
   - Other money set aside to buy something in the future.

A budget organized in this way clarifies what percentage of your total expenses is fixed and how much is variable or discretionary. Fixed expenses come each month whether one or both of you are working or unemployed. The lower your ratio of fixed costs to total cash outflow, the better you can withstand the unexpected bumps. Ideally, your fixed costs plus a cushion for food and clothes are covered by only one individual's net take-home pay. More discussion of the one-income versus two-income household follows in Chapter 3.

The budget process has two phases. First, complete a profile with names, addresses, ages, and the like and, after gathering together some documents, input salary and deductions, mortgage information, and insurance information. There are secure, password-protected online templates for Macs and PCs that can be stored online or downloaded from www.RetireYes.com. If you use the computerized templates, this information is automatically transferred to your budget. The second step is estimating your variable expenses. The templates are written so that as you input your data the computer does the rest of the work. When you correct a date or an amount, the program automatically corrects each place where that data applies. The computer program allows you to take these budgets, spread the information to other schedules, and bring the significance of the outcome home by using your own numbers.

This discussion uses simple budgets and dispenses with a full financial planning process in order to focus on selected big issues facing you rather than getting weighted down by the full process at this stage.

Suggestion: You may be questioning the value of preparing a budget at this time. If so, read the rest of the book and come back to the budget process. Understanding the dramatic impact of the savings and investment opportunities in this book will compel you to come back and develop your budget to start taking advantage of these strategies.

Personal Information

The personal information template, Template 1, gathers necessary information in one place and spreads it to various locations in the templates. All of this information will probably come into play at some point. None of this leaves your computer, and no one other than you will see it. You are asked for monthly information. The computer program will annualize the amounts when necessary and will stop deductions when they hit a maximum statutory limit, like the Social Security tax established by the Federal Insurance Contributions Act (FICA).

Budget Data Gathering

Template 2 gathers information about income and deductions. (See Table 2.1.) This information comes directly from your pay stubs showing gross pay and withholding amounts.

On Template 3, house payment information comes from the mortgage documents for your residence. (See Table 2.2.) You may remember what the monthly payment is, the interest rate, and the month and year the payments began, but you also need to state the loan number, the term until the rate will change, and other details. You require this information to get answers when you ask, "What if I had a different type of loan—how much could I save?" The computer loves numbers, so let it answer those questions for you.

A mortgage impound account is when your mortgage lender requires that they collect a portion of your property taxes, homeowners' insurance, and any private mortgage insurance each month by adding this amount to your monthly mortgage payment. If you are a disciplined saver, avoid this if you can—so you can earn the interest, not give it to your lender.

Insurance information on Template 4 comes from copies of all your insurance policies. (See Table 2.3.) Unfortunately, your insurance probably is spread among several insurance companies and the payment plans are usually different. You will want to list these and figure out the total monthly payments. There are two columns because some couples and family members have individual insurance with different companies—life insurance, for instance.

Template 5, your preliminary budget (Table 2.4), will be already partially filled in if you use the computer. The filled-in items are from information you entered in the previous fact gathering. The remaining entries can be done with collective knowledge. Otherwise, you will need to add up items from your checkbook(s) and credit card statement(s). If you highlight a cell and click the right mouse button, the help menu will summarize what you are expected to enter in that cell.

When you complete the budget, the number you want to look at is line

TABLE 2.1   Template 2—Income and Deduction Information

	Person 1	Person 2	Combined
Employment Earnings			
Regular pay			
Overtime			
Gross pay per month			
Deductions—Statutory			
Federal income tax			
Social Security tax (FICA)			
Medicare tax			
State income tax			
State disability or other tax			
City income tax, if any			
Total statutory deductions			
Other Deductions			
401(k) or retirement deduction			
Stock savings plan			
Health insurance			
Dental and vision insurance, if separate			
Life insurance, if separate			
Disability insurance, if separate			
Child care			
Garnishments			
Total other deductions			
Net pay per month			
Other Cash Received			
Alimony			
Child support			
Cashing out stock options			
(Less tax due on stock option cashout)			
Bonuses			
(Less tax withheld on bonuses—usually 20%)			
(Less extra tax due on bonuses)			
Dividends if not reinvested			
Interest income			
Capital gains on security sales if not reinvested			
(Less tax due on security sales)			
Net other income per month			

TABLE 2.2   Template 3—House Payment Information

	Mortgage 1	Mortgage 2
Name of lender		
Loan number		
Original loan amount		
Interest rate		
Loan term until rate changes		
Date first payment made		
Monthly principal + interest		
If impound—homeowners' insurance		
If impound—property taxes		
If impound—private mortgage insurance		
Total monthly payment		

39, estimated surplus or deficit. This should be zero or close to zero. If the result shows a surplus but you have no extra money, then it is time to go back and revise your budget. Do this in the revised estimate column so you can see where the differences were and what the net difference is when you have finished.

If you have a deficit (a negative number), go back and compare the balances you have run up on loans or credit cards over the past year to what your deficit is. This will help you revise your budget so the deficit approximates the run-up in credit card balances. Also do this in the revised estimate column so you can see where your budget amounts differed from your first estimate. When all else fails, go to the checkbook and credit card statements to figure out the differences.

When you get within $1,000, stop the process; that is close enough for our purposes.

Realist's Balance Sheet—Assets Minus Responsibilities

An accountant-prepared balance sheet is a snapshot in time that tells the net worth of an individual or a business (assets minus liabilities equals owner's equity). We are going to do it differently. Now that we have finished budgeting we know approximately how much extra money we have each year to add to our asset account. This is a good time to do a reality check and look at what your assets minus your responsibilities look like. Responsibilities are what you owe to others, plus obligations in the future. This forward-looking balance sheet tells you how prepared, or unprepared, your family is to meet its future obligations like the down payment for a house, college, and care of family members. This balance sheet does not consider retirement because that could involve changing your residence.

TABLE 2.3   Template 4—Insurance Information

	Person 1	Person 2
Homeowners' insurance		
Company name		
Policy number		
Renewal date		
Amount of coverage on structure		
Amount of coverage on contents		
Monthly premium		
Earthquake or flood insurance		
Company name		
Policy number		
Renewal date		
Amount of coverage		
Monthly premium		
Automobile insurance		
Company name		
Policy number		
Renewal date		
Collision deductible		
Liability limit		
Monthly premium		
Insurance on boat or other		
Company name		
Policy number		
Renewal date		
Amount of coverage		
Liability limit		
Monthly premium		
Umbrella liability insurance		
Company name		
Policy number		
Renewal date		
Liability limit		
Monthly premium		

TABLE 2.3   *(Continued)*

	Person 1	Person 2
Health insurance		
Company name		
Policy number		
Renewal date		
Monthly premium		
Dental and vision insurance, if separate		
Company name		
Policy number		
Renewal date		
Monthly premium		
Life insurance, if separate		
Company name		
Policy number		
Renewal date		
Face amount of coverage		
Policy Type—		
Whole-life, Term, Accidental death		
If whole-life, cash value		
Monthly premium		
Disability insurance, if separate		
Company name		
Policy number		
Renewal date		
Term of coverage		
Monthly premium		
Total monthly premiums		

TABLE 2.4 Template 5—Annual Budget

Names: _____

Prepared (Date of Data): _____

Estimated Annual Budget

The purpose of these questions is to help you see where your family spends your current income annually. Use good guesses—this is just an approximation. Amounts for mortgage payments, property taxes, income taxes, cash contributions, and other items have already been gathered and will be brought into the final budget.

	Monthly	Estimated Annual Amounts	Revised Estimated New Annual Amounts	Adjustments to Budget Difference + (−)
Household Fixed Expenses NOT Added in Automatically Below:				
1 If not a homeowner, annual rent paid	× 12			
2 Utilities (gas, electric, water, phone, garbage, etc.)	× 12			
3 Alimony and child support	× 12			
4 Annual unreimbursed medical and dental, usually your deductible plus co-pay				
5 Spent monthly on car installment or lease payments not reimbursed by a business	× 12			
6 Annual amounts spent to make minimum payments on credit card debt				
7 **Basic household fixed expenses**				
Household Variable Expenses:				
8 Groceries, spirits, and wine per month	× 12			
9 Spent annually by your family for clothing				
10 Personal care (e.g., hair appointments and products, etc.) per month	× 12			

11 Amount spent annually out of current income for home repairs, new furniture, gardening, etc.

12 Spent annually on car repairs and fuel not reimbursed by a business

13 Spent annually on child care, excluding babysitting added in lines 17, 18, and 19 below

14 Nondeductible consumer loan or student loan interest (not car loans incl. in line 5 above or credit cards in line 6)

15 Spent annually out of current income for tuition, college room/board, allowance, etc.

16 Annual support payments for parents, family members, or friends, not including college costs covered in 12

17 Annual amounts spent to pay down credit card or other debt in excess of minimums

Job-Related Variable Expenses:

	Person 1	Person 2
18 Monthly unreimbursed commuting and parking	× 12	× 12
19 Monthly unreimbursed lunches	× 12	× 12
20 Monthly job clothing purchases	× 12	× 12

21 Job-related variable expenses

Entertainment, Dining Out, and Vacation Variable Expenses:

	Person 1	Person 2
22 How many times per month do you go out for dinner at your own expense		× 12
23 What is the amount of your average dinner check for these meals, incl. babysitting		× 12
24 Amount spend out of current income annually on vacations		
25 Concerts, the ballet, movies, sporting events, dues etc. per month, including babysitting		× 12

26 Entertainment, dining out, and vacation variable expenses

(Continued)

31

TABLE 2.4 *(Continued)*

	Monthly	Estimated Annual Amounts	Revised Estimated New Annual Amounts	Adjustments to Budget Difference + (−)
Investments, Savings, and Retirement				
27 Annual contributions to IRA, other pensions NOT deducted from paycheck				
28 Annual bank or brokerage firm savings account additions net of withdrawals				
29 Annual investment additions, net of withdrawals, other than retirement on line 27 or savings on line 28				
30 Vacation fund				
31 Other expenses from income not shown elsewhere				
If available, below data was gathered electronically, if not please enter annual amounts				
32 Home mortgage payments, principal + interest				
33 Taxes paid: income tax (fed & state), Social Security, property taxes (home, autos, boats, etc.)				
34 Insurance from worksheet				
35 Annual contributions to IRA, Keogh, or other retirement plans deducted from paycheck				
36 Garnishments automatically taken from paycheck				
37 Estimated total cash outflow (items 1 through 36)				

32

	Person 1	Person 2
38 Net monthly cash flow income from pay stub		
39 Net monthly cash inflow from other sources		
Total monthly cash inflow		
40 Estimated surplus or (deficit)—**LOOK BACK AND MAKE ANY ADJUSTMENTS**		

Cash Flow Summary and Ratios

	Person 1	Person 2	Total Original	Total Revised
41 Gross pay and other income				
42 Less: Required taxes and other withholding				
43 Net pay				
44 Total household fixed costs				
45 Variable expenses				
46 Net before savings and retirement contributions				
47 Savings and retirement contributions				
48 Estimated surplus or (deficit)				
49 Fixed costs as a percent of either person's and total net income				
50 Savings and retirement contributions as a percent of net income				

Before we start to fill out this balance sheet, be forewarned that it will probably show how unprepared you are to meet future obligations. The reason for filling out the balance sheet is to help you understand how much you need to plan and have a strategy to meet these pending costs. Saving for the down payment to buy a home or to make the maximum contribution to your 401(k) type pension takes discipline, but if you set a realistic goal and do not skip payments, everything is possible given time. Table 2.5 is a simple chart indicating how much you need to save each month to reach a goal in any of several years in the future. The table assumes the money compounds at 4 percent per year, a reasonable after-tax net return.

To complete the forward-looking balance sheet in Table 2.6 you have to know how much surplus cash you generate each year. If there is none, just enter zero on the "possible additional cash" line. The other numbers will be your best estimate. This is not a balance sheet to show to the bank or anyone else, just a way of letting you know what is ahead of you. Almost no one will have a surplus on this balance sheet.

Trimming Your Budget—Finding New Money

Knowing where you spend your money today is the first step in challenging yourself to cut back without necessarily sacrificing the quality of your life. Table 2.7 lists suggested items for change and the probable

TABLE 2.5   Amount You Need to Save Monthly to Reach a Goal

Monthly Amount Saved	Years of Continuous Savings						
	1 Year	3 Years	5 Years	7 Years	10 Years	15 Years	20 Years
$ 25	$ 307	$ 956	$ 1,659	$ 2,420	$ 3,682	$ 6,152	$ 9,167
50	612	1,910	3,316	4,838	7,362	12,302	18,333
100	1,223	3,819	6,630	9,675	14,723	24,603	36,663
150	1,834	5,728	9,945	14,512	22,084	36,903	54,994
200	2,445	7,637	13,260	19,349	29,445	49,204	73,324
250	3,057	9,546	16,574	24,186	36,806	61,504	91,655
300	3,668	11,455	19,889	29,023	44,167	73,805	109,985
350	4,279	13,364	23,204	33,860	51,528	86,105	128,316
400	4,890	15,273	26,518	38,697	58,889	98,406	146,646
500	6,112	19,091	33,147	48,371	73,611	123,007	183,307
750	9,168	28,636	49,720	72,556	110,416	184,509	274,960
1,000	12,223	38,180	66,293	96,742	147,220	246,012	366,612
1,500	18,334	57,270	99,440	145,112	220,830	369,017	549,917
2,000	24,446	76,360	132,586	193,482	294,439	492,022	733,222
2,500	30,557	95,449	165,732	241,852	368,048	615,027	916,527

TABLE 2.6   Forward-Looking Balance Sheet

Name: _____

Date Prepared: _____

Forward-Looking Balance Sheet
(Assets Minus Responsibilities)

(Years until First Goal)   _____

Selected Assets

Cash in bank   _____

Cash in money market funds   _____

  Quick-access cash   _____

Nonpension security account balances   _____

Other assets held for investment   _____

Cash added to nonpension savings last year   _____

× Number of years until first big obligation   _____

Possible additional cash   ======== ⟶   _____

(A) Total usable assets   _____

Add:

Inheritance expected   _____

Second home or property   _____

Roth IRA balance   _____

Annual additions to Roth IRA, times years until first obligation   _____

(B) Total assets available for long-term obligations   ========

Selected Liabilities and Responsibilities

Credit card balance not paid off monthly   _____

Mortgage on second home   _____

Total vehicle loans outstanding   _____

Total boat and other loans outstanding   _____

(C) Total debt other than normal living and home mortgage   _____

(D) Net worth available to pay future obligations (B minus C)   ========

Selected Future Obligations

Down payment needed for first home   _____

College cost—first child   _____

College cost—second child   _____

College cost—third child   _____

Weddings—parent of the bride(s)   _____

(E) Selected future liabilities   ========

Surplus after paying future obligations (D Minus E)   ========

TABLE 2.7   Potential Yearly Savings

Lunches: Bag lunches came back into style with the stock market plunge of 2000–2002. Brown-bag it and save ...	$1,300
Buy the pre-owned vehicle: This trick from Chapter 1 will save on both the down payment and the overall monthly costs. This is money earmarked for your pension contribution.	$6,000
Cheaper gas: The price of gas varies widely. Watch prices and save 15 cents per gallon. If you commute 20,000 miles a year, you can save ...	$180
Car with better gas mileage: Trade the gas-guzzling SUV (14 miles/gallon) for a fuel-efficient car (25 miles/gallon). If you drive 15,000 miles a year, you save ...	$1,000
Car washes: Do your own car washes for two cars times 52 weeks of the year, and you save ...	$1,248
Espresso drinks versus plain coffee: Find the good coffee vendors and you'll be happy with a plain cup of coffee; try it and you can save ...	$520
Fewer dinners out: Eat at home and save ...	$2,000
Less expensive brands/same brands at lower prices: This can be summed up in one word: **Costco.** Costco has warehouses in 34 states.	$$$$
Plan your purchases and do not impulse buy.	$$$$$$

annual dollar impacts of making such changes. Some will make sense for you and others won't. As you look down the list, have in mind a positive idea of how you will use the savings to achieve a goal: pay off credit card debt, fund an IRA, or save toward the down payment on a house or a car.

The following is a list of the average markup over their cost that nondiscount retailers in various industries charge for products they purchase and resell to you. A 100 percent markup means they double their purchase price when they sell it to you. A 200 percent markup means they buy it for $10 and sell it to you for $30 (a 200 percent profit of $20), and so on. If it is a three-tiered market, the middleman's markup is part of the wholesale price paid by the retailer.

Women's fashions	200% to 350%
Men's fashions and clothing	250%
Furniture and home products	200% to 320%
Major chain grocery store food	100%
U.S. domestic automobiles	4%
U.S. hot-selling pickup trucks	4%
Foreign automobiles	6%
Lumber and home hardware	100%
Plants and garden supplies	100%

Costco (averages 11 percent markup)[1] is not necessarily the place where you have to buy a year's supply of ketchup or toilet paper at one time, although Costco does indeed sell some food and household products in oversized packages not suited for the small family. As manufacturers have come to accept Costco as another distribution channel, you now find great prices on electronics, appliances, and clothing as well as on food items. Costco's 312 warehouses in 34 states give it unprecedented buying power.[2] Another key element that allows Costco to control its prices is a lack of shrinkage due to spoilage or theft). Costco's business formula is a saving grace for vendors with an oversupply of a product; for their day in, day out merchandise lines, vendors compete to be featured at Costco. Costco, for example, examines the manufacturing costs and overhead for a vendor and states what it will pay for a product. This is a painful process for an inefficient producer because Costco really does know what the costs should be—after all, it is going through this same process with that vendor's major competitors. After buying a product, Costco marks items up no more than 14 percent[3] (11 percent average) and features them in warehouses the same way Safeway or Macy's merchandises products to match local trends. Costco often can buy a product and add its markup, and still sell the item for less than local single-store retailers can even buy that same item. On top of its buying power, Costco usually buys direct and knocks out the middleman's handling costs and profit. The Costco web site has a store locator index (www.costco.com).

Trader Joe's (60 percent to 65 percent markup) has 200 neighborhood grocery stores in 17 states. Its formula is slightly different from Costco's. Trader Joe's tries to buy manufacturer's overstocked or discontinued items, plus staples. The stores' average markup is higher, but they sell in individual-use quantities. This same formula holds true for **Smart & Final** and other discounters. It is amazing how smart businesspeople will dream up a product line; produce, package, and manufacture it in large quantities; and, before it comes to market, decide to dump it so their name is not associated with the product or poor package design. This phenomenon helps retailers like Trader Joe's thrive. Trader Joe's has a great monthly newsletter you can view on its web site at www.traderjoes.com, as well as a store locator index. The Smart & Final web site is at www.smartandfinal.com.

Not to be overlooked are **Wal-Mart** and *Sam's Clubs*. While Costco is in urban locations, Wal-Mart has until recently concentrated on more rural locations for its 532 Wal-Mart and Sam's Club stores. Wal-Mart has more sales volume than any other retailer in North America. However, it has no uniform markup policy, which make it difficult to describe an advantage other than usual low prices and lots of merchandise (www.walmart.com).

T. J. Maxx has 700 stores in 47 states that sell brand-name designer fashions and housewares for less. Because T. J. Maxx buys overstocked or discontinued brand-name merchandise, the way to save is just to keep coming back on a catch-as-catch-can basis (www.tjmaxx.com).

Health Savings Accounts

The Medicare Prescription Drug Act of 2003 created Health Savings Accounts (HSAs) that enable workers with high-deductible health insurance to make a pretax contribution of up to $2,600 each year ($5,150 for families) to cover medical costs. Monies withdrawn to pay deductibles and other medical costs are not included in taxable income. High-deductible medical insurance programs are defined as having a $1,000 annual deductible for one person or $2,000 for a family. To date the plans have been slow to be introduced because of the complexity of hiring an administrator to review and distribute amounts to claimants. This is unfortunate, because the plans that are available cost no more than low-deductible medical insurance. An advantage is that if you do not use the year's pretax contribution it carries over to future years.

Flexible Spending Accounts

Another way to save on dependent care, medical expenses, and commuter expenses is to contribute pretax dollars to a flexible spending account set up by your employer and administered at work. An advantage of these accounts is that the monies to fund them are deducted from your paycheck, so there is no temptation to rationalize and spend the cash first. Under Section 125 of the Internal Revenue Code, your employer can establish plans that allow you to voluntarily reduce your salary in exchange for your employer providing a reimbursement account for qualified expenses. These amounts are deducted from your paycheck over the year and put into any of three separate accounts for your use: dependent care, medical reimbursement, and commuting expenses. This means, depending on your federal income tax bracket (see Table 2.8), you can save 15 percent to 35 percent on qualified expenses up to the allowable contribution limits. If you do not use up the balances each year, though, they can *not* be carried over to next calendar year. These are calendar-year plans that require you to decide in December how much you want to contribute to the plan for the coming year. So you will have to do a little budgeting to decide how much you will spend in each in the three categories. We will look at them individually because they have different rules.

TABLE 2.8   2005 Federal Income Tax Brackets (Estimated)

Upper Limits of Taxable Income per Tax Bracket

Tax Bracket	Single Taxpayers	Head of Household	Joint Taxpayers	Married Filing Separately
15%	$ 29,050	$ 38,900	$ 58,100	$ 29,050
25%	$ 70,350	$100,500	$117,250	$ 58,625
28%	$146,750	$162,700	$178,650	$ 89,325
33%	$319,100	$319,100	$319,100	$159,550
35%	>$319,100	>$319,100	>$319,100	>$159,550

Dependent Care Plans

For year 2005 you are allowed to contribute per household $3,000 for one dependent and $6,000 for two or more. These may be children under age 13, dependent parents who live with you and who are in need of day care, or a disabled child or parent who lives with you. Only qualified expenses are eligible for reimbursement. These are day camp, preschool, and day care for an older parent. You must submit receipts, and the care must be provided by a day care center. Presumably this does not include a nanny.

The dependent care account does not provide reimbursement for overnight camps, day care for an older parent who is financially independent, or the cost of kindergarten or higher schooling.

Although the federal government also allows a tax credit for these same expenses, you cannot use the credit and the flexible spending plan in the same year. When you apply the numbers to the rules, the flexible spending plan usually offers a larger after-tax savings than does the credit. If you are in the 15 percent federal income tax bracket (taxable income of less than $29,050 for single taxpayers, $38,900 for heads of household, and $58,100 for joint filers) it is a breakeven—the credit and the pretax deduction provide the same benefit; however, if your employer makes the deduction before you see the money, there is no temptation to spend it. Above the 15 percent bracket you save 23 percent by using a flexible spending account.

Medical Reimbursement Plans

These plans allow you to contribute up to $1,000 of pretax income to be used for items not covered by your employer health plan. The federal government has recently included on the list of eligible items nonprescription cold medicines, antacids, pain relievers, and multiple pairs of prescription eyeglasses. Not included are vitamin C and Weight Watchers (unless physician prescribed), eye lifts, and health club dues to stay fit.

This benefit is per employer, and there is no offsetting federal credit to complicate your decision. Given the co-pay amount on your health insurance, plus the other qualified items you purchase over the year, participation in this account saves you whatever your tax bracket is: 15 percent, 25 percent, 28 percent, 33 percent, or 35 percent. If you are married and you both have employers, you can participate in both plans if your expenses amount to enough.

Transportation Reimbursement Account

If you commute using public transportation, you can contribute tax free to your employer's plan and be reimbursed up to $105 per month. Unused amounts carry forward to other months in the same calendar year.

If you pay parking you can contribute tax free and be reimbursed up to $195 per month tax free. These amounts cannot be used to maintain your vehicle. These amounts are per employer, so if you both work and commute to different employers, you can double up in the contributions if you have the costs.

What does this really mean? For example, if you are single and have taxable income over $68,000 and you provide day care for two kids, spend more than $1,000 on additional qualified medical items, and have to pay for parking when you drive to work, you could save $2,320 in taxes per year. If you are married and both work, your tax savings could range from $1,900 to $4,375, depending on your tax bracket, plus the state income tax benefit, if any.

If your employer does not offer Section 125 flexible spending accounts, rally support from fellow employees for these plans. From your employer's standpoint it means someone is going to have to administer the accounts and make the reimbursements to employees as they submit documented requests.

Buying a Car—Supply and Demand Works

This segment comes to you courtesy of an interview with Michael Mills, a respected independent car broker in Northern California. Most of Michael's work is finding high-end cars and negotiating price for buyers willing to pay a fee. Michael deals exclusively in high-end cars, he explains, because there is only $100 to $300 of gross profit to the dealer on most domestic and imported autos, SUVs, and trucks. Vehicles have become a commodity unless they are a hot new model, and then the savings to the consumer can be in the thousands of dollars. They have become so much of a commodity that the only way the manufacturers can manipulate profit margins is to shrink supply. Michael believes it is a buyer's market, but passes on tips to make you a smarter shopper:

- Go shopping armed with the actual dealer's cost. This is the *Kelly Blue Book* (www.kbb.com) or *Consumer Reports* invoice price, plus the dealer's advertising costs and destination charge. Kelly will also tell you what the typical selling price for a car is in your zip code.
- One of the first questions the salesperson will ask you is whether you want to lease or finance the vehicle. The dealer and thus the salesperson makes their money on the financing, not the price of the car. If you act like a high roller and say your going to pay cash, management will allow the salesperson only limited flexibility in pricing. However, if you say you are going to lease the car, the dealer may inflate the financing charges by 5 percent, which allows plenty of room (5 percent) to seemingly reduce the base price quoted to a price even below so-called dealer's cost. Now that you have the lowest negotiated price, switch your financing decision from leasing back to dealer financing and see if they will hold the price.
- An extension the preceding point is vehicle financing from the manufacturer. This 0.9 percent, 1.9 percent, or 2.9 percent financing is a sales tool that is too good to pass up. Many times these low interest rates also apply to vehicles coming off lease (money-saving technique in Chapter 1). Banks' and credit unions' rates are 6 percent to 8 percent and are not competitive.
- Used cars are a high-profit-margin item for dealers because consumers already think they are saving money and don't dicker as hard or come as well prepared with pricing information. Kelly Blue Book (www.kbb.com), Edmunds (www.edmunds.com), and others quote what a used model should sell for by zip code.
- Vehicles coming off lease are a particular problem for dealers. Three years ago car companies were competing to get customers to buy and lease vehicles. To attractively price leases, companies used unusually high end-of-lease values, also know as residual values. The higher end-of-lease value meant a higher end-of-lease resale value, allowing the current lease payments to be reduced. This all presumed the car company could resell the vehicle for that high value at the end of the lease. They were wrong and now are taking big losses on these vehicles coming off lease. This makes it doubly important that you know what the vehicle is really worth. The car company owns the vehicle if it was a manufacturer's lease program, but allows the dealer to sell the vehicle for whatever price the dealer can get.

Michael has another caution about the car-buying process. Because vehicles have become such a commodity and profit margins are so thin, he sees more dealers going out of business or consolidating in 18 to 24 months.

Automatic Payroll Deductions

The government requires payroll deductions for taxes and the amount you contribute to your 401(k) type plan to be automatically deducted from your paycheck. This same strategy can be applied to monies you want to save monthly. Most payroll services will do this, even routinely transferring money to your bank savings account, your rainy-day fund. This method of forced savings eliminates the temptation to use the money for something else—it's gone (saved) before you see it.

The flip side of forced savings is not adjusting your income tax withholding so that the correct amount comes out each pay period so you to owe nothing more when you file with your income tax returns. The reason people wait so long to prepare their tax returns is that they don't want to be shocked by what they may have to pay. Figuring out how much your tax bill is going to be at the end of a calendar year is simple because there are not very many moving parts. Very inexpensively, either a tax preparer or you with computer software can take last year's tax return plus any estimates of what will change and very closely estimate this year's taxes. If you do it yourself, buy Intuit's TurboTax. TurboTax basic (federal only) costs $20 (less at Costco or other discounters). This program has an extensive on-screen interview process to make sure you don't miss items. Input last year's tax return plus any salary increases, additional personal exemptions, and adjustments to mortgage interest and the like. This will approximate your tax liability. Now go to the Tax Forecaster, a planning tool for next year. It will take the amounts you previously put in and compute this year's tax at this year's rates. This is important because the tax rates are changing.

Now for the only tricky part. If you are using the templates on my web site, go to Template 7, Estimating Your Taxes. TurboTax also allows you to do this process.

1. Input your estimated current year's total tax liability on the top line.
2. From your pay stubs, add up the total federal and state taxes paid year-to-date, plus one more pay period, and put the result on the next line. The extra pay period is because after you tell your employer you want to make a change it will take several weeks for the change to become effective.
3. The balance of tax due after subtracting item 2 from item 1 must be divided by the number of remaining paychecks you will receive this calendar year, less the one added in step 2 above. If you are paid twice per month the yearly total is 24, 12 if you are paid once a month, and 26 if you are paid every two weeks.

4. The amount to be withheld each pay period is the net tax due divided by the number of remaining paychecks. This specified amount goes on line 6 of the Form W-4 your employer will send the payroll company and the government. Cross out line 5 because you are not computing withholding using allowances. There is a similar form to adjust your state income tax withholding.
5. Look at the amounts. If they are 10 percent above or below your current withholding there may be a mistake. If so, ask for help. Either a payroll person or a tax preparer can help you locate the error and determine the right withholding amounts.
6. If you get a pay increase or something major happens midyear, redo the process to adjust your withholding so you will owe nothing and have no surprises at tax time.

In this way there will be no surprises on April 15—either bad or good. After all, why worry for six months about whether you have enough withheld, and worse, why overpay and make a non-interest-bearing loan to the government as an excuse for forced savings?

3

Two-Income Households: Affording a Home and Retirement While Avoiding Bankruptcy

In the previous chapter, we looked at your family income, how it is spent, and what percentage of your cash outflow is for fixed costs. While the one-income household may bring in less money, it also has fewer opportunities to save for retirement. If you are a one-income household, the questions are easier:

- Am I living within my means, and if not how can I trim my costs to save for future obligations?
- Am I contributing enough to at least get the maximum matching employer contribution in my pension plan/savings plan at work?

Two-Income Households—Jump-Starting Your Future

The decision to stay a two-income household, especially a two-income household without children, for some period is probably today the key to having both the home of your choice and a pleasant retirement. By controlling your living expenses you have the maximum opportunity to put money away. This may be your last opportunity to have this luxury, so take advantage of it for as long as you can.

Two careers mean you have two people with two sets of skills and the opportunity to participate in two retirement programs and pick the health plan that provides the best coverage at the best price. The most significant savings opportunity of your lifetime comes from living on one paycheck and saving the other. The law allows people who file a joint tax return to both contribute the maximum to their employer-sponsored pension plans. No matter how early a one-income household starts contributing to a 401(k) type pension plan, the odds are you will not have enough put away to retire comfortably at age 65. The best argument to stay a two-income household is that you take the extra income and both contribute the maximum to your pension plans. The compounding of the tax-deferred contributions and the tax-free compounding of the investment returns over the years may well be what allow you to retire while others are still working way past age 65.

If you can afford to live on one income and save or put into retirement accounts the second income, you can put money away for a house. As you will see in Chapter 4, "Buying a Home," this discipline will pay off in more ways than you may originally think. Controlling your expenses and not running up credit card or other debt will dramatically improve your credit ratings while you amass the cash for a down payment. Because you have the cash plus a good credit rating, many more home-borrowing opportunities will become available. This means lower interest rates and types of loans that are not available to people with marginal or bad credit.

Net, Do Two Incomes Mean More Cash Flow?

Now to the downside of thinking your two incomes will let you live any way you want. If your fixed costs exceed either one of your two incomes, there should be big yellow caution flags.

After you have children there is a whole different set of considerations and complications. Let's look at this second income by asking two questions:

1. Does the second paycheck really add anything after additional job-related expenses? This takes looking at the numbers—a mini cash flow analysis.
2. Does the second income set you up for the trap of ballooning your fixed expenses beyond the level where you can ever go back to one income—voluntarily or involuntarily?

Job-Related Expenses

The first thing that happens when both partners work is that many job-related costs are doubled. The tax man is the first to come calling. Your combined incomes will usually push you into a higher marginal income tax bracket. This means that instead of the incremental second income being taxed at your 25 percent bracket, it may all get taxed at a higher rate, say 28 percent. The second income, added in on top of the first, will be taxed at a higher rate. This is because the tax rates are graduated. The second income will also have to pay additional Social Security and Medicare tax, either at the 2004 combined 7.7 percent if employed or 15.3 percent if self-employed. Next, add in work-related costs, dressing for success, and possibly a second car with insurance, fuel, and maintenance. The last two parts to this question are often the deciding factors:

1. Net of all the taxes I have to pay and the additional costs of being out there on the job, will I have to pay a house cleaning service more per hour than I am going to make net per hour from my job?
2. Will the cost of day care/preschool on top of the other costs leave us with any additional income each month?
   - Day care and preschool are usually funded by parents with after-tax dollars.
   - Preschool costs $300 to $500 per month, as much as a mid-range private K-through-12 school. These are already-taxed dollars.
   - Will one parent have to skip work and lose income when a child is sick?

Fixed Costs

In Chapter 2, we examined your fixed costs. Controlling your fixed costs is critical. If you are living on one income and saving the second, you are already on a successful track. The time-tested best way for a young couple without children to get ahead is for both of you to work and save, save, save for the down payment on a house. I will go a step further and suggest you keep the low-interest-rate, long-term student loans and pay them off over time. Don't forget that participating in both employers' pension plans for as many years as possible will give you the edge when considering retirement. In Chapter 6 on pension plans, some striking examples drive this point home. These are parts of the strategy you need to employ in the early years to have the things you want later.

Too often, however, the second income becomes the candy to be consumed. It is the trap that balloons your fixed cost spending to levels you can't get out from under later. Couples rationalize incurring more debt with the idea they will use the second income to pay it off. If you borrow the money for a down payment on a house from the Bank of Mom and Dad, they will probably be forgiving if payments don't come through as planned. The rest of the world is not as understanding.

Over the past 24 months, 2.7 million manufacturing jobs have gone away that are not coming back, because businesses can learn to do without those tasks. In Silicon Valley 200,000 jobs have been eliminated. The prediction is that it will take 10 years before these jobs reappear.[1]

Those are the practical questions. Elizabeth Warren and her daughter Amelia Warren Tyagi have said this so well in their book *The Two-Income Trap: Why Middle-Class Mothers and Fathers Are Going Broke* (Basic Books, 2003).

Their book is based on a national bankruptcy study co-authored by Elizabeth Warren, who is a chaired professor of bankruptcy at Harvard Law School. As they interviewed almost 1,000 families nationwide who had gone through personal bankruptcy, the survey uncovered patterns that led to unexpected conclusions.

The Two-Income Trap focuses on the same audience as this book— college-educated couples ages 25 through 55. The two most startling conclusions reached about the modern family are:

1. The biggest predictor of personal bankruptcy is having a child.[2]
2. More children will see their parents go through bankruptcy this year than a divorce.[3]

Amelia Warren Tyagi, herself a management consultant with McKinsey & Company, summarizes the book's findings thus:

- The beauty of the Over-Consumption Myth is that it squares neatly with our own intuitions. We see the malls packed with shoppers. We receive catalogs filled with outrageously expensive gadgets.
- And yet, when it is all added up, including the Tommy sweatshirts and Ray-Ban sunglasses, the average family of four today spends 21 percent *less* (inflation adjusted) on clothing than a similar family did in the early 1970s.
- They spend 44 percent less on major appliances today than they did a generation ago.[4]

Follow sensible advice, and credit card balances will vanish, bankruptcy filings will disappear, and mortgage foreclosures will cease to plague America. Reality is not nearly so neat. Sure, there are some families who buy too much stuff, but there is no evidence of any "epidemic" in overspending—"certainly nothing that could explain a 255 percent increase in the foreclosure rate, a 430 percent increase in the bankruptcy rolls, and a 570 percent increase in credit card debt."[5]

The authors document in their book that the culprit is the high cost of suburban housing caused by two-income families bidding up the cost of homes in good school districts. This is compounded by parents' desire to provide their children with a superior education—starting with preschool. This is made possible by consumer protection laws that allow, many would say encourage, lenders to count both incomes as one in qualifying for a mortgage. In tandem with the deregulation of the mortgage industry in the early 1980s, lenders have creative mortgage products that allow couples to spend more than half of their combined gross income on their mortgage. The sad part is that many of these couples get locked into a high-interest-rate mortgage when, with research, they could qualify for a market-rate mortgage and save hundred of dollars every month.

The two-income plan works, but often just barely until something goes wrong. When one partner stops working for whatever reason and that portion of the income vanishes, the problems begin. People usually stop working because of a pressing commitment that itself often means incurring costs:

- Providing care for a family member.
- Pregnancy and resulting infant care.
- A wage earner's own disability or long-term illness.

Lenders believe people with good credit will figure out a way to solve their financial problems and keep mortgage payments current. Credit card providers are eager for cardholders to build up balances and pay high interest rates while only requiring them to make minimum monthly payments. Each year they estimate what their losses will be from borrowers and cardholders who stop paying. This loan loss amount is eventually worked into the pricing of their products. Don't become one of their statistics.

Credit Theft

Maintaining your credit score is so important and so hard to fix when there are problems that the topic deserves its own chapter. Your credit report is your financial report card—or at least the one other people from lenders, credit card companies, and future employers use to judge you. Unfortunately, the commonly accepted belief is that the strength of your credit report mirrors the strength of your character and ability to be responsible.

Eighty percent of all credit reports have errors, and one in four have errors serious enough that credit could be denied. That statistic and the fact that under a new federal law credit reports from each of the three credit reporting agencies are now free should be enough to get you to check your credit. You may do this online or by writing directly to them. Because the process of correcting errors can take months, this is something you should start long before you apply for credit, especially for a large purchase such as a car or a home.

Whether you know it or not, companies that are interested in you spend a lot of time analyzing your credit report. There are three credit reporting agencies that receive data and maintain their own files. The items reported on a person's credit report include good items, black marks, and those that aren't even yours, and can differ from one credit reporting company to the next. Even small disputed items can have big consequences. Credit collection agencies report even questionable items to the reporting agencies. In fact, these collection agencies use the threat of reporting even a minor item as a common tactic to collect debts. Remember, they are paid on commission—a percentage of what they collect on each case given to them.

The process of correcting errors or clarifying entries sent in by creditors is time-consuming and may take up to six months. Documentation must be provided to the credit reporting agency to make corrections. It is important that you follow up to make sure the corrections were made. The three national credit agencies are:

1. Transunion: www.transunion.com; (800) 916-8800.
2. Equifax: www.equifax.com; (800) 685-1111.
3. Experian: www.experian.com; (800) 397-3742.

When you find an error, report the error in writing to each credit reporting agency that has the incorrect item. Provide details and supporting information. Credit reporting agencies are required to resolve disputes in 30 days. However, if the creditor won't budge, they will leave the item in the report. The company (creditor) that reported the item must report the dispute when making further reports to the reporting agencies. Ask the credit reporting agency to post a note in your file saying the item is being contested by you.

Credit card companies inquire about your credit to find periods of financial strain. They look at your payment history, particularly late payments and high balances relative to your income. Creditors also draw conclusions from customer profiles derived from your payment history with other lenders. Sometimes they do this monthly. A May 2003 article in the *New York Times*[6] reported on credit card issuers using credit reports to raise the interest rate on balances outstanding to as high as 29 percent. Any unusual borrowing or credit card activity will invariably bring a flood of high-priced credit card applications and other unwanted junk mail.

How much of your available credit you utilize is also very important. A $15,000 credit card limit where $3,000 gets used and paid each month is good. Three credit cards, each with a $5,000 limit, are not so good: multiple cards reduce your credit score. Each time the balance outstanding on a credit card exceeds more than one-half of the card's limit it reduces your credit rating. This is also true when you take out new credit cards to pay off the balances on other cards and to get a lower rate. The credit scoring system has no way of knowing you went for a lower rate, just that you have more credit cards. The solution is to voluntarily terminate the old credit cards.

Home equity lines of credit also affect your credit score. Remember, what the computer is looking at is how and how much you utilize your available credit. High loan balances on home equity lines of credit look like credit cards with large balances. These balances, even though used for good purposes, can have a dramatic negative effect on your credit score. Home equity loans, as opposed to lines of credit, are considered more like mortgage loans. What the computer scores here is whether monthly payments are made on time. So look for an equity line of credit that converts part of your balance to an equity loan with monthly payments. This shifts that part of the balance from available credit into the loan category and improves your score.

Lenders and companies granting credit to buy houses, cars, and so on rely on a score called your FICO score. This score is determined by a formula developed by the Fair Isaac Corporation. Reacting to consumer groups' demands, recently Fair Isaac explained the formula and made it available for use by the individual credit reporting agencies. Scores can range between 300 and 850. Your score is considered to be a predictor of how you will repay the money lent to you. Usually, if your FICO score is better than 680, you are in good shape. As with items on, or not on, your credit report, your FICO score often differs among the three credit reporting agencies and they all can differ from the score provided by Fair Isaac itself. Until recently a high number of inquiries about your credit history reduced your FICO score. Two of the four largest bank lenders in the country obtain your FICO score from each of the three credit reporting agencies and toss out the high and the low score. Unmarried couples are considered joint borrowers by most national lenders. The couple's combined income is used for income qualification. The credit history of the higher earner is used to select the credit report.

It is worthwhile to go to the www.myfico.com web site, pay the $12.95 fee, and avail yourself of the myFICO.com service. I paid the $12.95 and looked at my score and the comments several months ago. Recently I got an e-mail from myFICO.com informing me that "nearly 30 percent of myFICO users have scores that differ by more than 50 points between the three credit bureaus." This highlighted an error by one of the credit reporting agencies. This could be the "difference between a 7.39 percent interest rate and a 5.58 percent interest rate on a $150,000, 30-year fixed loan—a $180 per month payment difference," according to Fair Isaac. Superimposed on a vertical bar showing the FICO score range of 350 to 850 were my three scores spread over about a 50-point range. When you order your FICO score through Fair Isaac's myFICO service, you can:[7]

- Get the best in-depth explanation of what is driving your personal FICO score.
- Learn from the experts how you can improve your score over time.
- Use the FICO Score Simulator tool to see how actions you take, like paying down balances, could affect your future FICO score.

- Find out how you compare to the U.S. population in terms of credit risk.
- Gain insight into the five main kinds of credit information the FICO score evaluates and how important each one is.
- Learn how lenders use credit scoring in the loan review process.
- Review the credit report on which your FICO score was calculated to check the information for accuracy.

In today's world of desktop mortgage underwriting—that is, underwriting performed on a desktop computer with sophisticated software—qualifying for a mortgage is done almost entirely by the lender evaluating your FICO score. Your FICO score determines what the lender will ask you for and how it prices the loan:

Less than 620: You will have to provide tax returns, financial statements, pay stubs, and other support data, and probably have to explain away black marks on your credit report, plus pay more for the loan.

Between 620 and 680: Your credit is probably acceptable, but there will be questions, and some or full documentation will be required.

Between 680 and 720: Your credit is good and you probably qualify for a "low paper" or loan not requiring verification of financial and employment information.

Above 720: You probably qualify for interest-only loans and loans at the lender's best pricing.

Self-employed people are usually still required to provide financial statements and tax returns and show some continuity of income over several years.

For first-time home buyers, some lenders go so far as to examine the source of funds you intend to use for your down payment. They are looking for evidence of "off balance sheet" loans you have not reported but have an obligation to repay, which would affect the amount of monthly income you have available to repay their loan.

Lenders have large statistical databases from which their computer software draws conclusions about your financial characteristics and use of credit. This is in addition to the same type of analysis done by Fair Isaac (FICO) to produce your credit score. As your credit score goes up, lenders offer better loan pricing and higher loan-to-home value ratios. This can be attractive, as in buying your way into good school districts, but it can trap you into loan payments plus related costs that are more than just a stretch—they are more than you can afford.

4

Buying a Home

Before we get down to details, let's look at some basics about the housing market and the home loan process.

It is better at any age to save and buy a house than to pay rent. The keys are saving for the down payment and having high credit scores. Building up home equity and applying your talents to improve your home will be rewarding. If it is a starter house that you sell and then trade up from, your rewards are tangible and obvious if you keep your eye on the goal of getting into the right house. This chapter will take you through time-tested rules, pitfalls, and things to consider as you build a house-buying strategy.

Don't skip this chapter if you already own a house. Gaining a good tip or just applying the math in the refinancing examples to your situation is worth the time. If you don't have the money saved for a down payment plus the necessary closing costs, but you have a reasonable credit history, the Federal Housing Authority (FHA) probably has a loan program to meet your needs if the loan amount is between $172,632 and $312,895 for a single-family home in 2005, depending on local limits. If you are a first-time home buyer, a teacher, a public service police officer, a farmer, or a Native American, the government sponsors loan programs with no down payment or modest 3 percent to 5 percent down payment programs where the costs to qualify and close the loan are subsidized by the government. There are even programs sponsored by reputable nonprofit organizations that will gift you the down payment to move into a fixer-upper house.

Usually you are paying rent because either you have not decided where to settle down or you don't have enough money saved for the 10 percent or 20 percent down payment plus closing costs for a house. The usual rule of thumb is that if you live in your house for more than two years and then sell, you can break even and earn back the real estate selling fees and loan origination costs out of the appreciation in home value. Additionally, you are able to live in the house and enjoy it.

Your house will be your single largest purchase and the single largest expense of your life. Later in life, your home equity and your pension will generally be your two most valuable assets. You will have the option to downsize, buy a smaller home, and live on that equity in retirement, so consider that buildup of home equity as a pot of cash to be protected.

The Housing Markets

When private school costs are paid out-of-pocket, this is done with after-tax dollars. This means that for each $10,000 of annual educational cost you must earn close to $15,000 in that year to pay the bill. Depending on the quality of your local public schools, this hardship can begin in kindergarten or before. For parents, number one on your house-hunting checklist should be the quality of a community's schools.

The extra money you pay to live in these communities will pay dividends over the long haul. Buy the least expensive house in the most expensive neighborhood you can afford. Usually, but not always, there is a correlation between good schools and good neighborhoods. Remember, parents just like you are doing their homework and selecting the best school districts while bidding up home prices in that district. Take the risk and buy this house before the kids are born and while you have the luxury of a two-income family. If you buy in a neighborhood that will require you to send your kids to private schools, every $10,000 you spend annually on private schools, if added to the down payment, qualifies you for $50,000 more house. Take two kids K through 12 and do the math—$250,000 to $350,000, plus or minus, will be spent on K through 12 private schools.

> **Rule of Thumb:** Buy a less expensive house in the most expensive neighborhood you can afford that has good schools.

Put your money into the right house for you with good public schools rather than a private K through 12 education. If you are able t do this while you are young, the extra income you are earning 1 housing inflation in those neighborhoods with good public schools should allow you to refinance your mortgage and live within the constraints of a one-income household if you choose.

A careful choice, plus time and energy, and the house that is underpriced for the neighborhood will appreciate in value faster as it catches up to the more expensive houses around it. But this is where the greatest housing inequity in the United States begins. Housing prices in job centers on either coast have consistently grown faster than job-related incomes over the past 20 years. This is particularly true in coastal metropolitan areas and their satellite communities with less than a two-hour commute to city center jobs (Boston, New York, Los Angeles, and San Francisco). Ten years ago this would have read "one-hour commute" during normal commute drive times.

> **Reality:** To buy your first house or the house you want requires a commute. If you work in a major job center, expect a longer commute.

Employers, and especially global companies, continue to reward higher-paid strategic executives and their families by locating headquarters in metropolitan areas while relocating lower-paid clerical, systems, manufacturing, and noncritical administrative staff into areas with lower land cost (lower office rent) and lower cost of living where salaries can be better kept in check. For 20 years (and probably 20 more) this pattern has fed the escalation in housing prices in these job center areas. Academics continue to predict a flattening in housing prices there, but the trend for high-salaried people to concentrate in these areas doesn't change. In addition, because of tighter city planning, fewer homes are being built than are demanded by prospective new homeowners.

Another interesting phenomenon is that when recent college graduates are polled about where they want to work and live, the leading choices are Boston, New York City, Los Angeles, and San Francisco. See any patterns?

In these four metropolitan areas and in many other job centers another phenomenon exists where land is available for developing houses. As close-in land (short commute) gets developed, home builders build farther out where civic planners have built or intend to soon build freeways ⸺ᵒʳ new roads. Many of these roads are part of the federal Great So-
⸺ng boom conceived in the 1960s and 1970s. These are of-
or bypass roads that allow major throughways to go
enter, opening access to vast rural tracts of developable
is a summary of these ring and access roads that continue
⸺ development in selected cities.

TABLE 4.1   Ring and Access Roads

City	Interstate Highway
Atlanta	285
Boston	95, then 495
Dallas	635
Denver	470/E-470
Los Angeles	210, 215, and 5
Sacramento	505 and 80
San Francisco	580 and 680
San Diego	15 and 8
Washington, D.C.	495

The outlying land is cheaper, so the houses are often less expensive or bigger. Once this ring of the ripple is built out, the builders start over again further out. After all, to survive they have to continue to build homes that appeal to new buyers, often first-time home buyers. Eventually employers relocate plants or offices on land zoned for such uses by the civic planners for the Great Society.

The trick is to figure out which building wave is close enough to the city center to be a tolerable commute, while also having sufficient planned large business parks to become a magnet for large employers. As city-center costs continue to escalate and corporate management changes, new bosses will consider relocating company home offices to this new, less-expensive location. Examples of this abound in all industries, at all sizes, and will in all job center communities so long as land is available and property/city taxes keep going up.

In the *New York Times* on August 6, 2003, writer David Leonhardt of the *Times* teamed with Economy.com in an article entitled "In Most of the Nation, a House Is a Home and Not a Real Estate Bonanza."[1] They adjusted 1983 home prices to 2003 dollars and compared those to actual 2003 home values for 318 major metropolitan areas around the United States. The average home appreciation, adjusted for inflation, across the United States was 35 percent over the 20-year period. Cumulative consumer price index (CPI)–based inflation over that 20-year span was 100 percent—that is, inflation doubled the selling price of products and services to the consumer. This means home appreciation on average nationally went up 135 percent in absolute terms. However, locations in the Midwest and South making a transition away from agriculture or away from rust belt manufacturing showed almost no gains.

Job center metropolitan areas had cumulative inflation-adjusted home appreciation as high as 100 percent to 167 percent over the 20-year period.

In absolute terms this means home appreciation in these areas was 200 percent to 320 percent, twice the national average. These areas also had the most expensive housing, averaging $350,000, combined with the highest cost of living and relatively higher average incomes. The anomaly in the study is Portland, Maine, with 202 percent cumulative appreciation and average home values of under $200,000. According to a friend who lives there, Portland has been discovered as a second- or third-home area by residents of the Northeast. (See Tables 4.2 and 4.3.)

Debunking the Cautions about Overpriced Single-Family Homes

No discussion of housing prices would be complete without putting the notion of overpriced housing into geographic perspective. Home prices are tied to four fundamentals:

1. Local rents for same-kind single-family homes.
2. Local household incomes.
3. Geographic desirability.
4. Local balance of supply and demand for single-family homes.

Most statistical studies concentrate on the first two fundamentals: the gross rent multiplier (GRM) calculating what the same house would rent for in a particular area and what housing prices are supported by local household incomes. In an area of average desirability,

TABLE 4.2   Locations with Positive Inflation-Adjusted Home Appreciation during the Period from 1983 through 2003

Northeast		Midwest	
Portland, Maine	202%	Detroit	94%
Boston and southern New Hampshire	167%	Chicago	71%
Barnstable–Yarmouth, Massachusetts	163%	Ann Arbor, Michigan	70%
Southeast		**West**	
Wilmington, North Carolina	100%	Vallejo–Fairfield–Napa, California	145%
Asheville, North Carolina	87%	Santa Cruz–Watsonville, California	144%
Baltimore	72%	San Jose, California	143%
Southwest			
Denver	71%		
Flagstaff, Arizona, and southern Utah	67%		
Colorado Springs	53%		

Courtesy of economy.com, as reported in the *New York Times*.

**TABLE 4.3   Locations with Negative Inflation-
Adjusted Home Appreciation during the Period
from 1983 through 2003**

Houston, Texas	−4%	Rochester, New York	−5%
Casper, Wyoming	−1%	Enid, Oklahoma	−15%
Lafayette, Louisiana	−15%	Odessa–Midland, Texas	−22%

Courtesy of economy.com, as reported in the *New York Times*.

houses tend to be priced at 10 to 12 times what they would rent for annually. So a $2,000 monthly rent ($24,000 annually) translates to housing prices at $240,000 to $288,000. San Diego and Orange County are at the other end of the scale, with homes selling at 20 to 25 times annual rent. This is possible only because of a combination of high household income, creative (scary) lending practices, and a short supply of homes.

Several noted economists have for years been publishing often-quoted studies about overpriced housing markets and why they exist. Recently, several noteworthy rationales have crept into the studies that bear noting. But first, I concede that housing on both coasts is overpriced, but will stay that way because of the desirability factor. Many people want to live, work, and raise their kids in New England and California. These people are willing to pay the price, often playing the mortgage market to qualify for houses they otherwise can't afford. These markets also have a limited supply of housing, which also forces prices up beyond reason based on national averages.

Chip Case and Bob Shiller, economists at Wellesley College and Yale University, respectively, argue that the housing bubble-like characteristics are justified in 42 states because they mirror the rise in personal income.[2] However, they discount the desirability factor of the other eight overpriced states, which are in New England, California, and Hawaii. The desirability of living in these areas will continue to drive housing prices upward. Only rising interest rates will dampen demand and slow housing appreciation.

Shawn Tully, in "Is the Housing Boom Over?" (*Fortune*, September 20, 2004), presents the argument that the debt piled on by homeowners is the real fear when coupled with rising interest rates. Tully points out that $661 billion in home equity loans and refinances since 2001 have fueled our economy and consumer spending. Since 1995 this has pushed the average nationwide home price up by 47 percent. Rising interest rates on adjustable-rate mortgages that are beginning to lose their fixed-rate front-end provision will put a crimp in household incomes and thus demand. Worse yet, rising rates may force families into even more risky variable-rate loans at a time when they should be locking in a fixed mortgage rate, but can't afford the additional cash outflow each month. More on navigating this problem later in this chapter.

Preliminary Steps

Long before you start serious house hunting, take these six steps:

1. Assess your and your partner's willingness to learn about and undertake the jobs involved in fixing up the typical starter house. Do not forget to factor in the stress of living in a house that is being remodeled, often without heat or solid walls.
2. Order your free annual credit reports from each of the credit reporting agencies used by mortgage lenders in your area. Review them for the inevitable errors and blemishes on your credit. Contest in writing all errors and invest the three to six months it will take to clean up your credit report. As you will see later in this chapter, the higher your credit score the more loan products will be offered to you at lower pricing.
3. Use Template 9 on my web site, "Buying a House—How Much Can I Afford?," to estimate what price range house you will qualify for and what the down payment might be.
4. Have sufficient cash or money market funds in your bank account for at least 90 days before you start to prequalify for a loan. Money older than 90 days is considered to be yours. Recent new deposits look like additional debt borrowed from parents or others that prospective lenders will figure into your debt repayment calculations.
5. Get preapproved (prequalify) for several loan types so you know how much house the lender agrees you can afford to buy before you go out to buy.
6. Consider your timing. Seventy percent of all houses are bought and sold between April and September. This is tied to relocating school-aged children during the summer vacation months. Prices are not necessarily higher during this period, but they can be lower in the off season when there is less inventory and fewer shoppers.

Obtaining the Most Money at the Best Rate

How much money will I be able to borrow to buy a house?

My website, www.RetireYes.com, has three templates that you can use to arrive at conclusions that fit your home buying strategy:

1. Template 8 is the rent versus buy analysis using your own numbers. You will input your rent and use a 30-year conforming FHA interest rate to keep the example simple. Property tax will be held

constant at 1.5 percent. It is assumed you intend to stay in the house for 10 years.

2. Template 9 tells you how much house lenders will allow you to prequalify for. Prequalifying for a loan means going to the lender of your choice and applying for a loan without a specific house in mind. The lender will determine how much you qualify for and give you that guarantee in writing. These loan price quotations are time-sensitive and expire. Having a loan guarantee can be a big help if there are multiple offers to buy a particular house. Most offers to buy are made subject to the prospective buyer getting financing. If you have prequalified you have the advantage.

   Completing this template requires that you input the interest rates for various loan types. Because you do not know what you will find and how long you might stay in the house, get quotations on both variable-rate loans and 30-year fixed-rate loans. Later in this chapter, we will examine the pros and cons of various loan types to facilitate your home buying strategy. The amount of house you get from various scenarios using this template may be more than your budget and sanity can accommodate. Some lenders are willing to consider house payments that are so large relative to your income that there is nothing left to live on. Don't fall into this trap!

3. Template 10 allows you to examine how different types of loan products at their respective interest rates play into your strategy. This may require that you loop back to Template 2 to see how this expanded list of loan products affects the size of the loan for which you can prequalify. After we move further into this chapter and know more about different types of loans, you will see how important this can be. This template is also valuable for comparing loans when considering refinancing an existing mortgage.

Be careful when you check the Sunday newspaper or with your bank for the rates of various types of mortgages. Online, go to www.bankrate.com to get average interest rates for various loan products by zip code. Knowing the interest rates of various loan products will help you understand the following examples. Lenders have a price matrix for loan products, and prices vary based on how long the quote is good for, the type of loan, and numerous other factors such as your credit. Lenders often publish quotes for loans where the rates apply for only a short period of time. This makes them look good, but it is meaningless to you. A respected mortgage lender from a big bank once told me he hates to quote a loan rate to a customer on Friday because the customer invariably hears at a weekend dinner party about a better deal someone else got with a different lender. In the end this was usually a rate for a different type of loan with different features.

Basics of Real Estate Appraisal

Real estate professionals who for a fee and following strict procedures calculate the value of residential and commercial real estate are known as appraisers. Many belong to the nationally recognized Appraisal Institute and bear the Member of Appraisal Institute (MAI) designation. Their credentials ensure that equal standards are applied across the country. For residential appraisals there are three valuation methods used to value property for different purposes:

1. *Market value.* For buying and selling, market value indicates the most probable price at which a home should sell in a fair sale in a competitive market.
2. *Assessment value.* Real estate taxes are based on the assessed value of your home, as estimated by your local assessor. This value is usually based on market value at the time of a resale or major home addition.
3. *Insurable value.* The insurable value is the cost of replacing your property if it were destroyed or damaged. This method is used to underwrite fire and hazard insurance.

Market value is the most important number for real estate buyers and sellers. The appraiser uses various databases of recent home sales to find homes as comparable as possible to yours in size and location, usually within a half-mile radius, for analysis. Next comes an addition and subtraction process to match the homes' features even more closely. Your property is then valued at about the average of these three to five comparable homes that have sold in your area in fair market sales during the past six months. If your property is not fairly typical of surrounding homes, the appraiser may have to make some educated guesses in determining value (they tend to be conservative). In the purchase process, if you have paid for this appraisal you usually have the right to receive a copy of the appraisal upon demand. This will allow you to see which homes were used as comparables and how less desirable features of your property detracted from the value, at least in that appraiser's mind. Most lenders base their loan amount on the appraised value of the property, not the purchase price you have agreed to pay.

Basics of Home Equity Buildup

You usually build up equity or value in a home in two ways: (1) some portion of each monthly mortgage payment goes toward paying off the principal balance of the loan, and (2) the home appreciates in value. If you sell a property for more than the purchase price, plus the costs incurred to buy it combined with the costs when you sell the home, this profit is the result of having built up equity through home appreciation. Again, the rule of thumb is that you have to live in the house two years to break even. For example, if homes in your area appreciate in value at the national average of 4 percent per year, then two years would equal 8 percent appreciation. Assume your home cost $100,000 and two years later will sell for $108,000. You typically pay a 6 percent ($6,480) real estate sales commission and incur $1,500 in costs to purchase the house, so your $8,000 appreciation increase has been eaten up by costs. Local customs vary, but usually the seller pays the real estate commission and the buyer pays the other costs related to their mortgage—title insurance, tax fees, loan points, and the like. Loan points are a fee charged by the lender. One point on a $200,000 loan is a $2,000 fee. Each point is equivalent to a one-quarter percent higher interest rate for four years. If you have a choice and don't intend to refinance and do plan to stay in the house for more than four years, paying points is better than accepting the higher interest rate.

In the preceding example, had the homeowner stayed in the home for four years at 4 percent compounding appreciation, the home would have a value of $117,000. Let's assume our homeowner borrowed $90,000 or $80,000 to buy the house and had only 10 percent ($10,000) or 20 percent ($20,000) personally invested in the house. This is called leverage—using someone else's money. In this example, the actual annual rate of return on the invested down payment was 23 percent if the down payment was $10,000 or 12 percent if the down payment was $20,000. (To summarize, $117,000 value, less $100,000 purchase price and $8,000 of costs equals a $9,000 gain.)

One of the earlier *New York Times*/Economy.com examples was Wilmington, North Carolina, where homes had an inflation-adjusted price increase of 100 percent, plus a 100 percent price increase due to inflation over 20 years—a 200 percent actual increase in market value. A 200 percent increase over 20 years is 10 percent per year. Simple math says if the down payment was 20 percent (one-fifth) of the home value, then this application of leverage means the homeowner earned 50 percent per year on the investment. Because of compounding, the 10 percent per year is actually closer to 6 percent, but this still means a 30 percent per year return on your down payment. Although we are not looking at your residence as an investment, these examples make it clear why the right house in the right location is a very smart thing to do with your money.

Back in the mid-1980s in the San Francisco Bay Area a friend and I tested the 4 percent annual home appreciation assumption on two houses we had purchased in 1974. This assumption includes inflation and major home improvements, so the numbers are different from the *New York Times*/Economy.com numbers. We took the amount we paid for our houses and appreciated it at 4 percent annually. The cost of every addition or significant structural improvement was added to the cumulative appreciated value that year. We then continued to appreciate the new value at 4 percent per year up to the current year. Both houses came out to about the value we thought we could sell them for in the current year (in the mid-1980s). I redid this exercise in the early 1990s and the 4 percent rule held true. Not until the unusually high home appreciation in the mid-1990s into 2004 did this rule fall apart. Now the 4 percent rule undervalues the house by 60 percent, or, if we believe the experts, the house is 60 percent overvalued! All of the additional "value" came during 10 years of hyper house inflation. From a national perspective this means that even though there are years of high appreciation, there are enough years of low or no appreciation to average out to 4 percent.

Put into perspective, home appreciation makes home ownership look like a great investment, but relative to buying and holding index mutual funds that track the stock markets, housing is a distant second. Housing prices in the San Francisco Bay Area went up 340 percent over the 22 years from 1982 through 2003. During the same period the Dow Jones Industrial Average of 30 major companies went up 1,020 percent and the Nasdaq Composite index went up 840 percent.[3] If, however, you factor in the leverage due to home loans, house price gains in high-appreciation areas could arguably be said to equal stock market gains.

Where to Shop for a House

There are many factors influencing the directions taken by residential neighborhoods over time. Unless there is a big, already well-funded change coming, a neighborhood that has begun a downhill slide will probably continue downhill. Stable residential neighborhoods without an influx of unplanned commercial development tend to remain stable and improve in value along with the surrounding community. Your hardest job as a prospective buyer is to get a true feel for the community and where it will go in the future.

In the 1990s I was part of a large national financial services company that made thousands of reverse mortgages to seniors across the United States. A reverse mortgage is a loan allowing seniors to draw equity out of their home to supplement income while continuing to live in the home. When they move, the home is sold, the lender is paid off, and the balance goes to the borrowers or their heirs. These people have lived in their homes for at least 25 years and have paid off their original mortgage. Many retirees, especially in temperate climates, want to stay in their homes until they are compelled to move for health reasons. Part of our job was to assess where we thought these usually mature neighborhoods would be in about 10 years when the home would be sold and we, the lender, would be paid from the proceeds of the home's sale. We saw many homes in established neighborhoods where pride in home ownership was reflected in the exterior maintenance of the homes. Inside, however, the seniors' homes typically had antiquated bathrooms and kitchens. These are ideal fixer-upper houses because you can quickly evaluate the character of the neighborhood and feel confident of its future. The exceptions were in neighborhoods with creeping unplanned and usually scattered commercial development. Often these were on residential connector streets that have today become major high-traffic thoroughfares. Unless you are looking in exclusive residential neighborhoods with strictly enforced zoning laws, these patterns of "commercial creep" can be a threat.

After you scout the communities where you would like to live and in which you can afford to buy, start doing your homework. Most communities have web sites and general plans that forecast 10, 20, and 50 years into the future. Look at not only the general direction the community plans to take, but at how various neighborhoods in the community have been zoned to control, maintain, or encourage growth. Watch out for areas with mixed zoning, such as areas that are zoned R-1 (one residential house per lot) mixed in with lots that are zoned for multiple-unit apartment buildings or condominiums. As housing becomes scarce and land values rise, developers always want to build apartments and other high-density housing on any lot zoned for multiple units, even if it is currently occupied by a single-family house. Single-family homes in neighborhoods with apartments do not typically appreciate at as high a rate as do those in neighborhoods of all single-family homes.

Fixer-Upper Houses in Better Locations

As mentioned earlier, a mature neighborhood may be a source for the ideal fixer-upper house. These are fairly well-maintained houses with long-term owners who don't mind the outdated kitchens, bathrooms, and general wear and tear. Such factors probably make a negative first impression on prospective buyers who want to move into a perfect house requiring no work, and thus lower the selling price. This is where your educated eye and willingness to roll up your sleeves can pay off: Visualize the home's possibilities and its future potential price relative to the rest of the neighborhood. Bear in mind that you never want to own the most expensive home in any neighborhood where nothing will catch up, pricewise. Given that the house is in your price range, and you can make selected improvements and enjoy it while you are adding value, then you may have found a winner.

Undertaking the improvement of an older house can uncover lots of unexpected costs, though. Older houses may not comply with current electrical and other building codes. If this is the case, every time you open up a wall the building inspector can require you to bring the wiring and electrical panels up to code. Determine how the house complies with building codes before you buy it and certainly before you begin the project. This will help you budget each phase of the project and eliminate many surprises.

Over the years the real estate and home improvement industries have consistently studied which projects earn back their costs at time of resale. The big winners are what our aforementioned senior has learned to live without: modernizing old kitchens and bathrooms as well as adding bathrooms. All of these earn back at sale at least 80 percent of your remodeling cost, and sometimes more than 100 percent in the case of a remodeled kitchen.

The appraisal and real estate industry listings categorize properties by the number of bedrooms and bathrooms. Adding bedrooms and bathrooms may move you into a higher-priced category in the eyes of both potential purchasers and appraisers looking for comparable sales. Carefully choosing what to do to a fixer-upper can compound the value and more than earn back your improvement costs.

The National Appraisal Institute has pointed out on its web site some home improvements that are wise investments and has indicated the percentage of your investment that can be regained at resale.

- *Remodeled kitchen—100 percent*. The rule is: Keep it simple. Extra money on expensive finishes and appliances not in keeping with the rest of the house will reduce payback.
- *Landscape improvements—100 percent*. Garden pots/beds and/or lawns are what potential buyers see first.
- *Fireplace—100 percent*. Fireplaces should be energy efficient. Buyers will envision warm gatherings around the hearth.
- *Second bathroom—100 percent*. A simple five-by-nine-foot second bathroom will make life more civilized. This addition may move your house up a category with more expensive houses.
- *Room addition—90 percent*. For best return at resale, the added room should be an additional bedroom or a family room.
- *Master bathroom—60–80 percent*. This is important to most buyers. If redoing or adding this bathroom, install two sinks and separate the toilet.
- *Expanded master bedroom suite—70 percent*. Adding square feet will usually require structural work and will diminish your return. When possible, combine or rearrange existing rooms/spaces to create an expanded space, including walk-in closets.
- *Deck—70 percent*. Outdoor living space is a desirable asset no matter where the locale. Zero-maintenance decking materials are a plus.

- *Exterior paint—50 percent.* Sprucing up tired siding, trim, and so on can lift years from the appearance of an older house. This adds only 50 percent because people expect fresh paint.
- *Finished attic—50 percent.* This can be especially attractive as an additional bedroom in a small house. If possible also add an adjoining bathroom.
- *Finished basement—40 percent.* This is a great way to add living space without building a more costly addition. A basement that has outside access increases value.
- *New heating system.* Replace the heating system only if the old system is nonfunctional. If replacing, add an energy-efficient furnace.
- *New windows and doors—35 percent.* Buyers appreciate changes that improve the looks, so attractive new French doors, for example, may be a plus. Buyers seldom consider energy-efficient windows at time of purchase.
- *Garage—30 percent.* A garage is desirable in a harsh climate and as a place to keep cars and other items stored securely.
- *Swimming pool—0 percent.* Unless you live where the sun always shines, this high-maintenance luxury item can detract from your resale profit, especially for buyers with small children.

This is not on the National Appraisal Institute's list, but according to Jay P. DeCima in his book, *Investing in Fixer-Uppers: A Complete Guide to Buying Low, Fixing Smart, Adding Value, and Selling (or Renting) High* (McGraw-Hill, 2003), a white picket fence is the most important thing that brings success at resale.

New Houses Outside the Beltway

Another way to get good value for your money is to find and buy a home further out and usually with a longer commute to work. Depending on your location, this can be either a new home in a new development or an older home in an outlying community.

New homes in new developments bring with them all that the adjective implies. They are usually designed with the new family and first-time buyer in mind. The trend is to have smaller rooms, but more of them; often each bedroom has its own bath or a well-located shared bathroom. The lots are usually small, but they often have a protected yard in which small children can play. The other advantage is that, depending on the stage of construction, you can choose finishes on floors, cabinets, countertops, and the like. There are typically fewer new homes than buyers. For this reason, after you choose the development, style, and floor plan, you may still have to wait six months to a year to move in.

Where there is one new development there are usually more. Large home-building corporations buy land when the area is in the master planning phase. If the area being developed is large enough, this often means the master plan calls for shopping centers and possibly new schools. Confirm these plans with the city or county planning department.

Large corporate home builders have researched who their buyers will be. The prices of their homes are attuned to what locals or commuters can afford—albeit often the higher end of the range, so you may have to stretch to qualify. If interest rates have been rising, the builder may "buy down" the interest rate available to buyers with local lenders to gain a competitive advantage for the project. This means the builder has purchased from a lender the ability to offer you access to lower-interest-rate mortgages when you buy a new home from them. Beware: this may still not be the lowest interest rate available if you have good credit.

Depending on location, buying early within a new development with a financially strong builder can mean avoiding price increases as that project and others get built out. Prices tend to increase as much as 10 percent to 20 percent in the first several years as the project reaches completion. This may mean parting with your down payment and then waiting in line for your home to be completed, but remember: your purchase price is fixed at the day you sign the contract, not at six months to a year later when you move in. Your risk is that interest rates may go up faster than your ability to pay the additional monthly payment amounts. This is where the builder's buy-down of the interest rate can be the deciding factor.

Given that you are on your own with the installation of decks and gardens, utilize the classes and employee experience at Home Depot and Lowe's Home Improvement Warehouse. Putting in a sprinkler system and building a wood, stone, or concrete patio or deck is not outside anyone's reach or ability to learn.

The top best-selling home repair books according to the *Wall Street Journal* and Amazon.com are:

- *Dare to Repair: A Do-It-Herself Guide to Fixing (Almost) Anything in the Home*, by Julie Sussman and Stephanie Glakas-Tenet (HarperCollins, 2002).
- *New Complete Do-it-Yourself Manual*, by Reader's Digest Association, Inc. (Reader's Digest, 1991).
- *Investing in Fixer-Uppers*, by Jay P. DeDima (McGraw-Hill, 2003).
- *The Complete Guide to Home Wiring*, revised, by Black & Decker (Creative Publishing International, 2001).
- *Home Comforts: The Art and Science of Keeping House*, by Cheryl Mendelson (Simon & Schuster, 1999).

What Does It Take to Qualify for a Loan?

Lenders require a certain ratio between your monthly income and the amount of the monthly mortgage payment at the time you apply for the loan. Depending on the different rules applied by various individual lenders, mortgage payments range from 30 percent to 50 percent of your income. This is where you must exercise caution! As houses have become more expensive and mortgages larger, lenders have increased the percentage of your monthly income they will allow to be apportioned to your mortgage payment. This is easy for them to say, but much harder for you to live with. A good rule of thumb is to pay no more than 3.5 times your stable annual household income for a house. Needless to say, this rule gets broken on both coasts.

As mortgage interest rates rise so do monthly mortgage payments. The result is that fewer people can qualify for a loan to buy the house they want. Mortgage rates in 2005 are near a 45-year low, driving up competition among buyers and thus housing prices. Table 4.4 shows how rate increases affect monthly principal and interest payments on typical 30-year fixed-rate loans. The right-hand column shows the approximate annual household income received at each interest rate if your monthly mortgage payments are 30 percent of your gross income.

Another potential downfall is that lenders look at *total household income* at the time the loan is written. In the statistically typical American household with both partners working, this means the combined income. If one person becomes unemployed for any reason, there will be an interruption in this two-income cash flow.

Lenders differentiate between salaried wage earners and the self-employed. The FHA, in contrast, is conservative and says that total monthly housing costs cannot exceed 29 percent of gross income for either salaried workers or the self-employed. The FHA defines total housing

TABLE 4.4 $300,000 Fixed Rate 30-Year Mortgage

Interest Rate	Monthly Payment	Annual Gross Household Income
5.0%	$1,610	$ 64,400
6.0%	$1,799	$ 72,000
7.0%	$1,996	$ 79,800
8.0%	$2,202	$ 88,000
9.0%	$2,414	$ 96,500
10.0%	$2,633	$105,000

costs to be the total of (1) mortgage payments, (2) mortgage insurance, (3) hazard insurance, and (4) property taxes. This is for conforming loans of $312,895 or less, which will be explained later. Some major lenders allow the amount of the mortgage payment alone to be 30 percent of self-employed net income or 40 percent of salaried workers' gross income. The 10 percent less for the self-employed is because self-employed people pay both the employer and employee parts of Social Security and the Medicare tax, and their income is thought to be less stable. It is a good idea to not allow your total mortgage payment, principal, interest, home-owner's insurance, property taxes, and, if required, mortgage insurance to exceed 38 percent of your gross pay. If you are a two-income family, study the potential impact on your budget if one of you were to stop working, even temporarily for a pregnancy or family leave. The 50 percent mortgage payment situation is usually for people with exceptional credit and low loan-to-home-value ratios. The lender's reasoning is that these people will figure out how to make the payments and not allow the home go into foreclosure and force it to be sold.

We started this process by creating a budget. If you rent, your monthly rent is probably in the range of 30 percent to 40 percent of your gross income. But remember, your landlord is responsible for property maintenance and taxes, and some or all of the utilities.

Let's look at the worst-case scenario and see what happens to your cash flow if your mortgage payments alone are 40 percent of gross pay:

Total pay check	100%
Less: federal, state, and local income taxes	–25%
Less: Social Security and Medicare tax	–8%
	67%
Less: maximum contribution to 401(k)	–15%
	52%
Less: mortgage payment allowed by lender	–40%
Less: property taxes, insurance, and utilities	–10%
Balance to live on	2%

Obviously, this doesn't work. Your first reaction is to delay contributing to your pension plan. However, these contributions are directly deductible from your gross income. If your employer offers a 401(k) defined contribution benefit plan, for each $1.00 contribution that you make in your 25 percent tax bracket your net cost is only $.75. If your employer makes a 50 percent matching contribution, then for $.75 you get $1.50 added to your 401(k)—a 100 percent return on your contribution. Even if you reduce your 401(k) contribution, don't cut it below the level at which your employer makes a matching contribution—this is free money you will be passing up. Let's look at other possibilities for stretching your dollars.

The Federal National Mortgage Association (Fannie Mae) has national statistics profiling borrowers' attitudes. For example, 83 percent of all American families stated their goal is to own their own home. In a January 6, 1998, speech James A. Johnson, the former chairman and CEO of Fannie Mae, recounted statistics from a national study describing five things that people are willing to do or give up in order to buy a house:

1. Sixty-one percent say they'd be prepared to take a second job.
2. Eighty-one percent say that they are prepared to have a longer commute.
3. Ninety-one percent say they're prepared to own a less expensive car.
4. Eighty-five percent say they'd be prepared to take shorter vacations.
5. Sixty-seven percent say that they would be willing to put off retirement for up to 10 years if that allowed them to have their own home.

Earlier in this chapter you saw an argument to buy the least expensive house in a more expensive neighborhood and fix it up. In this way you can use your ingenuity and hard work to improve the house and turn sweat equity into hard dollars when you sell. The caution is that if you borrow to the maximum some lenders will allow, you will become house poor and have nothing left over with which to make home improvements, let alone to live on. Count on spending 1 percent to 2 percent of your annual income on routine home improvements, and more for a fixer-upper depending on what improvements you intend to make.

Aside from the five ways just cited to help your dollars go further, the type of home loan you choose is another critical ingredient to your home-buying strategy. If your decision is to suffer the longer commute and buy a less expensive house or a less expensive fixer-upper, then you have probably also made the decision to stay in that house for about five years, sell it, and move to a new or better location. If this is your decision, there are types of home mortgages that are tailored to this strategy and have lower monthly payments. These lower payments, combined with tempering your mortgage-to-income ratio toward the 30 percent side of the range, will make you less house poor. Another rule of thumb is that the combination of your mortgage payment and any car and boat payments should not exceed 36 percent of your gross income. You will probably also embrace some or all of the suggestions from the Fannie Mae study. So accept the reality of the five points. Every family is house poor when they first buy a house.

Types of Loans

In 1949, during the Truman administration, the National Housing Act was passed. This created the Federal Housing Authority (FHA) and two quasi-public companies to purchase and resell home loans—Fannie Mae and Freddie Mac. At the end of World War II, 44 percent of American families owned their own homes; in 1947, there were 15 million American homeowners. Today 69 million, or 68 percent, of American families own homes.[4] Seventy percent of those homes with conforming mortgages are financed by loans created under FHA programs. There are many types of mortgage loans and loan prices. It is important to choose the correct loan based on your overall strategy. The key elements to consider are how long you intend to stay in the house and what your risk tolerance is in carrying a good variable-rate loan.

Conforming Loans

A loan is conforming because it is less than the maximum-size single-family home mortgage that Congress allows the FHA to originate with government guarantees. Likewise, it is the maximum size that Fannie Mae and Freddie Mac are authorized to buy from the originating lender and put into pools of loans that can be sold as mortgage-backed securities. For 2005 the basic standard FHA-insured loan size for a single-family home is between $172,632 and $312,895, depending on housing costs and the cost of living in different areas. In higher-cost-of-living areas the single-family limit goes up to as much as $469,344 (Honolulu). To check the limits in your area on single-family up to owner-occupied four-unit buildings, go to the Department of Housing and Urban Development web site's FHA Mortgage Limits page at https://entp.hud.gov/idapp/html/hicostlook.cfm.

Nonconforming Loans

Larger loans, sometimes called jumbo loans, charge a higher interest rate and are also usually securitized. Securitizing is the process of pooling 1,000 loans together and selling them to an insurance company or a pension fund that wants investments with predictable rates of return. Your lender, the loan originator, makes its money from the fees and charges from originating the loan and usually doesn't want to take the interest rate risk of holding the loan.

Loan securitization shifts the interest rate risk on a loan from the individual homeowner to the international capital markets. Without securitization the lender would have to hold the loan in its portfolio. This would force it to either charge higher interest rates for that risk or constantly adjust your interest rate every time its cost of funds went up. Securitization is big business and earns Fannie Mae, Freddie Mac, and the lenders big fees. Since the early 1990s Fannie Mae has increased the upper limits on its conforming loans from $109,000 to $359,650 in order to capture more of the securitization business. This is great news for borrowers because it means lower interest rates on a bigger variety of larger loans.

Loans and Their Place in Your Strategy

First let's look at your home ownership strategy. If you are lucky enough to buy a house you may stay in for 10 years or more in the neighborhood you want, consider a 30-year fixed rate loan. Although rates are going up, they are as low as they have been in 30 to 40 years. Unfortunately, today that doesn't mean that variable rate loans are that much cheaper. Anticipating rising interest rates and because of unusually high demand for variable rate loans, their rates are only marginally less than for a 30-year fixed rate loan. If you might stay only three to five years, then it is still worth pricing variable rate loan products that optimize your cost within that time frame. For example, a common variable rate loan product is one that keeps the rate fixed for five years and then adjusts the rate annually each year thereafter. Let's say the rate on this type of variable rate conforming loan is 5.5 percent, while it is $1\frac{1}{8}$ percent higher on the 30-year fixed rate loan. Over five years you would save $5,625 per $100,000 of loan amount with the lower interest rate on the variable rate loan. The discussion later on variable rate loans points out pricing circumstances when certain types of variable rate loans are cheaper in the long run than fixed rate mortgages.

Thirty-, Twenty-, and Fifteen-Year Fixed Rate Mortgages

Thirty-, twenty-, and fifteen-year fixed rate loans are amortized, which means that the interest rate and the amount of the monthly payments are fixed over the term of the loan. In the early years of the loan most of each payment is interest and there is minimal equity buildup. Not until about the 20th year of a 30-year amortized mortgage does the monthly equity buildup begin to exceed the interest paid. If you refinance this type of loan to get a lower monthly interest rate, you start all over again with each payment being mostly interest. The advantage of a 30-year fixed rate loan is that you always know what your payments will be.

A 15-year fixed rate mortgage has monthly payments almost twice those of a 30-year mortgage. These are popular with people planning to have their home loan paid off when they retire.

Split Payments

By asking your lender to allow you to evenly split your monthly pay-ment into two equal payments each month, you are paying down the loan principal faster each month. This simple process means that a 30-year mortgage gets paid off in about 20 years with a huge savings in loan interest. Splitting the monthly payments on a 15-year amortized loan means it is paid off in about eight years. One caution: in the month you switch to two payments there will usually be a full extra mortgage pay-ment because the new split payments must be made in advance of the mortgage due date, usually the first of the month.

Fixed, Then Variable Rate Mortgages

These are a type of variable rate mortgages because the initial rate is fixed for one, three, or five years and then the rate and payment size varies ac-cording to the cost of money index used by that lender. These loans are quoted, for example, as 5/1, meaning the rate is fixed for five years and then adjusts annually thereafter based on some lending index. The ad-vantage of these loans is that the initial interest rate is lower than the rate on a comparable 30-year fixed rate mortgage. This lower rate may be what you need to qualify for the loan in your house price range. The risk to you is that if the rate is higher when the fixed term runs out you will have to pay more. Following this borrowing strategy requires that you look at the total cost of your borrowing, assuming you will refinance at the end of your fixed term. This means adding the loan closing costs into your total cost of borrowing and comparing it to your savings, if any, compared to a fixed rate loan.

Variable Rate Mortgages

These loans probably yield the lowest initial mortgage payments, but the rate of interest, and thus the mortgage payment, can go up each month or quarterly if the index to which the loan rate is tied goes up. Just like with credit card teaser interest rates that start low and then go up, these rates can be used to get you to qualify for more house than you can afford. I normally cannot recommend these loans to anyone because I was advis-ing clients in 1978 when the prime rate went from 7 percent to 17 percent. Families saw their mortgage payments double in six months. The only way they could stop the escalation was to lock in a fixed rate loan at a very high cost. Before you even consider a variable rate, factor a 50 per-cent increase in your mortgage payment into your budget and observe the negative results.

One type of variable rate loan can, however, be very advantageous. Variable rate loans where the interest rate adjusts (increases) no more than two percentage points annually and no more than five percentage points over the 15- or 30-year term of the mortgage can actually be cheaper than a fixed rate mortgage if the pricing is right. Referring to Table 4.5, let's assume you want a $300,000 mortgage. If the initial difference in rates (spread) between this type of variable rate mortgage and a fixed rate mortgage is 3.5 percent at the time of loan origination, you are $15,000 ahead in cumulative interest cost in the first two years and not until year six do you break even (the variable rate catches up to the fixed rate). At a 4.0 percent difference you break even in year nine, but saved $18,400 during the first three years. At a 4.5 percent difference you are $23,000 ahead in the first three years and the total cost of borrowing will always be less for a mortgage with this 4.5 percent lower starting rate than had you taken out a fixed rate mortgage at the higher rate. Although I am not trying to encourage you into a higher-priced house you can't afford, the reality is that these lower borrowing costs in the early years may help you qualify for that perfect house. This is especially important when you are starting out or when your income will go up by more than the usual 3 to 4 percent annual increases.

Interest-Only Loans

Interest-only home loans were originally designed for young professionals who want smaller payments up front and who expect their annual incomes to increase rapidly. Because the monthly payment is smaller, they are able to qualify for a larger loan and thus more house at their income level.

These loans are popular with financially savvy people with good credit who live in areas with high home appreciation and whose mortgage payments are not a high percentage of their income. These loans are usually interest-only for three or five years and then become fully amortized with larger principal and interest payments at the current interest rate after the interest-only period. This means you are probably refinancing every three to five years and risk having to pay higher interest rates at the time of refinance. Even though this risk is minimal, if your income is fairly constant the interest rate increase or the switch to the higher amortized payments could be a hardship.

In high home appreciation areas the advantage of these interest-only loans is that the equity buildup comes through home appreciation and the leverage gained by using the lender's money to grow the value of your property. We switched to the word *property* because people using this approach commonly consider their home as an investment they just happen to live in. For example, if you put a down payment of $20,000 and borrowed $100,000 in an area with annually high historic home appreciation of 8 percent, then you are making $8,000 on your $20,000 investment, or a 40 percent annual return. If you combined this with your

TABLE 4.5 Comparisons of Fixed Mortgage Costs to Variable Mortgage Costs at Different Interest Rate Spreads

Example 1: 3.5 Percent Initial Spread with 5 Percent Maximum Rate Increase

	Fixed Mortgage Interest Rate Fixed at 7.0 Percent				Adjustable Rate Mortgage Interest Rate Starts at 3.5 Percent				
Year	Beginning Loan Balance	Equity Buildup	Annual Interest Cost	Cumulative Interest Cost	Beginning Loan Balance	Equity Buildup	Annual Interest Cost	Cumulative Interest Cost	Interest Savings
1	$300,000	$ 3,047	$20,903	$ 20,903	$300,000	$ 5,757	$10,408	$ 10,408	$10,495
2	$296,953	$ 3,268	$20,683	$ 41,587	$294,243	$ 3,058	$16,135	$ 26,543	$ 4,549
3	$293,685	$ 3,504	$20,447	$ 62,034	$291,184	$ 2,013	$21,798	$ 48,341	($ 1,351)
4	$290,181	$ 3,757	$20,194	$ 82,227	$289,171	$ 1,706	$24,537	$ 72,878	($ 4,343)
5	$286,424	$ 4,029	$19,922	$102,149	$287,465	$ 2,383	$24,343	$ 97,221	($ 4,421)
6	$282,395	$ 4,320	$19,631	$121,780	$285,082	$ 2,594	$24,132	$121,353	($ 4,502)
		$21,925				$17,512			

Example 2: 4.0 Percent Initial Spread with 5 Percent Maximum Rate Increase

	Fixed Mortgage Interest Rate Fixed at 8.0 Percent				Adjustable Rate Mortgage Interest Rate Starts at 4.0 Percent				
Year	Beginning Loan Balance	Equity Buildup	Annual Interest Cost	Cumulative Interest Cost	Beginning Loan Balance	Equity Buildup	Annual Interest Cost	Cumulative Interest Cost	Interest Savings
1	$300,000	$2,268	$25,413	$25,413	$300,000	$4,840	$13,401	$13,401	$12,012
2	$297,732	$2,468	$25,213	$50,626	$295,160	$3,299	$19,088	$32,489	$ 6,124
3	$295,264	$2,687	$24,994	$75,620	$291,861	$2,206	$24,724	$57,213	$ 271

74

Year	Beginning Loan Balance	Equity Buildup	Annual Interest Cost	Cumulative Interest Cost		Beginning Loan Balance	Equity Buildup	Annual Interest Cost	Cumulative Interest Cost	Interest Savings
4	$292,577	$ 2,924	$24,757	$100,377	4	$289,655	$ 1,786	$27,441	$ 84,654	($2,684)
5	$289,653	$ 3,182	$24,498	$124,875	5	$287,869	$ 1,963	$27,264	$111,917	($2,765)
6	$286,471	$ 3,464	$24,217	$149,092	6	$285,905	$ 2,158	$27,069	$138,986	($2,851)
7	$283,007	$ 3,770	$23,911	$173,003	7	$283,747	$ 2,372	$26,854	$165,840	($2,943)
8	$279,237	$ 4,103	$23,578	$196,581	8	$281,375	$ 2,608	$26,619	$192,459	($3,041)
9	$275,134	$ 4,466	$23,215	$219,796	9	$278,767	$ 2,867	$26,360	$218,819	($3,145)
		$29,332					$24,100			

Example 3: 4.5 Percent Initial Spread with 5 Percent Maximum Rate Increase

	Fixed Mortgage Interest Rate Fixed at 9.0 Percent					Adjustable Rate Mortgage Interest Rate Starts at 4.5 Percent				
Year	Beginning Loan Balance	Equity Buildup	Annual Interest Cost	Cumulative Interest Cost	Year	Beginning Loan Balance	Equity Buildup	Annual Interest Cost	Cumulative Interest Cost	Interest Savings
1	$300,000	$ 2,050	$26,917	$ 26,917	1	$300,000	$4,840	$13,401	$ 13,401	$13,516
2	$297,950	$ 2,242	$26,725	$ 53,641	2	$295,160	$3,299	$19,088	$ 32,489	$ 7,636
3	$295,709	$ 2,452	$26,514	$ 80,156	3	$291,861	$2,206	$24,724	$ 57,213	$ 1,791
4	$293,256	$ 2,682	$26,284	$106,440	4	$289,655	$1,786	$27,441	$ 84,654	($ 1,157)
5	$290,574	$ 2,934	$26,033	$132,472	5	$287,869	$1,963	$27,264	$111,917	($ 1,231)
6	$287,640	$ 3,209	$25,757	$158,230	6	$285,905	$2,158	$27,069	$138,986	($ 1,311)
7	$284,431	$ 3,510	$25,456	$183,686	7	$283,747	$2,372	$26,854	$165,840	($ 1,398)
8	$280,921	$ 3,839	$25,127	$208,813	8	$281,375	$2,608	$26,619	$192,459	($1,492)
9	$277,082	$ 4,199	$24,767	$233,580	9	$278,767	$2,867	$26,360	$218,819	($1,593)
10	$272,883	$ 4,593	$24,373	$257,953	10	$275,900	$3,151	$26,076	$244,895	($1,703)
11	$268,289	$ 5,024	$23,942	$281,896	11	$272,749	$3,464	$25,763	$270,658	($1,821)
		$36,735					$30,715			

own fixer-upper skills and bought the low-priced home in the expensive neighborhood, you could possibly do much better. Some people go into real estate sales and successfully use this approach to make big profits in the residential real estate market.

Purchase-and-Renovate Loans

As the name implies, these are loans for people who want to buy a home and immediately begin renovating and adding value to the home. These loans are offered nationally by General Motors Acceptance Corporation (GMAC), Wells Fargo Bank, and other lenders. When you read the following issues (cautions) it will become clear that these loans are for people with home renovation experience. Although there are minor variations, this is how the loans work:

- You go to the lender with a set of preliminary plans or sketches of what you want to do with a particular house. The lender has the house appraised as if the work were completed and bases the loan amount on that higher value. The lender will usually want to approve the final plans.
- Lenders are experienced in making loans on new home construction through a succession of loan draws to pay invoices submitted by a contractor as predefined parts of the job are completed and signed off by the city building department. Expect this process to be more difficult on a remodel. Some lenders will automatically add a 10 percent cost overrun amount to the loan balance to cover additional unforeseen costs.
- Your loan amount, including the cost overrun reserve, had better be enough to complete the work included in the appraised value because any additional funds required to complete the work will not be available, if at all, until the work is done.
  - The timing of when funds are released varies among lenders, but usually will cause timing problems. You, the owner or owner/contractor, must advance the money for architectural drawings and any engineering while you apply to the city building department for a permit to do the work. It is important to know up front whether this will be an easy process or one involving variances to the building codes that can take time and add risk that your project will not be approved for construction.
  - The second difference among lenders is whether you can get monetary credit for any work you do yourself rather than hiring a contractor, subcontractor, or designer to do that part for you. If you cannot get credit for any work you do, then the loan amount must include all the contractor's fees and any overages.
  - A caution regarding overages: If you are improving an older house, expect to have wiring and plumbing that needs to be brought up to

current building code standards. These improvements may or may not add value to the appraisal, so make sure such hidden costs are included in the total.

Also expect to pay interest on the full loan amount even before the re-model begins. This will test your skill in getting the project approved and work completed on a timely basis and most importantly within the amount the lender has budgeted for completion.

Builder Buy-Downs

Large-scale new home builders often purchase a preferential interest rate for their buyers from a financial institution. This is called buying down the interest rate. It is a marketing tool and can be an advantage to the buyer if that institution in fact has the lowest rate.

Borrower Buy-Downs and Loan Points

Individual borrowers are also allowed to pay money up front and obtain a lower long-term fixed mortgage rate—thus buying down the rate. This is essentially the same thing as paying percentage points as part of the loan fee at loan closing. One point is the equivalent of one percentage point, or $1,000 per $100,000 of loan amount. This brings us back to the question of how long you intend to stay in the house, or how long before you intend to refinance the house. One point up front is the equivalent of a quarter-percentage-point decrease in the interest rate over four years on a 30-year mortgage. This means you have to stay in the house and not re-finance for four years to earn back the one point you paid up front. If you intend to stay in the house and think interest rates are going to go up and not down, this is a good idea.

Veterans Administration Loan Programs

Twenty-nine million veterans of the armed forces are eligible for Veterans Administration (VA) loans. These loans are made by a lender, such as a mortgage company, savings and loan, or bank. The VA's guarantee on the loan protects the lender against loss if the payments are not made, and is intended to encourage lenders to offer veterans loans with more favorable terms. The amount of guarantee on the loan depends on the loan amount and whether the veteran used some entitlement previously. With the current maximum guarantee, a veteran who hasn't previously used the benefit may be able to obtain a VA loan up to $359,650, depending on the borrower's income level and the appraised value of the property. The local VA office can provide more details on guarantee and entitlement amounts.

Two helpful web sites are www.valoans.com/va_facts_limits.cfm and www.homeloans.va.gov/veteran.htm.

According to the VA, veterans should consider some of the advantages of VA home loans before arranging for a new mortgage to finance a home purchase.

- The most important consideration is that no down payment is required in most cases.
- Loan maximum may be up to 100 percent of the VA-established reasonable value of the property. Due to secondary market requirements, however, loans generally may not exceed $359,650 with no down payment.
- Flexibility of negotiating interest rates with the lender.
- No monthly mortgage insurance premium to pay.
- Limitation on buyer's closing costs.
- An appraisal that informs the buyer of property value.
- Thirty-year loans with a choice of repayment plans:
  - Traditional fixed payment (constant principal and interest; increases or decreases may be expected in property taxes and homeowner's insurance coverage).
  - Graduated payment mortgage (GPM)—low initial payments, which gradually rise to a level payment starting in the sixth year.
  - In some areas, growing equity mortgage (GEM)—gradually increasing payments with all of the increase applied to principal, resulting in an early payoff of the loan.
- For most loans on new houses, construction is inspected at appropriate stages to ensure compliance with the approved plans, and a one-year warranty is required from the builder that the house is built in conformity with the approved plans and specifications. In those cases where the builder provides an acceptable 10-year warranty plan, only a final inspection may be required.
- An assumable mortgage, subject to VA approval of the assumer's credit.
- Right to prepay loan without penalty.
- VA performs personal loan servicing and offers financial counseling to help veterans avoid losing their homes during temporary financial difficulties.

To find out more go to: www.homeloans.va.gov/lgyinfo.htm.

Government-Subsidized First-Time Buyer Programs

The FHA sponsors a number of loan programs for first-time buyers using conforming loans ($172,632 up to $469,344 in high-cost areas). Many of these loan programs are done in conjunction with state authorities. These are spelled out in detail on the FHA web site (www.fha-home-loans.com).

An example is the FHA-insured "CHAFA" mortgage loan program operated by the California Housing Finance Authority (CHFA). This program and others like it are designed to provide up to 100 percent of home loan financing to prospective eligible first-time home buyers. The California Housing Finance Authority describes these loans:

> Generally, the loan consists of a standard 97 percent FHA–CHFA fixed-rate 30-year mortgage and a 3 percent CHFA down payment assistance second mortgage, which is also called a "sleeping" or "silent" second. The second mortgage is offered for 30 years at 3 percent simple interest. All payments are deferred on this second mortgage until one of the following happens: the CHAFA first mortgage becomes due and payable; the first mortgage is paid in full or refinanced; or, the property is sold.
>
> The CHFA 100 Percent Home Loan Program is available to all low-income home buyers in all 58 counties in California. Moderate-income home buyers are eligible only in certain counties.
>
> In order to qualify for a CHFA loan, certain eligibility requirements must be met:
>
> - Annual household/family income does not exceed income limits for the family size and county in which the home is located. These average county income statistics are available from your state housing authority, usually on its web site.
> - Property must be owner-occupied for the term of the loan or until sold.
> - Credit, income, and loan requirements of the CHFA lender and the mortgage insurer must be met.
> - Be a first-time home buyer, which is defined as a person(s) who has not had an ownership interest in their primary residence during the previous *three* years. This requirement is waived if property is located in a federally designated Target Area.
> - Have sufficient funds available to meet the required down payment: 3 to 5 percent plus closing costs. Some restrictions apply to gift funds.
> - Have the legal right to permanently reside in the United States.
>
> CHFA loans are subject to a federal income tax recapture that borrowers may have to pay if they sell or transfer their CHFA-financed home within nine years.[5]

Learn more about CHFA loans at www.fha-home-loans.com /chafa_fha_loan.htm.

Types of Lenders

Banks

Banks are not all created equal. Small community banks specialize in serving a local community. Regional banks operate in surrounding states and are similar, but offer more business-related services. Big national banks offer a full range of national and international services, many of which are of little or no interest to the average consumer. What you do want to know about a bank is the range of its ATM network and how many services are available to you for free or at a reduced fee.

The size of a bank's ATM network is important because when you go to another bank's ATM or a privately owned ATM, you pay a fee of $1 to $3 per transaction. If you use the ATM that does not belong to your bank often, these fees can add up significantly. It's better to stick with a bank in your community or travel radius that has lots of ATMs.

From a short list of banks in your locale with plenty of ATMs, ask what services they provide for free if you take out a home mortgage with them. This can include free home banking, no-fee credit cards with overdraft protection, and free checking. It also can include free automatic deposit of your paycheck. Often if you use automatic deposit and allow the bank to automatically debit (withdraw) mortgage payments from your account the bank reduces the interest rate on new home mortgages. Make sure you can specify the date of the automatic mortgage payment so it comes after your paycheck is deposited.

Mortgage Brokers

Mortgage brokers are individuals from organizations licensed by the state to originate home mortgages for a fee. They have a stable of banks and nonbank lenders for whom they originate loans. Their fee is usually higher than the origination fee (loan points) charged by a bank, but they can be invaluable if you have less than perfect credit or a hard-to-explain self-employment situation. Their fees are earned in finding you the best-priced loan for your situation. Mortgage brokerage companies may use the wholesale division of your bank and act as an agent to lend to you. They will typically obtain the money wholesale at a discount of one percentage point less than what the bank will charge you. The bank can justify this because it is not doing the work. The broker will then tell you it is adding a percent (one point) to the loan costs as its fee. Object to this and insist the broker cut its fee, because it was already paid by the bank. Except for its loan fee, which is usually an extra .5 percent (50 basis points or $5,000 for each $100,000 of loan amount), the rest of the broker's costs should be the same as those of a bank.

Nontraditional Banks

Nontraditional banks are corporations like Countrywide Mortgage, General Electric Finance, General Motors Acceptance Corporation, and large insurance companies that originate loans both directly and through mortgage brokers. Today Charles Schwab has a bank that underwrites mortgages. These lenders have started bank subsidiaries and are often very competitive with traditional banks. Just like traditional banks, Schwab wants to develop and expand a relationship with you.

Online Mortgage Quotes

Desktop loan underwriting, as is done on a desktop computer, combined with FICO scores, has made Internet loan quotes a reality. If you are salaried and have a good FICO score (650+), you can get numerous competitive quotes from www.lendingtree.com, www.e-loan.com, and others. If you are self-employed, many of the Internet lenders are far less attractive because you don't fit into a preconceived category that allows your loan to be easily securitized and sold.

Loan Closing Costs

When comparing loans, it is equally important to compare the costs imposed by the lender to originate and close the loan. These application and loan closing fees are a big source of income for lenders, but vary widely among types of lenders. Banks that want to encourage you to use multiple services may credit back fees for some of these services, especially if you are a premier or preferred banking customer. Whether these are costs that can be added to the loan balance or they must be paid in hard cash at the time of loan origination, they are still costs to be examined. Although Congress is putting pressure on lenders to control these costs, new costs seem to appear on loan closing statements.

If you do not have a history with a lender, it may require that you pay into an escrow account each month enough money to cover both your property taxes and your homeowner's insurance. Most of these escrow accounts don't pay interest on your balances. Another reason you don't want to escrow your property taxes is that for income tax planning reasons you may want to accelerate the second payment to take advantage of a higher income tax bracket and thus a larger deduction in the current year.

Congress enacted the Real Estate Settlement Procedures Act (RESPA) to give the U.S. Department of Housing and Urban Development (HUD) the authority to provide consumer protection in the real estate lending process. Lenders are required early in the process to provide a detailed estimate of the loan closing costs. Reputable lenders follow these rules because the penalties are harsh. The HUD web site has a great deal of valuable information (www.hud.gov/offices/hsg /sfh/res/respa_hm.cfm).

Private Mortgage Insurance

Private mortgage insurance (PMI) is required by the lender when a loan closes with less than a 20 percent down payment. This applies to loans on one- to four-unit residential housing. This insurance protects the lender from default losses in the event a loan becomes delinquent. By law PMI must be canceled when a homeowner's equity reaches 22 percent. Rates vary depending on the type of loan and the amount of the homeowner's down payment. There are also different PMI programs for loans defined as high-risk by Fannie Mae and Freddie Mac.

Home Inspection Services

When you buy a house, you should assume you will spend 1 percent to 2 percent of your annual income on home repairs and improvements. A new home will probably have a builder's one-year warranty, especially if the builder has uncompleted homes in the development. Older homes require that a professional inspect the house for potential problems before you sign. If problems are detected, you can probably obtain a price reduction or persuade the owner to fix them as part of your purchase contract. If you have the option, have repairs done now at the previous owner's expense. In this way you minimize your out-of-pocket costs.

Home inspection services that follow the standards of the American Society of Home Inspectors (ASHI) are a resource for home inspections for a fee (www.ashi.org). The inspectors examine 10 key elements of a home:

1. Attic
2. Crawl space
3. Floors
4. Insulation
5. Windows and doors
6. Appliances
7. Mechanical

8. Wiring
9. Plumbing
10. Foundation

Careful examination of the inspection reports is critical if repair work is recommended. There are numerous reports of disreputable contractors who use the inspection process as a way to generate work for themselves or for affiliated companies performing unnecessary repairs.

5

Paying for College with Other People's Money

I f your children are planning to go to college, you will have to consider how to fund their education as part of your retirement strategy. The funding strategies for the two are interdependent. Fortunately, funding the costs of a college education presents one of the best opportunities to use someone else's money to meet your goal.

The college planning process is about selecting schools that are a good financial and educational fit for the family. There are 2,450 four-year colleges in the United States.[1] Seventy-five percent of these are private schools costing $16,000 to $40,000 per year. Many state schools don't cost much less, especially if you pay out-of-state tuition because neither you nor the student are residents of that state. In-state public college costs have risen 7 percent per annum over the past 15 years and 14 percent this past year alone. Private college costs have risen only 6 percent in the past year.[2] As of this writing, tuition for in-state public colleges averages $15,000 per year. Out-of-state tuition is $20,000 to $30,000, similar to private college tuition. Elite private college tuition, however, is in the $35,000 to $40,000 range. Once you factor in that only 15 percent of students complete college in four years and 43 percent take more than five years, the sums needed to fund a college education are easily up into the six figures.

A six-year public college undergraduate completion track adds a new perspective to the cost of college:

	Per Year	Years	Total Cost
Public college in state	$15,000	6	$ 90,000
Public college out of state	$25,000	6	$150,000
Private college	$25,000	4	$100,000
Elite private college	$40,000	4	$160,000

Even if your children are young and won't be going to college for up to 15 more years, the amount you'll need to save is still pretty staggering.

Parents and students are desperate for information and practical guidance on how to cope with these spiraling costs. This desperation is understandable since half of American households have saved nothing toward college costs. They expect they can turn to college guidance counselors and financial aid counselors for advice. However, these counselors are busy and, at the high school level, may have as many as 1,000 college-bound students to advise in the course of a year. They are, as well, seldom trained in the complexities of college financial aid. Fortunately, there *is* money out there and you can take advantage of it if you know the ropes.

For starters, many middle-class and upper-middle-class parents wrongly assume that their incomes are too high for financial aid. In the 2003–2004 school year, colleges handed out $122 billion in financial aid,[3] much of it to people in middle and higher income brackets. This included $65.9 billion of low-interest-rate student loans that don't require any repayment until your student is out of college.[4] This allows you and the student to borrow and spread the cost of college over a number of years. The money borrowed is at tax-deductible low interest rates, and the repayment is made with inflation-reduced future dollars. By putting the money saved currently into tax-deductible retirement savings accounts that accumulate income tax free, you really make the system work for you!

One of the first things you need to know is that more than 95 percent of all financial aid is awarded by the individual colleges. Much of this is federal and state money filtered through the colleges in the form of gift aid—grants and scholarships. Private colleges tend to give out substantially more aid at the same income levels than public colleges. Why? Because the public colleges are bound to the Federal Methodology (FM) formula (more on that later); the private colleges, in contrast, have much more latitude to determine how the money is given out and to whom. This is particularly true of the second- and third-tier private colleges, according to Rick Darvis, founder of College Funding, Inc., whose network counsels thousands of students annually.[5]

Colleges are a multibillion-dollar business in the United States. They have marketing, sales, and production departments. Colleges compete for students to fill empty seats. The ratio between the acceptance letters issued and the number of students entering a college is as important in how a college is ranked as are the average test scores of entering freshmen. Except for a group of very prestigious schools, as much as you think your student is competing to get in, colleges are often competing with other colleges to get your student. If your student's test scores are within the school's acceptable range and the student writes a good essay, then you are more in the driver's seat than you may think.

The recent exception to this is public colleges in states under funding pressure because of budget problems. Cutbacks mean there may be more students qualified to be accepted than there are seats available. This is predicted to get worse as high school graduating classes grow. The graduating class of 2008 will be the largest in American history. This may alter or reduce your choices of schools, but not the availability of student aid.

Application Strategies

Applying only to colleges that are competing for the same students is risky. Stanford, Harvard, Princeton, and Brown Universities, the University of California at Berkeley, and the University of Michigan are all equally competitive in admissions. A good strategy is to balance your list of schools academically, financially, and socially. Include one or two that you can afford without aid. Your list should be balanced:

- So-called "reach" schools—25 percent.
- Likely to be admitted to schools—50 percent.
- Certain to be admitted to schools—25 percent.

Rule #1: Complete the college financial aid application as soon as possible after January 1st of your student's senior year in high school. This form must be completed annually by June 30th. Many schools require it be filed as early as February 1st (Duke University, Dartmouth College). Don't complete the application until after you have read this chapter.

To qualify for grants, scholarships, and loans, you must complete the federal government's Free Application for Federal Student Aid (FAFSA). Always complete a timely FAFSA application. This signals your interest in receiving financial aid, even if you think you do not qualify. Also consider including a private school that your student is certain to be admitted to and that is known to be liberal with financial aid. Once you receive a high financial aid grant letter, it can then give you some important leverage in approaching other schools for aid.[6] A word of caution if the student will be a first-year student. Acceptance letters from the colleges mostly come out at the same time and give you a short window in which to respond. You must be prepared to build a strategy and move quickly to contact colleges and plead your case. If your student is applying midyear or for other than the freshman year, this process is more difficult because acceptance letters seem to come out randomly.

When completing the FAFSA form, list at least six colleges in alphabetical order. These colleges will each get a copy of your financial aid request and see the other colleges to which you are applying. In addition to colleges you are interested in, list additional colleges with which your colleges of interest compete for students. The sidebar in the Princeton Review manual *The Best 357 Colleges* (Princeton Review, 2005), lists these colleges under three headings: "Applicants also look at and often prefer," "Sometimes prefer," and "Rarely prefer." This is another place where gamesmanship allows you to introduce competition between colleges into the application process.

According to Rick Darvis, applying for early decision will often cost you grant aid dollars. He likens applying for early decision to being overeager when you go to a new car dealer—you get the car, but not the best price.[7]

Remember that although applying for financial aid is formula-driven, after the formula establishes your family need for financial aid, the individual schools can reinterpret your need either on their own or because you appeal. Now, where is the money and how to get it?

What Is College Financial Aid?

Colleges no longer separate the admissions process from the granting of financial aid. Applying for and maneuvering to get financial aid are part of the admissions process. It is important to keep in mind that most financial aid for higher education is administered by the colleges and comes from a number of sources:

		2003–2004 Expenditures
Aid administered by colleges:		
Federal aid, grants, loans, tax credits	62%	$81.5 billion
State aid	6%	$ 5.6 billion
College aid (endowments)	17%	$23.2 billion
Nonfederal loans	7%	$11.3 billion
Subtotal	92%	$ 122 billion[8]

Aid administered by others:

Employer provided	5%
VA programs	2%
Private scholarships	1%
Total	100%

There are two types of financial aid:

1. *Self-help aid* consisting of interest-subsidized loans and work-study programs.
2. *Gift aid* consisting of grants and scholarships.

The amount and type of financial aid are based on two factors:

1. The student's *merit*—scholastic, athletic, musical, and so on.
2. The *financial need* of the student and his or her family. Most of the financial aid given by colleges and certainly by the government is based on financial need.

Top universities like Stanford, Harvard, and Princeton don't give scholastic merit aid. Their gift aid comes in the form of direct grants and tuition relief. The top private colleges price the cost of an education based on what the rich can afford to pay, and they discount to everyone else. Below the top tier of private schools, good students often get merit aid from the college's endowment funds.

Rule #2: If you don't ask for financial aid you usually don't get it.

Need-Based Financial Aid

Financial aid formulas are income-driven, not asset-driven. Need-based financial aid is awarded to families who demonstrate they are unable to pay their portion of the college bill based on federal government–mandated calculations to determine a family's expected family contribution (EFC). The EFC is a concept developed by Congress and the colleges that measures what the formula says families can afford to pay for college.

To determine whether you qualify for financial aid, start by taking a financial snapshot. You can do this at any time before your student starts the college selection process. Don't worry about inflation—the cost of college will probably go up faster than your income. But do not forget that it is your income the calendar year that begins while your child is a junior in high school that gets reported on the FAFSA form while they are

FIGURE 5.1   Flow Chart to Determine Adjusted Financial Need

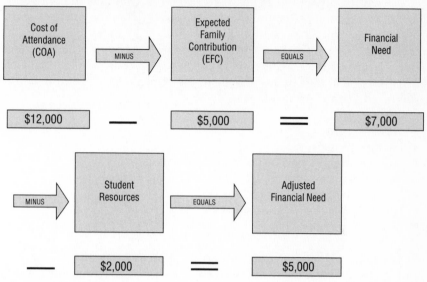

a senior. This will require you to estimate your income early in January the year they are a senior to get the form in on time. If your income turns out to be different when you compute it for income tax by April 15, you may amend the FAFSA form after your final tax return is completed. Assets, on the other hand, are a snapshot in time the day you sign the FAFSA forms. This means if you are going to divorce, transfer assets, come into an inheritance, or exercise stock options keep this date in mind.

As shown in Figure 5.1, the need-based analysis starts with what the college says is the annual cost of attendance (COA). Subtracted from the COA is the expected family contribution (EFC). Subtracted from this are any student resources available to the student other than parental assets used in determining the EFC. The adjusted financial need is the maximum amount of federal monies that can be distributed to the student to cover the cost of attendance. Private college endowment grants are in addition to federal monies. However, enrollment counselors at private and some public colleges have tremendous latitude to overlook or adjust income and asset items based on special circumstances and grant aid, especially when they think they are competing for a student.

Definitions

Cost of attendance (COA) consists of tuition, fees, room and board, books and supplies, personal expenses, cost of a computer, and transportation to and from college. The college must furnish the COA information, but colleges often do not include personal expenses (clothing and entertainment) and the transportation to and from college (airline or commuting by car). The true COA will enable the student to show more financial need. The COAs published by the colleges are used by Princeton Review (www.princetonreview.com) and Peterson's (www.petersons.com). Items usually not included by the college in the published COA, but that you should add in an appeal, are:

- Travel expenses.
- Phone expenses.
- Car on campus—gas, maintenance, insurance.
- Memberships—sorority/fraternity, clubs, professional groups.
- Fees and permits.
- Laundry, dry cleaning, personal sundries.
- Nighttime snacks—pizza fund.

The expected family contribution (EFC) measures what the formula says a family can afford to pay for college—in other words, how much the family is expected to contribute to the total cost of college for a single year. The complete U.S. Department of Education EFC computation forms for 2004–2005 are reproduced in an interactive computational format on my web site, www.RetireYes.com. The forms themselves do not contain much in the way of explanations or definitions, but definitions are organized from various sources on the following pages. From other sources you can access automated EFC forms, but the ones I have looked at don't show you enough detail to allow you to plan or shift assets between child and parents to maximize your benefit.

The expected family contribution (EFC) is computed from information you provide on the Free Application for Federal Student Aid (FAFSA). This form is used by most colleges and trade schools to gather the data that goes into other formulas. It must be completed and filed on time in order to qualify for any need-based aid and parental or student loans. The application should be completed online at www.fafsa.ed.gov to avoid input errors at the service center. This form should be completed as soon as possible after January 1 of your student's senior year in high school. The income of the parents and the student is assessed using the year-end data of what is called the base year—the calendar year prior to the year in which the student is entering college. For a student starting college in fall 2006, this would mean the prior year's income tax returns—the 2005 federal Form 1040. Even if you don't think you will qualify for gifts in aid you must still fill out the FAFSA form *on time* to qualify for student loans.

The assets of the parents and the student are assessed at the time the form is signed. This is critical in the timing of business valuations or divorce settlements. If possible, sign the divorce settlement before submitting the FAFSA. You will show less income and assets and be single. Also, don't convert an asset like your retirement account or home equity or sell your business for cash the day before you sign the form.

There are two formulas that can be used to calculate the EFC. These are the Federal Methodology (FM) formula and the Institutional Methodology (IM) formula. These same formulas apply to junior colleges, colleges, postgraduate schools, and trade schools.

The Federal Methodology (FM) formula is used by every accredited college to determine the amount of federal monies that can be distributed by the college to cover the student's COA. Income is 100 percent verified and assets are verified on 30 percent of the applications.[9] It is important to note that retirement account balances, home equity, and farm equity are exempt from consideration in this formula. Critical factors are income (when earned and by whom—family or student?) and assets (who owns?). Hence, you need to start the planning process early.

The Institutional Methodology (IM) formula was developed by the College Board, a trade association, and is an alternative formula used by 300 elite private colleges to calculate EFC. This formula includes home equity, equity in a family farm, and even siblings' assets. Some private schools add the value of an annuity and cash value of life insurance when totaling assets. This additional information is collected on their own financial aid forms and/or the College Scholarship Service (CSS) Financial Aid PROFILE application administered by the College Board. Most require federal income tax returns with all schedules attached, plus W-2s. Private college financial aid offices have considerable latitude in how they interpret items in this nongovernment formula when considering the granting of awards from their own pockets, including endowment and private scholarship funds.

Student Resources

This is the category that hurts, because the federal formula works dollar for dollar against students who are recognized by private scholarships and against well-intended parents who contributed to prepaid 529 plans. Student resources include:

- Employer-provided educational assistance.
- Private scholarships or grants.
- Veterans Administration benefits.
- Payments from prepaid tuition plans (prepaid 529 plans).
- Assets in Uniform Gifts to Minors Trusts.
- Payments for educational assistance other than family income and assets.

- Any sources other than immediate family income and assets (for example, grandparents' gifts).

These formulas are complex because of the different ways they classify income, assets, family size, and how close the parents are to retirement. Each element has a different percentage weighting to ultimately come up with your family's EFC. Once the EFC is calculated, it is compared by each school with the cost of attendance. The difference between cost of attendance and the EFC, less any student resources, is the family's financial need. This is the maximum amount of need-based federal grants-in-aid you will likely receive.

Figure 5.2 shows how the expected family contribution is computed. The elements are coded 1 through 4, and explanations of how each of

FIGURE 5.2 Expected Family Contribution (EFC) Computation

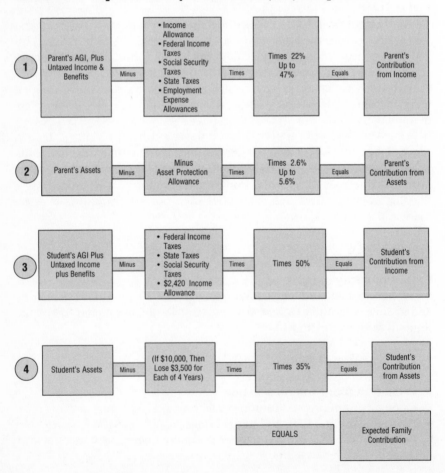

these elements is calculated follow. Employees who are participants in company 401(k) plans will be able to closely estimate their EFC if other income and their assets are not complicated. This will help you predict whether you qualify for financial aid. My web site has a template for this calculation based on the Department of Education's EFC formula, 2004–2005. Because of the variances in the formula for valuing a closely held business, the EFC you calculate may vary from the EFC returned to you and the colleges by the Department of Education's analysis. Also, the government calculates everything to three decimal points and then rounds to two decimal points at the end, which will cause differences.

Element 1—Parent's Contribution from Income

Parent's income is typically the adjusted gross income (AGI), line 35 at the bottom of the first page of your joint federal Form 1040, plus any untaxed income. If the parent is single, divorced, or a head of household it is the AGI on their individual return. Added back into income are untaxed income and benefits for that tax year:[10]

- Employee contributions to 401(k), 403(b), IRA, simplified employee pension (SEP), or Keogh retirement plans shown on that year's return.
- Tax-exempt interest.
- Workmen's compensation benefits.
- Child support received.
- Income exclusions (gain on a personal residence sold).
- Untaxed portion of retirement, pension, or life insurance withdrawals or benefits, excluding rollovers. This includes withdrawals from Coverdell Education Savings Accounts.
- Veteran's benefits.
- Social Security.

Items that are not included in income are:

- Loan proceeds.
- Gifts and support other than money.
- Contributions to flexible spending plans, including medical savings accounts and cafeteria plans.
- Federal and state disaster funds.
- Financial aid proceeds.

From your income you deduct the following items:

- Federal income taxes paid on the return, not including alternative minimum tax (AMT). The Hope and Lifetime Learning credits, which reduce the federal income tax, are added back.

- Any employment expense allowance shown on the W-2.
- Child support paid.
- Taxable grants and scholarships.
- Social Security tax—this is done by the Department of Education's EFC formula.
- State tax allowance—this is also done by the formula.
- Income protection allowance—this is automatically calculated by the formula based on the number of members in the household and the number of household members enrolled in college. Members of the household include anyone receiving more than half of their support. This can include foreign exchange students, student's or parent's unborn children, and grandparents in a nursing home. The definition is different from exemptions on a tax return.
- Employment expense allowance—a maximum of $3,000 for 2005–2006. It is calculated by multiplying the lesser of the father's or mother's earned income times 35 percent.

The resulting number is multiplied by a factor between 22 percent and 47 percent. Generally if your adjusted gross income from your federal 1040 is $65,000 or more the factor is 47 percent.[11] This amount is the parent's contribution from income.

Element 2—Parent's Contribution from Assets

Parent's assets are the current market value of your assets *on the day you sign the form*. For the Federal Methodology these assets are principally savings accounts, securities, second homes, businesses, and investment farms. Current market value means proceeds from a forced sale within 30 days. Although you report these at the current value, the Department of Education subtracts a discount of 40 percent on the first $100,000, 50 percent of the next $195,000, and 60 percent of the next $195,000, and excludes all value above $490,001 because of presumed lack of marketability, future tax liability, and any minority interests.[12] If you have a material participation in a business, farm, vineyard, orchard, and so on, it should be classified as a business to get the deepest discount in value.

For the Institutional Methodology (IM), the personal residence is considered an asset. Also included in assets under the IM formula are the value of annuities, the cash surrender value of life insurance and siblings' assets.

Not included as assets in the Federal Methodology formula are:[13]

- Balances in a 401(k), 403(b), IRA, and defined benefit Keogh, SEP, or other qualified retirement plan(s).
- Equity in your home or a family farm. Equity here means the fair market value, less related debt.

- Defined benefit pension plans are also not included because they are a promise by your employer to make *future* payments to you.
- Annuities.
- Life insurance.
- Financial aid.
- Personal items including collectibles.

From this net assets number the formula subtracts an Education Savings and Asset Protection Allowance. This is weighted based on the older parent's age and whether there are two parents. This is a sliding scale: the older you are, the more you move toward the 2.6 percent of the 5.6 percent to 2.6 percent range. Some examples are shown in Table 5.1.

Element 3—Student's Contribution from Income

Student's income is the adjusted gross income from his/her federal income tax return, plus any untaxed child support paid directly to the student. For the student, as is the case for the parents, this is the income earned in the tax year that began while they were a junior in high school (that is, the year before the FAFSA is filed when they are a senior). The student must add back into income any tax-deductible contributions made to a traditional non-Roth IRA.[14]

TABLE 5.1   Education Savings and Asset Protection Allowance, Selected Values

Age of Older Parent	Allowance If There Are Two Parents	Allowance If There Is Only One Parent	Age of Older Parent	Allowance If There Are Two Parents	Allowance If There Is Only One Parent
40	$37,300	$18,600	53	$51,700	$24,800
41	$38,200	$19,000	54	$53,200	$25,400
42	$39,200	$19,400	55	$54,500	$26,200
43	$40,200	$19,800	56	$56,200	$26,800
44	$41,200	$20,300	57	$57,900	$27,400
45	$42,200	$20,700	58	$59,600	$28,200
46	$43,300	$21,100	59	$61,400	$28,900
47	$44,300	$21,600	60	$63,200	$29,700
48	$45,400	$22,200	61	$65,100	$30,500
49	$46,600	$22,600	62	$67,300	$31,200
50	$47,700	$23,100	63	$69,200	$32,100
51	$49,200	$23,700	64	$71,600	$33,100
52	$50,400	$24,200	65 & over	$74,000	$34,100

Source: The EFC Formula, 2004–2005, U.S. Department of Education, page 19.

Deductible from this amount are:[15]

- Federal income taxes paid on the return, not including alternative minimum tax (AMT). The Hope and Lifetime Learning credits, which reduce the federal income tax, are added back.
- State tax factor plus Social Security taxes are computed by the formula.

The following four items may be deducted from income, but are considered student resources and have a dollar-for-dollar negative impact on financial aid eligibility:[16]

1. Child support paid by parents directly to the student.
2. Federal work-study or other need-based work programs if included in adjusted gross income (AGI).
3. Taxable grants and scholarships in excess of tuition, fees, books, and required supplies if included in AGI.
4. Allowances and benefits from AmeriCorps if included in AGI.

The student is also allowed a $2,420 income allowance. The student can have income up to this limit, but any income above $2,420 costs the student 50 cents on the dollar of eligibility for financial aid.[17]

Element 4—Student's Contribution from Assets

Student assets are any assets in custodial accounts and investment assets. Typically, the student has no other assets. Because any amount in this category is multiplied by a 35 percent factor, any assets in a student's own name can be costly: $10,000 of assets would cost $14,000 in aid eligibility over four years ($10,000 × 35% = $3,500 × 4). For the Federal Methodology, Coverdell Education Savings Account balances are considered the student's asset and the 35 percent factor applies.[18] If financial aid looks possible, or you are applying to private colleges and your student has assets in a Uniform Gift to Minors Trust, consider spending that money on a computer and a car for the student. If there is a large sum and your student is likely to go a school and stay there for four years, consider using the money for the down payment on a house or flat.

When these four elements are added up and munched by the formula, your expected family contribution (EFC) is the resulting number. This amount is returned to you with a cryptic explanation on the FAFSA Student Aid Report (SAR) form. If something clearly appears wrong, you should file a formal appeal.

Table 5.2 looks at comparative expected family contributions at various parental income and asset levels with either one or two students

TABLE 5.2   Expected Family Contribution: Effect of Multiple Students in School at Various Income Levels for a Five-Member Family (Federal Methodology Formula Only)

Parents' income	$75,000	$75,000	$100,000	$100,000	$150,000	$150,000	$200,000	$200,000
Assets	$50,000	$50,000	$ 50,000	$ 50,000	$100,000	$100,000	$100,000	$100,000
Number in college	1	2	1	2	1	2	1	2
EFC	$10,720	$ 5,350	$ 19,460	$ 9,730	$39,080	$ 19,540	$ 53,500	$ 26,750

in college at the same time. Assume in the column where the EFC is $5,350 you are looking at a state college with a COA of $18,000. In this state college example, the $12,650 of annual aid would come in the form of student loans payable after college is completed. The cutoff point above which no federal aid grants are available is an EFC of $3,800 (2003–2005).[19]

As mentioned, college planning and retirement planning are interdependent. Had you put $6,000 into your employer-provided 401(k) plan with a 50 percent employer match, you would have saved $5,540 from the combination of $1,100 tax savings from a lower taxable income, $1,440 in your reduced EFC, and $3,000 in employer matching. This works particularly well when household income is less than $100,000.

The columns show the striking difference in parental EFC (approximately one-half), when the second student starts college. The lower EFC could expand your list of possible schools to include private colleges that may previously have been outside your financial reach. Remember that private colleges have endowment funds available that public colleges do not.

A third observation is that even when the EFC is $53,500, don't assume because you do not qualify for financial aid that you never will. Your family circumstances may change because of divorce, death, unemployment, or disability. These are also special circumstances that can be documented and explained to the financial aid officer at the college, even after you have been rejected for financial aid or received an award letter. If your income went from $200,000 to $100,000, your EFC would drop by $34,068 to $19,432. If this happened midyear you could petition, but only if you had filled out the FAFSA form before the March deadline the previous year. Complete and file the form to be safe.

Emancipate Your Student

If a student is or becomes a so-called independent student, the family income and assets are not considered in the Federal Methodology EFC formula. Emancipating your child has many significant advantages at all parental income tax levels. Although support provided by parents is considered income to the student in the EFC formula, proper planning can minimize the negative impact. An independent student is someone who meets one of the following seven criteria:

1. Is at least age 24 by December 31 of the school year and is not a dependent of someone else (parents) based on the IRS definition of support. Support includes:[20]
   - Rental value of lodging furnished.
   - Cost of all items paid out directly or for the benefit of the dependent: clothing and food, education, medical and dental care and insurance, gifts, transportation, entertainment and recreation, and capital expenditures for automobiles, furniture, appliances, and so on.
2. Is a veteran of the U.S. armed services or one of the service academies. You must have been on active duty. This does not include the National Guard or a reserve enlistee.
3. Is a graduate or professional student. Most medical (M.D. and D.D.S.) programs still require the inclusion of parental assets.
4. Is a married student.
5. Is a ward of the court, unless a legal guardian has been appointed and required to provide support. Neither foster parents or stepparents are considered when determining a student's dependency status.
6. Both parents are deceased.
7. Has legal dependents other than a spouse. A legal dependent is any person who lives with the student, including an unborn child, and receives more than one-half of their support from the student and will continue to receive that support during the school year. This may be a natural or adopted child or a child for whom the student is legal guardian.

The student's income, minus federal income taxes and Social Security taxes paid, an allowance for state taxes, and an income protection allowance of $5,490 for a single independent student, is multiplied by a .50 factor. Education credits (Hope and Lifetime Learning tax credits) are added back into income, as are taxable earnings from need-based workstudy and employment portions of fellowships. Also added back into income are distributions taken from an IRA for education expenses.

Investment assets, plus cash in the bank, are multiplied by a .35 factor. Student loan proceeds put in your bank account are not considered an assessable asset. The sum of these two amounts (income and assets) is the student's EFC. FAFSA Worksheet 2 requires that cash received or any money paid on the student's behalf, not reported elsewhere, be added to income. For married students and students married with children, the income protection allowance goes up.

It is worth repeating that student resources reduce aid availability dollar for dollar. Any employer-provided benefits are considered a student resource and reduce eligibility for aid dollar for dollar.

Parental contributions can reduce aid by 50 cents on the dollar, as shown in Table 5.3. A single student may earn $20,000 per year by working 26 hours a week during school months and 40 hours per week in the summer earning $15 per hour. After income taxes and Social Security tax, this leaves approximately $1,300 per month from earnings to live on. Notice the effect of a $9,500 parental contribution. This $9,500 of assistance could reduce possible financial aid by $4,750—50 cents on the dollar.

It is also worth repeating that the 300 top private schools that use the institutional method (IM) formula and require the CSS/Financial Aid PROFILE form add back additional items into both income and assets, but this varies by school.

Higher-income parents who with an AGI above $53,000 (2005) if single and $107,000 (2005)[21] if filing jointly lose the benefit of the Hope and Lifetime Learning credit and lose the benefit of the dependent exemption above $142,700 if single, $178,350 if head of household, and $214,050 if filing jointly in 2004.[22] The examples in Table 5.3 have the parents providing less than half of the now-independent child's support. Students with income below $29,050 are in the 15 percent federal income tax bracket. If the college has a COA above their income level (EFC), they demonstrate a financial need and qualify for need-based loans and, if a private college, endowment grants. Our independent student earning $20,000 qualifies to use the Hope or Lifetime Learning tax credit, even if it has to be added back into income. In the 15 percent tax bracket this student still nets almost $1,000. The subsidized federal loan he or she qualifies for is interest-free until after leaving school. Any unsubsidized loan is at a very low interest rate.

Another avenue for self-employed parents and small business owners is to hire their child, presuming they can prove the child is productively working. The parent deducts the wages as a business expense and the child

TABLE 5.3 Expected Family Contribution—Independent Student with Assets of $3,000, EFC at Various Income Levels (Federal Methodology Formula Only)

Student's income	$15,000	$15,000	$20,000	$20,000	$25,000	$25,000	$30,000	$30,000
Provided by parents	$ 0	$ 7,400	$ 0	$ 9,500	$ 0	$12,000	$ 0	$14,000
EFC	$ 728	$ 4,428	$ 2,541	$ 7,291	$ 4,350	$10,350	$ 6,158	$13,158

is in a low 10 or 15 percent tax bracket. In this example, our student working in the family business and earning $25,000 can save the parents about $3,000: the tax savings minus Social Security taxes paid on the employee. Additional savings can come from medical and other benefit programs provided by the employer/parent, but not considered income to the student.

Appeal Letters to Correct or Clarify Your Financial Situation

After you have completed the FAFSA applications and have your EFC, you may find errors or experience a change requiring an appeal. This should be done in writing directly to the college financial aid officer. Financial aid officers are able to use their professional judgment to reclassify items and restate income if it was reported incorrectly or has changed. Professional judgment is not limited to the items cited on the financial aid application. This is particularly important when you might be considered for merit aid. Additional special circumstances include:

- Ask to adjust your EFC if you or the student has unusual nonrecurring items on your income tax return such as a one-time bonus or stock transaction included in income.
- Independent students should ask to have their income adjusted to reflect a lower earned income while attending school.
- Ask to adjust the COA to reflect actual costs of attendance including travel and extras that are not included in the published number. (You will not be the first to request this.)
- Ask to be changed from dependent to independent student status because of a change in circumstances. (Compute this first on your own to see the effect.)
- Ask to have your income and assets reduced if there has been damage due to a federally recognized disaster.
- Ask to have a younger child's elementary or high school tuition deducted from your income.
- Ask to have excessive medical and dental costs subtracted.
- Ask to have income adjusted if you or your spouse is transferred or unemployed.
- Ask for consideration if there is a divorce, separation, or the death of a parent.
- Present any other special circumstances that will allow you to negotiate directly with the financial aid officer.

Hope and Lifetime Learning Credits

Your eligibility or that of your student for these credits depends on how a college applies grants and scholarships; these credits are phased out at higher levels of adjusted gross income. However, one-third of these credits, or $3.8 billion, goes to taxpayers earning more than $60,000.[23]

The Hope scholarship credit provides a maximum $1,500 federal income tax credit for the first two years of postsecondary education. This credit is equal to 100 percent of the first $1,000 of qualified tuition paid by the taxpayer and 50 percent of the next $1,000. The maximum Hope credit allowed per student is $1,500.[24]

The Lifetime Learning credit allows a federal income tax credit of 20 percent of the first $5,000 of total qualified tuition paid by the taxpayer for any year the Hope credit is not claimed.[25] Qualified tuition and related expenses do not include room and board, books, student health, food, or transportation. Critical to note is that the amount of qualified tuition paid and related expenses paid is reduced dollar for dollar with any tax-free funds (such as scholarships or Pell grants) in computing the credit for both the Hope and Lifetime Learning credits.

Colleges often allow you to apply the scholarship monies to either tuition or room and board. Apply only enough to room and board to get the full Hope credit. This portion of the grant applied to room and board will become taxable income, but the credit is usually more valuable from a tax standpoint.

These credits phase out in 2003 for single taxpayers with an AGI above $53,000 and married taxpayers filing jointly with AGI above $107,000.[26] Investigate moving any expenses from itemized deductions to business or farm expenses where they will reduce AGI.

You may elect not to take the Hope or Lifetime Learning credits in order to take full advantage of distributions from Coverdell Education Savings Accounts and other qualified tuition plans.

Grants and Scholarships

A federal Pell grant is a gift ranging up to $4,050 per year for undergraduate students. The EFC must be less than $3,800 to qualify. The minimum grant is $400.[27] In 2005 these grants will total $12 billion and account for 12 percent of all federal student aid. For 2005 the income restrictions have been tightened for parents earning more than $15,000.

Loans—Government-Subsidized

Federally subsidized Stafford loans are variable-rate, need-based undergraduate loans with maximum amounts that vary by school year. If you're a dependent student, each year you can borrow:

- Up to $2,625 if you are a first-year student enrolled in a program of study that is at least a full academic year.

- Up to $3,500 if you have completed your first year of study and the remainder of your program is at least a full academic year.
- Up to $5,500 if you have completed two years of study and the remainder of your program is at least a full academic year.
- Up to $8,500 per year for graduate and professional students.

The need-based amount is determined by subtracting from the school's COA your EFC and any Pell grant monies. The remainder is your financial need. To qualify, your EFC must be below $3,800.

The interest is paid (subsidized) by the federal government until six months after the student leaves school. The interest rate is currently (2005) 2.77 percent and is capped at 8.25 percent. If the student makes the first 48 monthly payments on time, the rate is dropped by 1 percent.

Federal Perkins loans are low-interest-rate need-based loans ranging up to $4,000 per year. The amount of the loan is determined by the college. These loans are in the student's name. Repayment begins after the student leaves school.

Loans—Nonsubsidized

Nonsubsidized Stafford loans to students, Parent Loans for Undergraduate Students (PLUS loans), and federal income tax credits account for 45 percent of all federal aid to postsecondary students and their parents.[28]

Unsubsidized Stafford loans are not need-based. They require the completion of a timely FAFSA application. The interest is not subsidized by the federal government and starts accruing immediately while the student is in school. The current rate is 2.77 percent. Repayment begins six months after the student leaves school. If you are a dependent student, each year you can borrow:

- Up to $2,625 if you are a first-year student enrolled in a program of study that is at least a full academic year.
- Up to $3,500 if you have completed your first year of study and the remainder of your program is at least a full academic year.
- Up to $5,500 if you have completed two years of study and the remainder of your program is at least a full academic year.
- Up to $8,500 per year for graduate and professional students.

If you are an independent undergraduate student or a dependent student whose parents have applied for and were unable to get a PLUS loan (a parent loan—see the next section), each year you can borrow:

- Up to $6,625 if you're a first-year student enrolled in a program of study that is at least a full academic year (at least $4,000 of this amount must be in unsubsidized loans).

- Up to $7,500 if you've completed your first year of study and the remainder of your program is at least a full academic year (at least $4,000 of this amount must be in unsubsidized loans).
- Up to $10,500 if you've completed two years of study and the remainder of your program is at least a full academic year (at least $5,000 of this amount must be in unsubsidized loans).
- Up to $18,500 per year for graduate and professional schools.

More information about Stafford student loans can be found on the Department of Education's web site at http://studentaid.ed.gov/PORTALS WebApp/students/english/index.jsp.

Federal Parent Loan for Undergraduate Students (PLUS) program loans are not need-based loans. The interest is not paid for by the government, and repayment begins immediately. The first payment is due within 60 days after the final loan disbursement for the period of enrollment for which you borrowed. Repayment is both loan principal and interest. The interest rate adjusts annually in July (2005 = 4.17 percent) with a maximum rate of 9 percent. The amount of federal PLUS monies a parent can borrow is limited to the cost of attendance (COA) minus the financial aid award offered the student. For example, if the COA is $16,000 and financial aid equals $4,000, then the amount that the parents can borrow is $12,000. These are signature loans by the parent with no collateral required. Only one parent must sign. If the signatory parent dies or becomes disabled before the loan is repaid, the remaining balance is forgiven. PLUS loans may be consolidated and repaid over 30 years. If the first 48 payments are on time and the payments are automatically deducted from your bank account, the rate is dropped 2 percent. Learn more about PLUS loans at the Department of Education's web site at http://studentaid.ed.gov/students/publications /FYE/2003_2004/english/plus-loansparents.htm.

Sallie Mae has a student PLUS loan program called Signature Student Loan. These loans are in the student's name, but the parents must co-sign. These loans are not repaid until after the student leaves school. These are an alternative for students who do not qualify for subsidized loans. The interest rate is prime plus 2 percent. This means 7.25 percent as opposed to 4.17 percent on a Stafford or federal PLUS loan. For details go to the Sallie Mae web site at www.salliemae.org. These rates change in July each year.

Most states have student loan programs. **State loan programs** vary, so contact the state's higher education department for details.

College Saving Alternatives

State Section 529 College Savings Plans

Section 529 plans, named after the section of the Internal Revenue Code that governs them, are college savings plans authorized by the states, but administered by outside investment firms. Section 529 savings plans allow each donor to gift as much as $55,000 in cash per student in a one-time contribution and avoid gift tax. After this "front loading" provision expires, normally you can gift $11,000 for each donor per year free of gift tax. The contributions are made with after-tax dollars, but the income accumulates and distributions are tax-free if used for qualified postsecondary school educational purposes at any accredited college. Taxpayers in the highest tax brackets benefit the most from 529 plans. There is no income restriction on contributions. The tax-free status of investment income withdrawals is scheduled to end in 2011. Some states allow some offset against state income taxes for 529 contributions to their state plans. These are considered parental assets and assessed at the 5.6 percent rate in the EFC computation.

If funds are withdrawn in excess of qualified educational expenses (the COA set by the college) the excess distributions are included in the gross income of the recipient, plus there is a 10 percent penalty tax. Unused amounts can be transferred to another beneficiary in the same family to be used for qualified educational expenses.

In 2003, Americans put $38 billion into state 529 plans. By 2007, contributions are expected to reach $200 billion. Recently, states have allowed mutual funds sold by investment advisers to increase their fees into the 5 percent range to encourage financial planners to recommend these state 529 plans. These commissions, plus annual fund expenses and state management fees, mean the first-year load is about 6 percent to 7 percent. Funds purchased directly from Vanguard or TIAA-CREF or purchased through your employer can reduce these fees. The TIAA-CREF 529 plan available in New York has a low 0.60 percent annual fee.[29] TIAA-CREF also offers 529 plans in 11 other states with a slightly higher expense ratio, but also with no sales load (commission). Check the www.tiaa-cref.org web site for more information. Vanguard offers plans in Iowa and Nevada with a 0.65 percent fee and no load. Do a Google search on 529 plans to find what is available in your state.

These 529 plans offered by major mutual fund companies and administered by the states have limited investment options. Many of the plans use age-based investment portfolios. As the student gets closer to starting school the asset allocation shifts to bonds.

Prepaid 529 Plans

Not all states offer prepaid 529 plans, and some states that initiated them have suspended the plans due to unusually high increases in tuition costs coupled with low investment yields on plan assets. These plans allow you to buy future tuition at today's prices, but only for state colleges in your state of residence. Colorado and Texas are among the states that have suspended their plans. Perhaps the biggest downside is that assets in these plans are considered a student resource and reduce qualification for financial aid dollar for dollar.

Independent 529 Plans

Approximately 240 private colleges in 38 states will allow you to invest in independent 529 plans and get future tuition at a discounted rate. Among them are Princeton, Notre Dame, Stanford, Rice, and Southern Methodist Universities, the University of Chicago, Amherst College, Boston College, and Middlebury College. The full list is at www.indepen dent529plan.org. Here is how it works: If you contribute $10,000 in hopes of sending your student to a college that now charges $20,000, you have locked in one-half of one year's cost. If next year you contribute another $10,000 when costs have gone to $25,000, you have locked in an additional 40 percent, totaling 90 percent of one year's future costs. Many allow you to invest up to $200,000. I take this to mean that they anticipate the average $35,000 annual cost today will grow to $50,000 a year in six to seven years.

These plans may work for your family if the private college of your choice is on the list. Monies invested in these plans may be shifted to another beneficiary in the same family. You may also withdraw the funds at a capped 2 percent earnings or annual loss rate and put them into a state 529 plan. These monies also are a dollar-for-dollar deduction against eligible financial aid.

Coverdell Education Savings Accounts

Formerly called Education IRAs, these plans allow families with an adjusted gross income up to $220,000 ($110,000 for separate return filers) to save $2,000 per year for educational expenses. The amount of your annual contribution starts to phase out when your joint AGI goes above $190,000 ($95,000 for separate return filers). Distributions are tax-free and can be used for K through 12 educational expenses. The assets belong to the beneficiary at majority at either age 18 or 21, depending on state law. These plans allow more investment options.

Custodial Accounts—Trusts

These trusts are created under the Uniform Gifts and Transfers to Minors Act. Under the new tax rules, dividends and capital gains are taxed at the new low 5 percent rate in the child's tax bracket. Until age 14, the first $750 of investment income would be tax-free thanks to the child's standard deduction. The next $750 would be taxed at 5 percent. Investment income in excess of $1,500 for the child under 14 is taxed at the parent's income tax rate, the so-called "kiddie tax."[30] After age 14, the 5 percent rate on investment income applies up to $29,050 when the child moves out of the 15 percent income tax bracket.

An interesting strategy is to transfer appreciated stock to the trust for a child who is age 14 and older. Provided their income remains below $29,050 where the 15 percent tax rate peaks, the capital gains tax on their sales will be only at the 5 percent rate, instead of at your 15 percent. This also would work if they are under age 14, but at least 14 when the stock is sold. The 5 percent capital gains rate is applicable until 2007 and falls to 0 percent in 2008 before it reverts to whatever Congress dreams up next.

The biggest drawback of these trusts is that the assets are irrevocably transferred to the child, who has access to the assets after reaching the age of majority, either 18 or 21 depending on the state. For the financial aid EFC computation, these assets are assessed at the student's 35 percent rate. If you qualify for financial aid, it would be more prudent to use the trust assets for the benefit of the child *before* the taxable year during which the student becomes a senior in high school. This will keep them out of the EFC computation.

Income tax returns due April 15 the year your child is completing senior year in high school determine financial aid qualification. This means income earned the prior calendar year (when they completed junior year and began senior year). If you intend to seek early admission to college in fall of your child's senior year in high school, this shifts the income-earned year to one year earlier if you also intend to seek financial aid as part of that application process. Assets, on the other hand, are a snapshot in time the day you sign the FAFSA forms.

The bottom line on all these strategies that transfer assets is that as a parent if you think your student might qualify for financial aid, keep the money in your own name. Remember, your assets are assessed at the 5.6 percent rate and the student's assets are assessed at 35 percent, all as part of the same EFC formula. A quick FAFSA computation using your current income and today's college costs could answer all your questions. Remember, the college costs will go up faster than will your income. Student loans are a cheap fallback position that allows you to use that cash to make the maximum contributions to your 401(k) or other pension plan (where your investment income can grow and compound tax-free until withdrawal) and keeps the asset out of the FAFSA EFC computation.

Helpful Web Sites

- FinAid! (www.finaid.org) has all the information about the financial aid process, but it is about as easy to read as the Internal Revenue Code.
- FastWeb! (www.fastweb.com) lists schools and what they offer in the way of financial aid.

- College Money (www.collegemoney.com) is a commercial site that sells college financial planning tools and lists the COAs for colleges across the country.
- CollegeBoard.com (www.collegeboard.com/pay) is a good site on which to research merit scholarships.
- Thomson Peterson's (www.petersons.com) is the web site for the Peterson's College Guides company. If you buy the hard copy of the four-year guide you also get all the information about 2,100 four-year colleges on an easy-to-use CD-ROM.
- The Princeton Review (www.PrincetonReview.com) is the web site of a test preparation company that has good online detail about colleges. They also stick their neck out and rank colleges by academics, hardest to get into, best bang for the buck, social life, demographics, and more and more.
- Federal Student Aid (FSA) (http://studentaid.ed.gov) provides Stafford loan borrowing limits and PLUS loan information at the U.S. Department of Education's web site.
- CollegeSmart.com (www.collegesmart.com) offers advice on how to rearrange assets and other issues on FAFSA.

Books with Additional Information and Insights

Two books by Michele A. Hernandez, ex-financial aid administrator at Dartmouth College, are: *A is for Admission: The Insider's Guide to Getting into the Ivy League and Other Top Colleges* (Warner Books, 1999) and *Acing the College Application: How to Maximize Your Chances for Admission to the College of Your Choice* (Random House, 2002).

6

Your Pension Plan = Your Retirement Lifeline

Fact: The oldest baby boomers, born in 1946, will reach age 65 in 2011, six years from now. For workers in their 60s the average 401(k) account balance is only $146, 211.[1]

For people in 401(k) type plans, the self-employed, or the potentially self-employed, this chapter is your lifeline to retirement. Your pension plan should be one of your two largest assets at the time you retire. Assuming you want to keep your house, then your pension plan plus any other income-producing investments are the source of cash flow in retirement. Ideally, you would live on the equivalent of 100 percent of your final annual income for your first five years in retirement and 80 percent each year thereafter. Inflation-adjusted, that means you start at 100 percent, and after five years 80 percent plus inflation equals 100 percent five years earlier. And inflation keeps on going.

Most American families will simply not achieve that retirement income level without a great deal of additional saving. Even retiring at age 70 may be a problem. This chapter will explain the maximum contribution rules and why you should squeeze that level of contribution from your paycheck. For employees who have switched from plans where a large corporate employer made the contributions to a smaller employer where employees must make contributions for themselves, we will learn how to maximize these plan benefits. Lastly, we will examine plans for the self-employed, which allow for more creativity, but only if your business makes extra profits you can stash in a plan pretax.

Policy Makers and the Bean Counters Changed Your Future

Until the early 1980s, the average retirement age had been declining for decades. From the 1940s and 1950s when it was age 70, the average retirement age had declined to 63 by 1980,[2] and has remained flat since then. This trend directly relates to the shift in who funds retirement benefits:

- The 1940s and 1950s saw the introduction of union and corporate defined benefit pension plans (monthly annuities) designed to retire workers at age 65 and often giving favorable benefits to workers who retired as early as age 55. A relative degree of security was attained because funding retirement was supposed to come from three sources: monies from Social Security, payments from defined benefit pension plans, and withdrawals from personal savings.
- By 1981 large employers had begun shifting the funding responsibility away from the company and to the employees via the new defined contribution type pension plans. This cost-cutting move coincided with a new trend toward permanent layoffs brought about by a soft economy.[3]

This caused a dramatic redistribution of the responsibility for both who funds pension benefits and who is responsible for directing how investment decisions are made in these self-directed contributory pension assets. As shown in Figure 6.1, in 1981 58 percent of workers' pensions were provided through corporate defined-benefit pension plans funded entirely by corporate employers. By 2001 corporate defined benefit plans accounted for less than 20 percent of worker retirement plans. Workers who have changed employers and have a mixture of plans are in the "both" category.[4]

These two types of pension plans have different financial incentives, different ways of paying benefits, and different types of risk: defined benefit plans cover 44 million union and corporate employees, and defined contribution plans cover another 70 million corporate, small business workers, teachers, and government employees. The word *pension* refers to plans where the required contribution rules are defined by Internal Revenue Code Section 401. Subsection (k) of the Code defines a particular type of plan, 401(k) plans. In addition to these plans, there

FIGURE 6.1   Percentage of Wage and Salary Workers with Pension Coverage by Type of Plan, 1981–2001

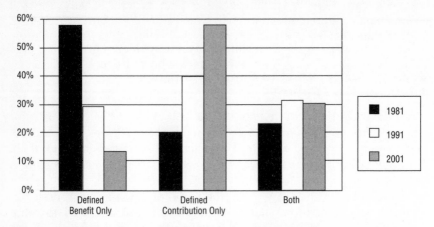

Source: *How Has the Shift to 401(k)s Affected the Retirement Age?* by Alicia H. Munnell, Kevin E. Cahill, and Natalia A. Jivan, Issue Brief 13, Center for Retirement Research at Boston College, September 2003.

are individual retirement accounts (IRAs), which have different rules but have 70 million participants who may also be in defined benefit and/or defined contribution plans. Participants in all types of defined contribution pension plans account for 80 percent of the American workforce.

This redistribution of both the management and investment responsibility over an individual's pension assets will become more significant if any of the various plans being discussed by government to privatize Social Security become reality. Disinterested employees will be forced to learn a whole new lingo about pensions and how to invest retirement assets to maximize their after-inflation return. This probability is what makes comprehending the rest of this book critically important.

Defined Benefit Pension Plans

These traditional defined benefit pension plans are typically offered by big, old-line companies. Of the Standard & Poor's 500 companies, 348 offer these plans and they cover 44 million American workers, 20 percent of the workforce.[5] Thirty-five million workers (13 percent) are covered by pensions paid for by a single employer. Nine and a half million workers (7 percent) participate in multiemployer plans typical of union collective bargaining agreements.[6] You do not usually make contributions to a defined benefit pension plan and you are paid a monthly income at retirement. The amount of a worker's benefit is determined by a benefit formula and is usually the sum of years of service (to the company) times some function of final salary or an average of the worker's salary over some number of final years, or a fixed percentage for each year of service. The annual contribution by the company to the plan is determined by an actuary. These plans are designed to reward long-term employees who retire at age 65. Sometimes employees are allowed to retire early by taking a discount or a lesser amount per month. During downsizing some employees may be given a sweetheart deal with less of a discount so as to remove the older, usually more highly compensated employees from the payroll and thereby reduce current operating expenses by utilizing younger, lower-compensated employees.

From the employee's standpoint four things are important to know about typical defined benefit pension plans:

1. How is your benefit calculated?
2. How many years of continuous service must you have before your benefits vest? Vesting means you have a right to a payout at retirement of benefits earned up to that point. A common waiting period before vesting is 10 years. At vesting these benefits and benefits earned from additional continuous service accumulate until normal retirement at age 65. If you leave before retirement but have vested, you get some reduced benefit at retirement.
3. How are your benefits reduced if you leave the company before retirement?
4. Once you begin receiving benefits, are these benefits cost of living adjusted?

For a long-service employee, these plans typically pay out 40 percent to 70 percent of the average of the highest three to five years of pay. For example, if your final pay or final average pay is $90,000 annually in today's dollars, your benefit could be between $40,500 (40 percent) up to $63,000 (70 percent). Many of these plans are integrated with Social Security, meaning that the Social Security benefit you will receive is subtracted from the calculated pension benefit. Plans for teachers are not integrated with Social Security because teachers do not participate. For this reason, teachers can often earn 2 percent per year for up to 35 years of service, or a 70 percent pension. The features are spelled out in the plan documents.

An advantage of these defined benefit plans is that the monthly benefits up to $3,698 (2005) for each worker retiring at age 65 are insured by the federal government through the Pension Benefit Guaranty Corporation (PBGC). The PBGC is funded by assessments to the corporate employers, assumedly a fee passed on to consumers in the form of price increases. At year-end 2004 the PBGC had a $23.3 billion deficit incurred paying benefits to employees in plans where the employers had filed for bankruptcy. The $9.8 billion takeover of the United Airlines defined benefit pension plan in April 2005 pushed the total to $33.1 billion. An agreement by the PBGC to take over the plans of other airlines will most likely force a taxpayer bailout of this fund. Ultimately this would cost the government (taxpayers) more than $110 million, more than the savings and loan scandal of the 1980s. What this means is that the 80 percent of workers (consumers) in uninsured defined contribution pensions are and will continue paying to insure (and maybe pay) the benefits of the 13 percent of workers in company-provided defined benefit plans.

Any emphasis in this book on defined benefit pension plans will be for employees who have left an employer with a defined benefit plan and now must start saving for their own retirement. The ex-employee must obtain from the employer answers to the above four questions to know what his/her expected benefits will be at age 65. These answers, plus whether or not the benefits will be reduced by Social Security, give you a starting point to understand how much you will have to save in other types of pension plans for your retirement.

Defined Contribution Pension Plans

Defined contribution plans cover 70 million American workers and are offered by companies, school districts, and governments of all sizes. Some companies may have both defined benefit and defined contribution plans. Defined contribution plans are profit-sharing plans, stock bonus plans, 401(k) plans, 403(b) plans for teachers, 457 plans for government workers, simplified employee pension (SEP) plans, and employee stock ownership plans (ESOPs). The employer contribution each year may be based on a written formula (a money purchase plan—for example, percentage of income) or may be determined annually at the employer's sole discretion (a profit-sharing plan). What these plans all have in common is that the individual employee has an account balance, at least for bookkeeping purposes. Typically these plans impose a waiting period before new employees may participate. Historically this has caused a hardship for people who frequently switched jobs because they left before the one-to-three year waiting period allowed them to participate in the plan. The growing trend today is for employers to shorten or eliminate the waiting period to entice new workers to their company. Once an employee becomes a participant, a distinct advantage is that the account balance is portable after some vesting period, allowing the employee to take the balance with him/her when leaving the employer. Employer matching contributions are still subject to a waiting period before they vest and become part of your portable account balance.

The benefits the employee will receive from these plans depend solely upon:

- The amount of the employee and employer contributions.
- Any forfeitures from other plan participants credited to the employee's account balance.
- The plan's investment income, expenses, gains, or losses.

There are three common types of defined contribution plans, but the 401(k) is the most common.

Profit-Sharing Plans

A plan must specifically state that it is a profit-sharing plan. Employer contributions are usually based on the employer's profits or tied to a discretionary formula. Employers, except for the self-employed, are not required to have a profit to contribute.

Stock Bonus Plans

Stock bonus plans are similar to profit-sharing plans, except the benefits are distributed in stock of the employer.

Section 401(k) Plans

This is a profit-sharing plan or stock bonus plan that includes a cash or deferred arrangement (CODA). Employee contributions into these plans are made on a pretax basis as a reduction to salary. The CODA is a deferral feature that allows a participant the option to defer compensation and have the employer contribute that deferral to the plan. For calendar year 2005, the maximum employee deferral/contribution is $14,000. A husband and wife who both work for employers who offer 401(k) plans may each contribute up to that limit, for a total of $28,000. Employees who reach the age of 50 before the end of a calendar year may make catch-up contributions that are also deferrals with pretax dollars if the plan allows for them. (See Table 6.1.)

TABLE 6.1   401(k) Contribution Limits

Year	Age 49 and Below	Age 50 and Above
2005	$14,000	$18,000
2006	$15,000	$20,000

There are limitation rules on contributions by highly compensated (more than $95,000 of annual compensation) employees if an insufficient number of lower-paid employees do not participate in the 401(k) plan. These antidiscrimination rules are one reason many employers encourage contributions from non–highly paid employees in the company's 401(k) plan. When more low-paid employees participate in the plan, the restriction limits for the higher-compensated employees are relaxed. In addition, and not to be overlooked, there is a growing sense of employer responsibility recognizing the need to encourage employees to save for retirement no matter how small the amount at the start.

An easier way for employers to ensure that highly compensated employees are able to participate fully is to modify their plan to be a Safe Harbor 401(k). The restrictions on highly compensated employees are removed if *either* of two conditions is met:

1. The employer contributes up to 3 percent of pay for all eligible participants whether or not the employee makes any contributions.
2. The employer matches employee contributions dollar for dollar up to 3 percent of a participant's pay, and then 50 cents on the dollar up to 5 percent of pay.

In 2003, employer matching contributions averaged 50 cents on the dollar up to 7 percent of employee compensation, according to a recent Hewitt and Associates study.[7] However, contribution matching can vary widely, from a low of 25 percent matching on the first 3 percent of salary up to 75 percent or 100 percent on the full annual maximum. So whether or not a prospective employer has a 401(k) plan is only part of the question.

Although the employee's contributions vest immediately, employer contributions usually vest ratably over three years. Employees may make excess contributions to the 401(k) plan, but they are not tax-deductible and are usually not matched by the employer. There are better places to put your money than into nondeductible excess contributions—for example, tax-deductible traditional IRAs.

You should contribute at least up to the limit of the employer matching in a 401(k) plan. For example, if you earn $90,000 and your employer matches 50 cents on the dollar up to 7 percent of your salary, your contribution would be $6,300 and the 50 percent match is $3,150. By making the contribution you do not have to include it in taxable income, thus saving the income tax bite now. In the 25 percent tax bracket (if you're filing jointly or as a head of household), this means that had you not made the contribution you would have put only $4,750 in your pocket after taxes. On this basis, your employer's $3,150 contribution amounts to a 66 percent return on your investment in that year. If you're single in the same example, you are in the 28 percent tax bracket and receive a 70 percent return on this employer contribution. If your employer matches 50 cents on the dollar all the way to $14,000 of earnings and you are in the 35 percent tax bracket, you receive a 77 percent return on your employer contribution. Any of these yields are too good to pass up.

Section 401(k) plans that are invested in employer stock don't seem to go away, even after employees at Enron, WorldCom, and companies as far back as Studebaker lost their retirement savings when the companies went bankrupt and the stock price went to zero.[8] Your employer may require that their matching contributions be invested in company stock, but you are entitled to invest your contribution in mutual funds and other choices provided by the plan administrator.

Don't be a chump. A recent study by Hewitt Associates reports that "a majority of employees (84 percent) invest employee contributions in employer stock and 86 percent [of companies] place no restriction on the percentage of employee contributions in employer stock."[9] Your paycheck is already dependent on the company's performance, so why put your retirement in the same bucket? We will talk about investments later, but employers cite "not diversifying investments adequately" as the most common mistake employees make in investing in their 401(k) accounts.[10]

Stock options are not discussed in this book, but if you do have stock options as part of your pay package, these are also potential future compensation dollars tied up in company stock. Diversification out of employer stock does not suggest you lack confidence in your employer's future. It is just prudent asset allocation into other industry sectors.

Table 6.2 shows the dramatic effect of contributing as much as you can as early in life as possible to your 401(k) plan at work. Each of the four examples show account balances and expected annual income draws in today's dollars by years of continuous plan participation.

The table is an expanded example of 401(k) account balances we looked at in Chapter 1. It is hard to go much further because we do not know how much the government will increase the cost of living index allowable for 401(k) contributions. However, if the $3,000 catch-up contributions for people over 50 is any indicator, tax-deductible cost of living adjustments will not allow you to contribute enough to fulfill your retirement goals.

You must gather your pension information and total it in today's dollars. You may have as many as four pension components. Input them into the pension template on my web site—be realistic about what you will actually contribute each year in the future, and assume only

TABLE 6.2 Typical 401(k) Pension Plan Balances and Annual Income Distributions by Years of Participation

Continuous Contributions	Year 1	Year 5	Year 10	Year 15	Year 20	Year 25	Year 30	Year 35	Year 45
Example 1 $6,000 per year with 50% employer match	$ 9,225	$ 48,490	$103,351	$165,422	$235,649	$315,105	$405,002	$ 506,713	$ 751,986
Starting retirement income if retire at age 65 with these years of continuous contributions			$ 4,134	$ 6,617	$ 9,426	$ 12,604	$ 16,200	$ 20,269	$ 30,079
Starting retirement income if retire at age 70 with these years of continuous contributions			$ 4,651	$ 7,444	$ 10,604	$ 14,180	$ 18,225	$ 22,802	$ 33,839
Example 2 $9,000 per year with 50% employer match	$13,838	$ 72,734	$155,027	$248,133	$353,474	$472,658	$607,504	$ 760,069	$1,127,979
Starting retirement income if retire at age 65 with these years of continuous contributions		$ 2,909	$ 6,201	$ 9,925	$ 14,139	$ 18,906	$ 24,300	$ 30,403	$ 45,119
Starting retirement income if retire at age 70 with these continuous contributions		$ 3,273	$ 6,976	$ 11,166	$ 15,906	$ 21,270	$ 27,338	$ 34,203	$ 50,759

Example 3 $14,000 per year with 50% employer match	$21,525	$113,142	$241,153	$385,985	$549,849	$735,246	$945,006	$1,182,330	$1,745,635
Starting retirement income if retire at age 65 with these years of continuous contributions		$ 4,526	$ 9,646	$ 15,439	$ 21,994	$ 29,410	$ 37,800	$ 47,293	$ 69,825
Starting retirement income if retire at age 70 with these years of continuous contributions		$ 5,091	$ 10,852	$ 17,369	$ 24,743	$ 33,086	$ 42,525	$ 53,205	$ 78,554
Example 4 $14,000 per year with 50% employer match for ten years and then full catch-up		$ 80,816	$186,279	$371,537	$570,937	$859,102	$1,149,163		
Starting retirement income if retire at age 65 with these years of continuous contributions		$ 3,233	$ 7,451	$ 14,861	$ 22,837	$ 34,364			
Starting retirement income if retire at age 70 with these years of continuous contributions		$ 3,637	$ 8,383	$ 16,719	$ 25,692	$ 38,660	$ 51,712		

Notes:
- All amounts are inflation-adjusted today's dollars. Investment return averages 8% with 3% inflation, a net 5% per year investment return.
- Starting income annual amounts are in 2005 dollars. As in the other examples, income is assumed to annually increase by 3%.
- Starting income for retirement at age 65 is 4% of the account balance. Income will run out at about age 100.
- Starting income for retirement at age 70 is 4.5% of the account balance. Income will run out at about age 100.
- In example 4, participant is age 50 in 2005 and contributions represent known annual maximum amounts before and after that date.

the contribution limits as they are today. Don't assume more than a 5 percent annual growth rate (8 percent investment return minus 3 percent annual inflation). Look at the outcome at ages 65 and 70 and see if you have enough to retire. If you do not have enough in your balances to retire, go back to your budget and see if you can increase your 401(k) contribution to the maximum. If you are already contributing at the maximum and still do not have enough for retirement, look at your other assets.

Your four possible pension components are:

1. Any expected payout from an ex-employer's defined benefit pension plan.
2. Any anticipated balances from an IRA and a rollover IRA.
3. Anticipated balances from your contributory plans like your 401(k), 403(b), 457, or stock bonus plan.
4. Any anticipated balances from an individual or small business defined benefit plan, if you have one or can start one.

How Much Income Can I Draw per Year?

How much you can draw down on the balance in your retirement accounts depends on five factors:

1. How long you and your spouse/partner are going to live.
2. How long until you want to run out of money.
   - What your investment rate of return will be.
   - What the inflation rate will be that reduces the effective value of your investments.
3. What inflation rate you want to use to increase the money available to you each year in retirement.
4. The value of other assets you can draw on for support when your investment pool is gone.
5. Whether or not you want to leave anything to your heirs or to charity when you die.

Americans are living longer and remaining in better health. Actuarially, you have a good chance of living to be 100. There are more people over the age of 100 living today than have ever reached the age of 100 in history.[11] Of an actuarial sampling of 100,000 persons born in 1953, 94,200 are still alive today. Seventy percent of those will reach age 75, and 20 percent will still be alive at age 90.[12]

There are two common methods for showing you how much you can safely draw down on your retirement savings and not run out of money until age 100.

Method 1

Throughout the early chapters of this book we have used the model that assumes you draw down 4 percent per year starting at age 65. Each year in retirement we assume you are going to increase your annual draw by 3 percent to account for inflation. This is based on an 8 percent annual investment return that is eroded annually by 3 percent inflation. In today's inflation-adjusted dollars, we are assuming you will need as much money your tenth or twentieth year in retirement as you spend in your first retirement years. Under these assumptions, you run out of money the year you turn 100.

If you retire at age 70, you can draw down 4.5 percent each year under the same assumptions. Because you were adding to your retirement account for an extra five years, your draw will be larger. If your investments do not hit the 8 percent target rate of return or inflation goes above 3 percent, it is time to look at method 2.

Although the assumption of an 8 percent annual investment rate of return is commonly used for retirement planning accumulation projections, some advisers suggest retirees shift principally to bonds in retirement. Historical bond performance has typically been less than 8 percent. By doing this the investor limits their annual yield and forfeits most or all future portfolio appreciation.

In Chapter 7, I introduce you to the proven concept of buying only low-fee/low-cost index-tracking mutual funds and exchange-traded funds (ETFs). If during the past 28 years you had bought and held a balanced portfolio of no-load, low-fee index tracking products over time you would have averaged 12 percent pre-inflation-adjusted returns. This kind of portfolio yield will dramatically increase your retirement nest egg and allow you to draw down double the income in retirement (8 percent inflation adjusted) while your account balance continues to grow.

Method 2

The alternative pre-enlightened method is to draw down 5 percent of the outstanding balance each year. At an 8 percent average investment yield (5 percent after inflation), this erodes your income unless you are able to make up the difference with good investments. The good thing about this method is that it forces you to focus each year on how your investments are doing. After a good year you can take out a little more and after a bad year a little less. However, if your investment yields average 8 percent in a 3 percent inflationary world and you retires at age 65, you will run out of money when you turn 90. At a 10 or 12 percent annual yield this method produces income until age 100. More on this in the next chapter.

Rolling Over Your 401(k)

When you leave an employer and have a balance in your 401(k) plan, you may leave it with the old employer or roll it over into an IRA or a new employer's 401(k). Employers are now required to roll over your 401(k) into an IRA unless you instruct them otherwise. To avoid taxation, this rollover must generally be done within 60 days. Avoid cashing out your 401(k) if you are under age 59½, or you generally must pay the income tax on the amount distributed, plus a 10 percent penalty tax. If you remove your balance from the old employer's plan and do not roll the balance into an IRA, there is a required 20 percent withholding for income taxes. Sadly, nearly half of all workers who changed jobs in 2002 cashed out their 401(k)s and subjected themselves to the tax and the penalties.[13] The decision whether to leave your balance with the old employer, transfer it to the new employer's 401(k), or put it into an IRA depends on the investment choices each offers. If you choose an IRA, set up a new rollover IRA to keep the amount separate. Set up your rollover IRA at a mutual fund company or investment firm that offers no-load, low-fee, index-tracking mutual funds and exchange-traded funds (ETFs).

If your old employer had your 401(k) balance or even only its part invested in company stock, this is the ideal time to sell that stock. You do this by rolling the account into a rollover IRA, then selling the stock and reinvesting the cash into a balance of other stocks, bonds, mutual funds, or exchange-traded funds.

Stock options are not a subject we are taking on in this book, but it is important to mention here that stock options usually expire 30 days after you leave an employer, if not at the instant you resign. Be sure you understand the stock option plan if you intend to resign. If the options expire at resignation, exercise them by allowing the personnel department to cash them out before you submit your resignation. If you are being terminated, make sure your employer gives you, in writing, a long enough window to cash out of the options.

Individual Retirement Account (IRA)

The original or traditional individual retirement account (traditional IRA) is a type of savings account that allows investors to make tax-deductible contributions. (See Table 6.3.) To make contributions to an IRA, you must have income from employment or alimony. Investment income does not qualify. The money can be invested in mutual funds, stocks, bonds, and so on, and the earnings grow tax free until withdrawal. You can begin withdrawing at age 59½; withdrawals *must* be started before the account owner reaches 70½ years of age. Whether or

TABLE 6.3   IRA Contribution Limits

Year	Age 49 and Below	Age 50 and Above
2005	$4,000	$4,500
2006 and 2007	$4,000	$5,000
2008	$5,000	$6,000

not your contribution to an IRA is tax deductible depends on whether you or your spouse were active participants in a company-sponsored defined benefit or defined contribution plan at any time during the year. Deductibility is dependent on the amount of your modified adjusted gross income (AGI). Adjusted gross income is usually the line by that name on your tax return with certain adjustments. The only adjustments you may encounter are that you must add back into income deductions for student loan interest, passive investment losses, and the IRA deduction itself. There are three different scenarios in determining whether or not your IRA contributions are deductible:

1. If you were not an active participant in an employer-sponsored plan, your maximum contribution is deductible so long as your AGI is less than $60,000 for 2005[14] for a single filer or head of household and $75,000 for 2005[15] for a married couple filing a joint return.
2. If you were an active participant in a plan at any time during the taxable year and your AGI is below the aforementioned limits, you may deduct payments to an IRA if your employer's qualified plan allows you to make a contribution to a "deemed IRA."[16] The employee's contribution will count toward the maximum allowable IRA contribution.
3. If your spouse was an active participant in a plan but you were not a plan participant and you file a joint income tax return, you may "borrow"[17] some of his/her income to reach the maximum contribution. Tax deductibility of the IRA contribution phases out starting at $150,000 of joint AGI and is gone at $160,000.[18]

One limitation is that if you are contributing to a 401(k) at work or to a self-employed pension plan, the total of those contributions plus your IRA contributions cannot exceed the maximum allowable in your employer's plan. This means that for 2005, your upper limit on contributions if you are covered by an employer's 401(k) is $14,000 or $18,000, depending on whether you are under or over age 50. The law also allows modest IRA catch-up contributions for people age 50 and above.

Your goal should be to invest at least enough in your 401(k) to get the maximum employer matching contribution. It is best to invest up to the maximum in your 401(k) if the investment choices are good. Another reason to make an IRA your second choice is that IRAs are not qualified retirement plans and are not protected in bankruptcy and from attachment by creditors in a lawsuit. The treatment of IRAs is left up to state law, at least until there is federal bankruptcy reform.[19]

There are several exceptions to the strict distribution rules that allow you to draw monies out of a traditional IRA, pay the income tax, but avoid paying the 10 percent penalty:

1. Payment of certain medical insurance premiums.
2. Payment of qualified higher-education expenses for yourself, your spouse, your children, and your grandchildren. Qualified expenses for postsecondary education are tuition, books, fees, supplies, and equipment.
3. First-time home buyer expenses. There is a lifetime withdrawal limit of $10,000 each for you and your spouse. The monies must be spent for acquisition costs, settlement costs, and closing costs, but the first-time residence can be for you or your spouse, children, or grandchildren. The only limitation is that the so-called first-time homebuyer cannot have had an ownership interest in a principal residence for the prior two years.

If your spouse or partner dies and has an IRA where you are the beneficiary, it is usually a good idea to elect to put the IRA into your own name, especially if you are under age 59½. This solves the problem of cashing it out and paying tax and any penalties. In this way you can draw it down for your own retirement after age 59½ and only start to pay taxes then.

Figure 6.2 shows the inflation-adjusted outcome of a student starting an IRA at age 22 upon finishing college in 1998. The original $2,000 contributions started in 1998, adjusted for known government increases in contribution limits or just 2.5 percent inflation, would total $415,000 by age 65. At age 65, the account balance in today's dollars would be $1 million. Under the conservative, high-cost mutual fund assumptions this would produce $40,000 per year of income with today's spending power. However, had this money been invested under the low-cost/low-fee index investing strategy, this $1 million would be $2.7 million and allow for $215,000 of annual income, cost of living adjusted. If the saver started at age 35, the balance would be only $235,000. Again, observe the miracle of compound interest! Imagine if this had been a 401(k) with $6,000 annual

FIGURE 6.2   Benefit of Starting Your IRA Early

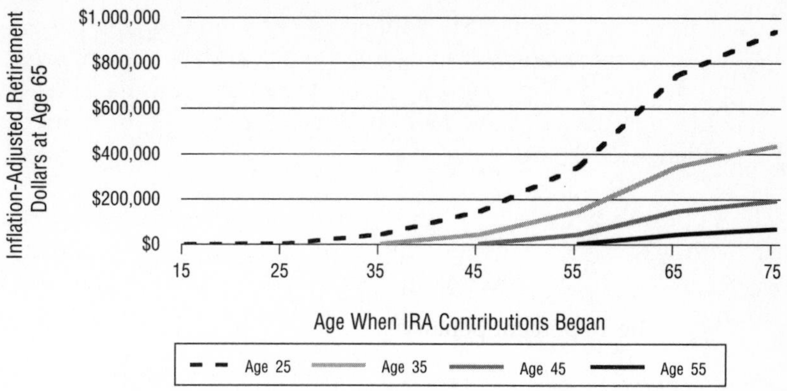

Y-axis: Inflation-Adjusted Retirement Dollars at Age 65

Values: $1,000,000 / $800,000 / $600,000 / $400,000 / $200,000 / $0

X-axis: Age When IRA Contributions Began — 15, 25, 35, 45, 55, 65, 75

Legend: - - Age 25   ▨ Age 35   — Age 45   — Age 55

contributions and 50 percent employer matching. Had it been a 401(k), our 22-year-old, under the high-cost mutual fund assumption, would have $1.5 million in today's dollars at retirement, enough for an inflation-adjusted lifetime income of $60,000 annually. This would be $4 million under the low-cost mutual fund assumption and yield an eye-popping $320,000 million of annual income.

Roth Individual Retirement Accounts (Roth IRAs)

The newer form of individual retirement accounts, Roth IRAs differ from the older traditional IRAs because the initial contributions are made with after-tax dollars and the contributions and investment income are both tax-free when withdrawn at retirement. The annual contribution limits are the same as with a traditional IRA. The Roth IRA is a valuable short- and long-term investment tool because of the liberal withdrawal rules. Because contributions to a Roth IRA are made with after-tax (nondeductible) dollars, you may withdraw your contributions at any time without tax or penalty. Provided the account has been open for five years and the account holder is at least $59\frac{1}{2}$ years of age, the earnings may be withdrawn tax free. And provided the five-year limitation is met, regardless of age, the earnings can be withdrawn tax free for the same three exceptions that apply to the traditional IRA:

1. Payment of certain medical insurance premiums.
2. Payment of qualified higher-education expenses for yourself, your spouse, your children, and your grandchildren. Qualified expenses for postsecondary education are tuition, books, fees, supplies, and equipment.

3. First-time home buyer expenses. There is a lifetime withdrawal limit of $10,000 each for you and your spouse. The monies must be spent for acquisition costs, settlement costs, and closing costs, but the first-time residence can be for you or your spouse, children, or grandchildren. The only limitation is that the so-called first-time homebuyer cannot have had an ownership interest in a principal residence for the prior two years.[20]

The opportunity here is to anticipate your expenditures and fund them with a Roth IRA where earnings accumulate tax free during the five-year or longer required holding period. This would be the case for first-time home buyer expenses and going back to college or graduate school.

Contributions to a Roth IRA are not permitted if your modified adjusted gross income is above $110,000 for a single taxpayer/head of household and $160,000 for joint taxpayers.[21]

Individual 401(k) Plans

New in 2002 were individual 401(k) plans for the self-employed with no full-time employees other than a spouse. These plans have the same higher contribution limits ($14,000 for 2005) as corporate 410(k) plans and are easy and relatively inexpensive to administer. Your business may be organized as a sole proprietorship, C corporation, S corporation, or limited liability company (LLC). Contribution limits are 100 percent of compensation or $14,000, plus catch-up contributions if you are over age 50. This means a husband and wife, age 50 plus, provided each has $17,000 in compensation, can put away a maximum of $34,000 in 2005 ($36,000 for 2006). All contributions are 100 percent vested, and IRS Form 5500 is not required until plan assets reach $100,000. Institutional plan providers usually require that you invest in mutual funds, so if you intend to invest in real estate or individual stocks, look for a provider that has flexible documents.

Creative Pension Plans When You Are the Boss

Catch-up contributions to a pension plan can take on new meaning if you are the boss at a small company or are self-employed. There are types of defined benefit plans that allow you to establish a desired annual retirement benefit that is the lesser of $170,000 per year or 100 percent of the average of your three highest-compensated years while you were employed.[22] These are 2005 limits and they should go up over time. Then the actuary determines how much you can fund and take a tax deduction for each year to get to the benefit level. There are some limiting factors such as not having been part of an employer-qualified plan recently, but if that is the case, there are individual 401(k) plans that allow you to contribute up to $42,000 per participant (2005) each year, tax deductible. The obvious problem with these plans is: how do I earn enough taxable income to contribute enough to make these plans work for me and still be able to pay the bills?

A commitment to these defined benefit plans has some real questions attached:

- How much income can you spare to contribute to the plan each year?
- How many years do you expect to earn this income, and how consistent will it be?
- What is your ability and propensity to save?
- What is your age, and what are those of your employees?
- If a small company, how many employees do you have?

Defined Benefit Plans for Individuals

The simplest example is the creation of a defined benefit plan for a self-employed person. You can contribute enough to get you to the expected pension benefit that is the lesser of $170,000 per year or the average of your three highest consecutive years of compensation while an employee.[23] Pension actuaries say that after the age of 42 contributions become disproportionately larger because you can play catch-up. I have a defined benefit plan that I established at age 55. The plan was created late in the year and funded before year-end with $100,000. This reduced my federal tax bill by $39,000 for that year and reduced my estimated taxes for the next year. This meant I saved $78,000 over two plan years in federal income taxes, but all compressed into several months. Although it depends on the facts, you should keep this up for a minimum of two years to avoid possible audit by the IRS.

Your annual contribution amount will be determined by the actuary, based on your age and a retirement income level you select. I suggest you turn the process around and tell the actuary/plan administrator how much you can tolerate in annual contributions. With this number, the actuary can tell what the retirement benefit will be. If your self-employment income is unusually high and you had three high years as an employee, and you can tolerate high annual contributions for two or more years, you can sock away a lot of tax-deferred money that you can draw down at retirement. Make the maximum contribution possible. If your earnings change, the actuary can recompute the benefit and reduce the annual contributions to match your revised situation. In the meantime you have enjoyed the tax deductibility of the contributions. Because of conflicting regulations it is critically important to have properly prepared plan documents.

Plan documents for these defined benefit plans, and also for many defined contribution plans, for individuals are often boilerplate documents preapproved by the IRS. Plan documents used by financial institutions usually require you to invest monies through them and do not allow outside investments. Fee-only pension and profit sharing administrators create more flexible plan documents, can tailor the plan to your needs, and don't care where the investments are made as long as they are allowed by the Internal Revenue Code and are allowed by the plan documents. Make sure the documents allow you both to borrow from the plan and to make investments other than in stocks and bonds, such as rental real estate that you can fix up and sell or keep as rental property. If you are so inclined, this allows you to diversify out of mutual funds, for example, and into fixer-upper real estate where you can use sweat equity and your skills in another form of inflation hedge. The law prohibits you using pension monies to buy vacation homes for personal use.

I have come to know and value the services of fee-only pension and profit-sharing plan consultants and administrators. Mark Clark, a partner at Benefit Associates, Inc., in Orange, California, is an excellent example. A lecturer and author, Mark specializes in these types of exotic pension plans and shares his insights with lawyers and CPAs nationwide. Mark's plan documents are typically designed around an individual's or group's unique situation. The cost of plan design and documentation depends on the complexity. Mark can be reached at (714) 538-5220, e-mail: mclark@benefitassoc.com.

Another excellent fee-only choice is John Cheplick, of Pensionalysis, in Northern California. Plans implemented and administered by John are primarily off-the-shelf documents, and the assets are placed at Charles Schwab or Salomon Smith Barney. The fee for an IRS-preapproved defined benefit plan and its annual administration is $2,500. John can be reached at (415) 459-0504, e-mail: john@pension alysis.com.

Table 6.4 is an example of what your annual income draw could be if you start and stick with a self-directed defined benefit pension plan. To these hypothetical balances you must add any monies in other pension plans and IRAs. The retirement income level goes above $170,000 in some of the long-lived plan examples because at 20 to 25 years in the future the limit will have gone up.

Defined Contribution Plans for Individuals and Small Groups

Defined contribution plans for individuals or small groups are profit-sharing plans and/or 401(k) plans that are combined with a profit-sharing plan. Certain plan limits apply to highly compensated

TABLE 6.4 Self-Directed Defined Benefit Pension Plan Balances and Annual Income Distributions by Years of Participation

	Continuous Contributions	Year 1	Year 5	Year 10	Year 15	Year 20	Year 25
Example 1	$25,000 per year continuous contributions	$ 26,250	$145,048	$330,170	$ 566,437	$ 867,981	$1,252,836
	Starting retirement income if retire at age 65 with these years of continuous contributions		$ 5,802	$ 13,207	$ 22,657	$ 34,719	$ 50,113
	Starting retirement income if retire at age 70 with these years of continuous contributions		$ 6,527	$ 14,858	$ 25,490	$ 39,059	$ 56,378
Example 2	$50,000 per year continuous contributions	$ 52,500	$290,096	$660,339	$1,132,875	$1,735,963	$2,505,673
	Starting retirement income if retire at age 65 with these years of continuous contributions		$ 11,604	$ 26,414	$ 45,315	$ 69,439	$ 100,227
	Starting retirement income if retire at age 70 with these years of continuous contributions		$ 13,054	$ 29,715	$ 50,979	$ 78,118	$ 112,755

(Continued)

127

TABLE 6.4 *(Continued)*

Continuous Contributions	Year 1	Year 5	Year 10	Year 15	Year 20	Year 25
Example 3 — $75,000 per year continuous contributions	$ 78,750	$435,143	$ 990,509	$1,699,312	$2,603,944	$3,758,509
Starting retirement income if retire at age 65 with these years of continuous contributions		$ 17,406	$ 39,620	$ 67,972	$ 104,158	$ 150,340
Starting retirement income if retire at age 70 with these years of continuous contributions		$ 19,581	$ 44,573	$ 76,469	$ 117,177	$ 169,133
Example 4 — $100,000 per year continuous contributions	$105,000	$580,191	$1,320,679	$2,265,749	$3,471,925	$5,011,345
Starting retirement income if retire at age 65 with these years of continuous contributions		$ 23,208	$ 52,827	$ 90,630	$ 138,877	$ 200,454
Starting retirement income if retire at age 70 with these years of continuous contributions		$ 26,109	$ 59,431	$ 101,959	$ 156,237	$ 225,511

Notes:
- All amounts are inflation-adjusted today's dollars. Investment return averages 8% with 3% inflation, a net 5% per year investment return.
- Starting income annual amounts are in 2005 dollars. Income is assumed to annually increase by 3%.
- Starting income for retirement at age 65 is 4% of the account balance. Income will run out at about age 100.
- Starting income for retirement at age 70 is 4.5% of the account balance. Income will run out at about age 100.

individuals. The Internal Revenue Code defines a highly compensated employee as any shareholder who owns more than 5 percent and/or anyone whose compensation exceeds $95,000.[24] If you use a personal 401(k), it must fully vest and provide the 3 percent guaranteed match to all participating employees. In this way the highly compensated employees/owners may contribute up to the maximum without running up against the antidiscrimination rules that limit their contributions. Let us assume our goal here is to get the maximum $42,000 (2005) contribution for the employee/owner(s) and limit the contribution to other employees. All contributions must be in cash and cannot exceed a participant's income.

Profit-Sharing Plan Examples

First, let's look at the simple profit sharing example. The Internal Revenue Code limits total annual profit sharing deductible contributions to 25 percent of the total pay for all participating employees.[25] The nondiscriminatory formula permits an allocation to the owner(s) of $42,000 (2005).[26] If the plan is "top heavy"—that is, it has highly compensated employee(s)—then other employees must receive a minimum of 3 percent of pay.[27] However, if we integrate Social Security benefits into the profit-sharing plan we are able to deduct the future Social Security payments to be received from the amounts allocated to the employees, thus reducing the employer-required contributions. This means allocating $42,000 to the employee/owner(s) and less to everyone else.

The example in Table 6.5 is a simple profit-sharing plan. The typical

TABLE 6.5   Hypothetical Simple Profit-Sharing Plan

Participant	Age	Compensation	Profit Sharing Pro Rata	
			Maximum Percent of Pay	Amount
Owner	59	$210,000	Maximum	$42,000
Employee	47	$ 81,500	20%	$16,300
Employee	30	$ 42,000	20%	$ 8,400
Employee	41	$ 27,600	20%	$ 5,520
Employee	27	$ 22,800	20%	$ 4,560
Total		$383,900		$76,780
25% profit sharing limitation		$ 95,975		
Percent to owner in this example				54%

simple plan with an employee who has compensation in excess of the $90,000 (2005) taxable wage base allocates 5.5 percent of the excess contribution as plan benefits to that employee. The balance of the plan contribution, not to exceed 25 percent of total participant pay, is allocated pro rata to the employees. This is further explained in the computation in Table 6.6. The net result is that the maximum of $42,000 has been allocated to the highly compensated owner and a lesser amount to each of the employees based on their wages as a percent of total wages, but not in excess of 20 percent of their salaries. This yields an example in which the owner has 54 percent of the plan allocated to him/her. Only $76,780 of the potential maximum plan contributions of $95,975 has been allocated. This is not an ideal solution.

Next, in Table 6.7, is an example of a plan in which employee contributions are age weighted. This reduces contributions to younger employees while allowing maximum contribution to the highly

TABLE 6.6   Simple Profit-Sharing Plan, Computation of Benefit Distribution

Highly compensated salaries	$210,000
Social Security taxable wage base (TWB)	$ 90,000
Excess salary above TWB	$120,000
Excess salary × plan document factor	0.055
Excess allocated to highly compensated employees	$ 6,600
Less total plan contribution	$ 95,975
Balance to distribute pro rata to employees	$ 89,375

Participant	Age	Compensation	Percent of Total Salary	Pro Rata Distribution	Maximum Plan Contribution	Limits Applied
Owner	59	$210,000	54.70%	$48,888	$55,488	$42,000
Employee	47	$ 81,500	21.22%	$18,965	$18,965	$16,300
Employee	30	$ 42,000	10.95%	$ 9,787	$ 9,787	$ 8,400
Employee	41	$ 27,600	7.19%	$ 6,426	$ 6,426	$ 5,520
Employee	27	$ 22,800	5.94%	$ 5,309	$ 5,309	$ 4,560
Total		$383,900	100.00%	$89,375	$95,975	$76,780

TABLE 6.7 Hypothetical Profit-Sharing Plan Integrated with Social Security (Age Weighted for Employees)

Participant	Age	Compensation	Profit Sharing Pro Rata		Profit Sharing Integrated with Social Security		Profit Sharing Final Result	
			Amount	% Pay	Amount	% Pay	Amount	% Pay
Owner	59	$210,000	$42,000	20%	$42,000	20%	$42,000	20%
Employee	47	$ 81,500	$16,300	20%	$13,633	17%	$ 4,077	5%
Employee	30	$ 42,000	$ 8,400	20%	$ 7,022	17%	$ 2,100	5%
Employee	41	$ 27,600	$ 5,520	20%	$ 4,615	17%	$ 1,380	5%
Employee	27	$ 22,800	$ 4,560	20%	$ 3,812	17%	$ 1,140	5%
Total		$383,900	$76,780		$70,082		$50,697	
25% profit sharing limitation	$95,975							
Percent to owner in this example					58%		83%	

131

compensated owner. Plans like this and the one that follows require using a skilled plan administrator and actuary. The result here is not bad from the owner's standpoint—83 percent of the total plan contributions are allocated to the owner—assuming that result is what he/she wants.

But a skilled plan designer can increase the tax-deductible contribution if we age weight the contributions and have two owners and more employees as in the example in Table 6.8. To be safe and because we have an employee in the age-weighted group who makes more than $95,000 and is thus highly compensated for tax law purposes, we will put a floor of 3 percent on the contributions. Even with this 3 percent floor, 84 percent of all contributions into the plan go to the two owners.

Safe Harbor 401(k) and One-Life 401(k) Plans

Safe Harbor 401(k) plans require that the employer make a matching contribution up to 3 percent of income. This characteristic permits the plan to avoid the antidiscrimination rules that prohibit full funding to highly compensated employees. Combining a Safe Harbor 401(k) plan with a profit-sharing plan allows participants to exceed the $14,000 401(k) contribution limit and make annual contributions of $42,000. In these plans we are also able to integrate the profit-sharing portion with Social Security and reduce the plan contributions for other employees. The beauty of this combination is that if you have an employee/owner and a spouse/partner, you are able to allocate 100 percent of the contributions to them. Another advantage of this type of plan is that because the profit-sharing portion is fully discretionary, you do not have to make contributions each year. Table 6.9 illustrates how it is done. (Remember that contributions cannot exceed, but can equal 100 percent of compensation.)

In this fictional example, contrived to show the limits of this plan type, each of the employee participants contributes the maximum $14,000 in the 401(k). The owner receives $28,000 in profit sharing to reach the maximum $42,000 allowed by the plan. The balance of $28,000 goes to the spouse/partner because the plan documents allow excess contributions to be allocated to other participants, such as the spouse/partner. The spouse/partner is at the contribution limit because contributions equal income. The total profit sharing contributions equal the 25 percent limit.

These special types of plans require expert advice from actuaries and

TABLE 6.8 Hypothetical Profit-Sharing Plan Integrated with Social Security (Age Weighted for Employees)

Participant	Age	Compensation	Profit Sharing Pro Rata		Profit Sharing Integrated with Social Security		Profit Sharing Final Result	
			Amount	% Pay	Amount	% Pay	Amount	% Pay
Owner 1	56	$210,000	$ 42,000	20%	$ 42,000	21%	$42,000	21%
Owner 2	42	$210,000	$ 42,000	20%	$ 42,000	21%	$42,000	21%
Employee	37	$118,000	$ 23,600	20%	$ 21,600	18%	$ 3,540	3%
Employee	44	$ 54,000	$ 10,800	20%	$ 9,000	17%	$ 2,700	5%
Employee	31	$ 45,000	$ 9,000	20%	$ 7,500	17%	$ 2,250	5%
Employee	60	$ 49,000	$ 9,800	20%	$ 8,200	17%	$ 2,450	5%
Employee	31	$ 41,500	$ 8,300	20%	$ 7,000	17%	$ 2,075	5%
Employee	31	$ 54,400	$ 10,880	20%	$ 9,000	17%	$ 2,720	5%
Total		$781,900	$156,380		$146,300		$99,735	
25% profit sharing limitation		$195,475						
Percent to owners this example			54%		57%		84%	

133

TABLE 6.9   Hypothetical One-Life 401(k) with Integrated Profit-Sharing Plan

Participant	Age	Compensation	Profit Sharing	401(k)	Total Allocation	Percent of Pay
Owner	40	$182,000	$28,000	$14,000	$42,000	22.30%
Spouse/Partner	40	$ 42,000	$28,000	$14,000	$42,000	100.00%
Total		$224,000	$56,000	$28,000	$84,000	
25% profit sharing limitation		$ 56,000				

lawyers who specialize in designing a plan to fit the circumstances of your small business.

Types of Plan Documents

There are three types of pension plan documents, and the type you have will control both your investment flexibility and the portability of your plan.

1. *Individually designed documents.* As the name implies, these documents have been designed to fit your wishes and give you the most flexibility. They are also the most expensive and must be individually approved by the IRS. However, if you want your defined benefit or contributory plan to invest in real estate, these may be necessary.
2. *Volume submitter plan documents.* These are preapproved by the IRS and are typically used by pension consultants who will tailor the choice of documents to best fit your needs. Ask questions and review the documents to make sure they fit. Although the cost of plan administration will be higher than for prototype documents, these are usually used for personal defined benefit or defined contribution plans requiring an actuary anyway.
3. *Prototype documents.* These are one-size-fits-all, usually free, but only if you invest in what the plan administrator is selling. These are the type offered by brokerage firms and insurance companies. Typically if you want to move your IRA, Keogh, individual 401(k), small business 410(k), or personal defined bene-

fit plan, you must get new documents or risk the plan being disqualified.

Protection from Creditors

In March 2004, the Supreme Court ruled that a sole proprietor who maintains a qualified retirement plan that also covers a common-law employee (other than the sole proprietor's spouse) enjoys the protection of his or her plan assets from creditors under federal Employee Retirement Income Security Act (ERISA) pension laws. This protection also applies to a sole proprietor with a Keogh plan if there is at least one nonspouse employee. This may not sound important until you get sued for more than the limits on your insurance policies. IRA assets and those of sole proprietors are still subject to creditor attachment.

A Call for 401(k) Pension Reform

The extent to which baby boomers are underfunded for retirement now has quantified evidence. A September 2003 study by the Employee Benefit Research Institute (EBRI) and the Investment Company Institute (ICI) presents a sobering view of how ill prepared many American workers are for retirement. The 2002 EBRI/ICI database contains 46,310 401(k) plans with $618.6 billion of assets and 15,509,185 participants.[28] Although this study accounts for only one-third of American workers in 401(k) plans, the data is five years more current than U.S. government data. The study looks at relationships among the plan participant ages, tenure at the employer, investment asset allocations, and average account balances across the entire database. Participants in their 60s with more than 30 years of employment tenure have average account balances of only $146,211.[29] The authors allow that this may not represent their entire retirement nest egg, but with 30 years of continuous employment this must represent the majority of their retirement savings. For participants in their 60s earning $80,000 to $90,000 per year with 20 years or more of tenure, their average account balances are 285 percent[30] of salary, or $230,000 to $250,000. If retirement comes at age 65 and we apply the 4 percent annual drawdown formula, this will yield annual retirement income of only $10,000. Combined with Social Security, this provides retirement income of only 33 percent of final salary. Participants in their 60s with 10 to 20 years of tenure have average balances equal to only 180 percent of salary for the $60,000 through $90,000 salary range.[31]

Account balances and plan participation for plan participants in their 30s, 40s, and 50s is equally sobering.[32] Plans with fewer than 1,000 participants average about 10 percent participation. Participation is only slightly better at 20 percent for plans with 1,001 through 5,000 participants, and 60 percent for plans with more than 5,000 participants. Although the study does not attribute this higher participation to any one factor, clearly larger plans have administrators with the resources to educate and encourage company employees to participate. Sadly, even this produces only 60 percent participation. Only 32 percent of participants in their 40s take advantage of the plan and only 22 percent in their 50s. The worst part is that 45 percent of all plan participants have account balances of less than $10,000.[33] Account balances between $50,000 and $100,000 account for 7 percent of participants, while balances in excess of $100,000 represent 10 percent of participants.[34]

No matter how you look at the data, very few employees seem to understand both the need to save for retirement and that by not participating they are forgoing the employer matching contributions. Beyond the lack of education about the need for participation, those who are participating need to have the ability to put more money aside on a tax-deferred basis.

When you argue to give a benefit that costs tax dollars, you have to balance it by taking in more tax dollars someplace else. The 47 million Americans who are being asked to fund their own pension plans need to be able to put away more money than the government now allows. By this point, you must understand the dismal prospects most Americans face in retirement. No matter how much you squeeze out of your income, life's adventures like buying a house, funding education, and paying the bills mean that until a certain age, retirement funding does not gain your full attention.

I propose that starting at age 40, Americans be allowed to begin making tax-deferred catch-up contributions to their 401(k) plans. And the older these plan participants get, the larger the tax-deferred catch-up contributions should be. As employees, they do not have the same opportunities the self-employed and business owners have for creative

TABLE 6.10   Proposed Additional Tax-Deferred 401(k) Contributions by Age Bracket

Age 40 to 44	Age 45 to 48	Age 49 to 52	Age 53 to 56	Age 57 and over
$7,000	$12,000	$18,000	$25,000	$30,000

pension planning. No matter how hard the 40- or 50-year-old tries, he/she will not attain a comfortable level of retirement income with the current limits on contributions. Unfortunately, almost no one starts making contributions to their company's 401(k) when they are in their 20s, and certainly not to the maximum possible.

I propose, in today's dollars, the tax-deferred 401(k) and 403(b) catch-up contribution schedule with high current income limitations shown in Table 6.10. These amounts would be in addition to the regular tax-deferred contribution limit, which is $14,000 this year.

The Winning Investment Strategy for the Twenty-First Century

Most investors . . . will find that the best way to own common stocks is through an index fund that charges minimal fees. Those following this path are sure to beat the net results (after fees and expenses) by the great majority of investment professionals.
   —Warren Buffett, from his letter to shareholders in the 1996
      Berkshire Hathaway Annual Report

Most investors would be better off in an index fund rather than investing in an actively managed equity mutual fund.[1]
   —Peter Lynch, retired manager of the then-largest actively
      managed mutual fund, Fidelity Investments Magellan Fund

The ultimate beauty of index funds is that they get you utterly out of the business of guessing what will happen next. They enable you to say seven magic words: "I don't know, and I don't care."[2]
   —Jason Zweig, mutual fund columnist, *Money* magazine

When we buy an actively managed [mutual] fund, we are like gamblers in Vegas. We know it is likely to be a losing proposition, yet somehow we feel we are getting our money's worth.[3]
   —Alex Frino and David Gallagher, mutual fund authorities
      from the University of Sydney, Australia, quoted in the *Wall
      Street Journal*, 2001

If you are one of the 80 percent of 401(k) type pension plan participants who recently reported that they either are uncertain about their plan investments or are reluctant to oversee the investments in their retirement account,[4] are one of the almost half of plan participants who did not adjust their investment mix over the past three years,[5] or are an individual investor who bought go-go mutual funds in 1999 and stared at the headlights as your nest egg disappeared, it's time to address a way to successfully invest and remain uninvolved. Computer models and many of the best investment minds agree that index funds will navigate you through market fluctuations and ultimately deliver desired returns. I offer the evidence and if you agree we can proceed to develop an investment strategy that you can maintain.

The strategy is to buy and hold a balance of index funds or exchange-traded funds (ETF). Your portfolio will outperform a portfolio of actively managed mutual funds for three key reasons:

1. Eight out of 10 actively managed mutual funds neither equal nor outperform the index they strive to match.[6] Professional money managers trade against each other in an efficient market in which the sum of their daily activity establishes the price of each respective index. They underperform the indexes by almost 3 percent on average, or approximately twice their 1.5 percent average annual management fee.[7]
2. Buying and holding index funds or exchange-traded funds will save you a minimum of 3 percent annually in lower management fees and trading costs. In this way you will approximate the market indexes, thus beating most of the pros.
3. Individual investors often buy and sell for all the wrong reasons and usually at the wrong time. To make a trade there must be a buyer and a seller—you versus the professionals. They profit from your mistakes while they cannot even beat the indexes.

Buying and holding investment products that track the indexes may sound either too simple or too good to be true, but the idea is not a new one. However, Wall Street brokerage firms spend billions of dollars annually on advertising to direct your attention to the active buying and selling of stocks and mutual funds to help you beat the market. Meanwhile legendary investment experts and professors lecture on indexing at institutional investment conferences. The evidence is irrefutable: 43 percent of all institutional money (big pensions and endowments) is invested in index products, while only 7 percent of individual or 401(k) type plan monies are invested in index products.[8] Professional managers are paid to squeeze every last ounce of profit and costs out of the funds they manage—so why shouldn't you?

The average investor/retiree can utilize the many examples and graphs in this chapter, which translate portfolio theory to individual reality with sample portfolios based on 28 years of Vanguard 500 and other index-tracking results. This simple presentation displays the cumulative result from better investment returns and the miracle of compound interest, which together allow retirees to draw down twice their expected income while their portfolio continues to grow. So, instead of $40,000 of income per year per million dollars of indexed retirement portfolio assets, you can take out $80,000 per year in inflation-adjusted today's dollars. Indexing may not be as intellectually stimulating as plotting your next trade in order to beat the markets, but it will add significantly more to your portfolio.

Decoding the Lingo

Let's get acquainted with the following classes of investment assets, because these financial instruments are available to self-directed pension investors:

- *Common stocks* are individual shares you purchase that represent ownership in a company. The future price of each share of common stock depends on that company's performance and how it is perceived by other investors. Common stock has no preference in the event of bankruptcy.
- *Bonds* represent money you lend to a company and for which you receive a specific, preestablished rate of interest. Because you receive a preferential investment return in the form of interest, you can expect a lower or no capital appreciation on bond investments. As overall interest rates go up relative to your bond's fixed rate, your bond's value, if you were to sell it, goes down. Conversely, if overall interest rates go down relative to your bond's fixed rate, your bond's value, if you were sell it, will increase.
- *Money market accounts* are savings-type accounts paying a nominal interest rate and functioning as a temporary parking place or cash reserve. Often you can designate that any cash in your brokerage account be put into a money market account so it will earn interest, while remaining available for investment at any time.
- *Certificates of deposit (CDs)* are issued by banks and brokerage firms and offer a fixed rate of interest income in exchange for your promise to leave the money in the CD for six months, one year, or longer. You earn a low but secure interest, but inflation erodes the value of your asset.
- *Mutual funds* offer investors a way to own a well-diversified portfolio of common stocks, bonds, or both by using economies of scale to buy large quantities of stock at low transaction costs. Mutual funds are organized by financial companies to track indexes of various sectors and

styles in domestic U.S. or foreign markets. Although historic returns are no indicator of a mutual fund's future performance, the consistent tenure of a long-standing manager is important. As we have already discussed, fees and turnover in the portfolio affect your return.

- *Exchange-traded funds (ETFs)* are actually index-tracking stocks (like mutual funds) traded on the American Stock Exchange. A relatively recent and successful investment vehicle created in the late 1990s, they buy all of the stocks or bonds that make up a particular index in the same ratio they represent on the index. Except for minor tracking errors they closely follow the index.

Asset Classes Suitable for Self-Directed Retirement Accounts

For our purposes I suggest we look at only three classes (types) of assets for use in your 401(k) type retirement accounts:

1. Domestic U.S. common stock, index-tracking mutual funds, and exchange-traded funds.
2. Domestic U.S. taxable high grade corporate bond funds and funds that follow the Lehman Aggregate Bond Index, which includes mortgage-backed securities and some government bonds.
3. Common stocks of non-U.S. corporations in developed countries that make up the Morgan Stanley Capital International Europe, Australasia, Far East (EAFE) Index.

These are three classes of assets you can purchase in low-cost index-tracking products. We will not consider real estate investment trusts (REITs) because they are difficult to evaluate, and common stocks in lesser developed countries because of unstable political issues. Also unsuitable domestic common stocks that have a share price of less than $1 and stocks that are not actively traded, as well as variable annuities and other life insurance–based products designed to provide you guaranteed income but at an enormous monetary and inflation-adjusted cost.

No-Load, Low-Fee Mutual Funds versus Exchange-Traded Funds: Which Should I Buy?

If you have a 401(k) type contributory pension plan, buying indexed mutual funds may be the only indexing option available to you. Both index mutual funds and exchange-traded funds offer investors a well-diversified indexed portfolio by using economies of scale to buy large quantities of stock at low transaction costs. While no-load, low-cost index mutual funds have lower acquisition costs, even the low-fee Vanguard 500 index fund loses its low-cost advantage in a direct one-year comparison with an ETF tracking the same index, due to the ETF's even lower management fees. I did this comparison using actual commissions charged on a $60,000 transaction in my Schwab account.[9] More important to your investment strategy is choosing the right allocation of indexed products and not getting lured into buying mutual funds that track individual industry sectors or growth-versus-value sector funds. Growth and value mutual funds limit your ability to be in the right sector at the right time without jumping around and paying excessive fees. Index-tracking products are made up of both growth and value companies and allow you to balance out being in the wrong place at the wrong time. What you save on trading costs will put you ahead of trying to pick sectors.

Costs and Fees

Brokerage firms, banks, commission-based financial planners, 401(k) type providers, and other mass marketers of mutual funds keep you in the dark about what it really costs you annually to buy and own mutual funds.[10] The average actively traded domestic stock fund has an annual management fee of 1.5 percent, taken out monthly. This is, however, only part of the total possible fees, disclosed or buried in excessive transaction costs paid to brokers and used to trade for investment research. Research expenses would add to reported management costs, but hiding them in soft-dollar arrangements allows fund advisers to skirt reporting rules and keep their reported fees lower than they actually are.[11]

Let's suppose you have been convinced to move your $100,000 401(k) type balance to a new provider with a whole new and supposedly better family of mutual funds. A detailed statement of your costs might look like Table 7.1.

Not all but most of these costs are involved in the transaction, either as up-front fees or as redemption charges when you sell the mutual funds. If all these typical costs were charged, you would have to make a 9.75 percent rate of return ($9,750) the first year just to stay even with the day you made this move. After paying those first-year fees and commissions, you are left with $90,250. But you are still going to be overpaying in fees

TABLE 7.1 Typical High Fee 401(k) Transaction Costs

Commission to buy funds	6.00%	$6,000
Annual management fee	1.50%	$1,500
Cost to execute trades each year	1.50%	$1,500
12(b)(1) ongoing advertising and deferred commission fees	0.75%	$ 750
Total fees in year of purchase	9.75%	$9,750

each year by 2 percent, even if you make no trades. After fees and front-end charges, assuming a prefee 8 percent annual return, at the end of 35 years your $90,250 will grow to $517,000 in inflation-adjusted today's dollars. By contrast, had you bought $100,000 of the no-load Vanguard 500 index fund with its 0.18 percent management fee, which holds a weighted average of the stocks that make up the Standard & Poor's 500 index, your money would have grown to $1,388,181 at the same assumed prefee 8 percent annual return. The difference is in the costs over the 35-year period, plus the first-year commissions:

	Annual Management Fee	Total 35-Year Management Fees
Vanguard 500 index fund	0.18%	$ 90,353
Average domestic stock fund	1.51%	$610,461

In 2004 Fidelity Investments reduced the fees on many of its index-tracking funds to 10 basis points. Vanguard Group followed in 2005 and reduced the minimum investment account size for its Admiral Shares funds to $100,000 from $250,000 to open these buy-and-hold type index funds with their 9 basis points fee to more investors. This kind of price war is good for the buy-and-hold investor.

It is much easier to decide to buy index funds or exchange-traded funds that have 2 percent lower fees and trading costs than to play the market and try to squeeze out a 2 percent higher annual investment yield. Depending on the market, a 2 percent greater yield means you have to make a 20 percent to 25 percent higher rate of return. The outcome is the same as Figure 7.1 shows. If 8 out of 10 managers of actively

FIGURE 7.1 Portfolio Gain by Squeezing Additional Annual Yield by Either Lower Expenses or Better Return

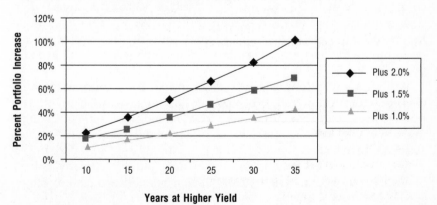

Years at Higher Yield

traded mutual funds can't beat the indexes, why should you think you can do any better?

Redemption fees are a big reason you need to be comfortable when you buy mutual funds that you intend to hold and not sell. Selling a fund within six months to five years can invoke redemption fees of from 1 percent to 4 percent at the time of sale. These are back-loaded sales fees. Check at the time of purchase, but mutual fund companies often charge a 1 percent redemption fee on mutual funds bought and then sold within six months. The Principal Group, a large 401(k) provider, has a sliding scale of 4 percent redemption fees on its no-commission mutual funds if they are sold in less than five years.[12] On top of fees imposed by the mutual fund family, Charles Schwab & Company charges an additional fee of 1 percent if funds from its no-load Select List are sold in less than six months.[13] Schwab, too, wants to discourage you from churning in your account. Buying and selling to match the mood of the markets may actually cause you to lose money in an up market.

Market timing your trades in mutual funds requires a strong under-standing of the markets but also constant attention to market indicators. This latter point is the great equalizer on this playing field. Almost every mutual fund investor can and does tell the story of how they hit one or more trends and rode them up: growth technology in 1999 or again in 2003. But did they tell you how late in the cycle they bought, or when they sold and how far down the fund had gone before they sold? The point is: average investors neither know what the sell signs are nor pay attention and take action.

Can Active Managers Measure Up?

For active fund managers to add value for investors they must outper-form passive investments like index-tracking funds and stocks. First, they must earn back their management fees (1.5 percent), plus trading costs (1.0 percent to 2.0 percent), or roughly 3 percent. On a year-after-year sustained basis this is extremely difficult. Very seldom does a mu-tual fund that outperforms its benchmark index in one year equal that performance the next year. Picking successive trends is difficult even for the professionals.

With few exceptions equity (stock) markets are efficient because decision-critical information is available instantaneously to investment professionals, who account for more than 75 percent of trading. Changes in the market price of equities (stocks) represent the change in the consen-sus of active investors about what the price should be. The sum of the ac-tions by these professionals makes up the daily indexes. As early as 1966, Nobel laureate in economics (1990) Bill Sharpe published a study showing that the average mutual fund underperformed the market by 40 basis points[14] (100 basis points is 1 percentage point).[15] By late 1999, Jonathan Clements of the *Wall Street Journal* believed "the average mutual fund underperformed its risk-adjusted benchmark [index] by 140 basis points [1.4 percent] a year."[16] Charles Ellis, founder of the institutional investment consultants Greenwich Associates, first published the following accepted fact in 1975: "The evidence is deeply disturbing: 85 percent of professionally managed funds underperformed the S&P 500 [index] during the past 10 years."[17]

Ellis, in the fourth edition of his famous book *Winning the Loser's Game* (2002), notes every individual investor's wish that they could invest with the guidance of "The Dream Team." Ellis correctly allows you to choose the best: Warren Buffett, Peter Lynch, the best at Fidelity, Vanguard, Merrill Lynch, and the other big Wall Street firms. Setting costs aside, these people get to tell you how to beat the market. Mountains of documentation later, Ellis observes, "All you do is index—because an index fund replicates the market and today's professional-dominated stock market reflects their accumulated expertise."[18]

Why Are We All Bad Active Investors?

Much has been written about the question of whether it is easier to buy or easier to sell a stock or mutual fund. Hands down the answer is that it is easier for individual investors to make a buy decision than a decision to sell. Social psychologists say investors develop an emotional attachment to what they have bought. When it is going up in price they see no reason to sell, and when it drops in price they want to wait for it to come back up. Psychologists also claim we are optimists about things turning around and too proud to admit we have made mistakes. These social psychologists may be right, but they discount the fact that American workers are often too busy with their jobs and families to even recognize that the price has gone down. Forty-one percent of plan participants surveyed in mid-2003 by Hewitt Associates said they had not made any investment changes in their plan assets for three years.[19] Had they originally bought a balance of securities tied to indexes that track different segments of the economy, this buy-and-hold strategy would have cushioned the shock over the past four years. (More on this later in the chapter.)

Beyond our emotionally driven stupidity as humans, the factor that erodes our investment portfolios the most is our impatience. Individual investors buy and sell mutual funds as they chase higher investment returns. By doing so they wipe out gains and often create losses because of front-end trading fees and/or back-end redemption fees charged by the fund and the brokerage house.

What Makes Markets Move?

There are four key factors or indicators to watch that broadly control the up-and-down movement of stock markets:

1. Anticipated and then announced corporate earnings.
2. The direction the Federal Reserve moves interest rates.
3. The world situation.
4. Investor sentiment and confidence.

Corporate Earnings

As corporate earnings move, so moves the market. Corporations issue estimates of future earnings and are required to tell the public about both good and bad events affecting the company. Securities analysts who follow particular companies estimate future earnings. When corporations do not meet or exceed analyst expectations, the stock price usually suffers. Most stocks are bought and sold based on estimates of future earnings. Think about how your company's stock price moves around, sometimes for no apparent reason. The reason is there are always buyers and sellers with different motivations for their actions.

The equity markets identify most companies as belonging to particular sectors of the economy. Not all companies in a sector will gain or lose share value at the same time, but the sectors are cyclical. This means that some sectors are expected to have price gains early in an economic cycle and some later. The 10 sectors are:

1. Energy	6. Health care
2. Financials	7. Materials
3. Information technology	8. Industrials
4. Telecommunication services	9. Consumer discretionary
5. Utilities	10. Consumer staples

Industrials (airlines, railroads, automobiles); materials (steel and building supplies); and information technology (computers and networking) are examples of cyclical sectors and industries in those sectors. Sales by companies in these industry groups are tied to performance in other industry groups or the economy as a whole. Professional investors use a great deal of research hoping to buy stocks of companies that have strong earnings potential, but where the stock is underpriced relative to the sector. Likewise, they sell when they think a stock is overpriced relative to the anticipated future earnings potential of the company.

The professionals started a big sell-off in March 2000 when they decided technology stocks and Internet stocks were overpriced based on unfounded expectations of future earnings and growth. The March 2000 tech bust was quickly followed by industrial customers putting the brakes on technology purchases. This further drove down the stock prices of computer and networking manufacturers and their suppliers. This is partially why the technology-heavy Nasdaq went down 50 percent in 2000 while the S&P 500 and Dow Jones Industrial Average were both flat or off less than 10 percent. By not making expenditures on technology, the customer companies in the S&P 500 and the Dow were actually implementing cost savings that buoyed their stock prices, at least for a while.

This isolated example of stock prices not being supported by sufficient anticipated company earnings growth reversed itself in 2003. One of the first stock market indicators that the economy and the price of tech stocks were turning in February/March of 2003 was increased orders for computer and networking hardware. Increased productivity by industrial companies was putting a strain on three-year-old computer hardware that needed to be replaced.

Isolating the relationship of these industry cyclical trends is critical if you are going to buy mutual funds that follow industry sectors. Remember that not all companies in a group will move at the same time. You need steel and aluminum to build automobiles and don't need them when automobile sales slow. Considering that most components in vehicles manufactured in the United States come from offshore, where worldwide are the steel and aluminum being mined, processed, and fabricated? The best guess is not in America and probably not by companies traded on our stock exchanges. Computer processor speed in new hardware makes the same old software work faster and move data acceptably well over an existing computer network. Much of industry is still absorbing computer software purchased in the year 2000.

Direction of Interest Rates

The Federal Reserve's Open Market Committee meets monthly to consider whether to raise or lower the interest rate that banks charge one another on monies borrowed overnight. These rate increases or decreases signal the Fed's optimism and pessimism about how the economy is moving and whether they need to put on the brakes or prime the pump. Higher interest rates mean higher borrowing costs. This is particularly damaging to small companies because the higher interest expense erodes their profits faster than those of big industrial companies, which usually get their funding from many sources not tied to short-term interest rates. These Fed meetings are eagerly anticipated by market watchers who know that rate changes will affect certain sectors of the economy more than others. The Federal Reserve often telegraphs the likelihood of a change to soften the reaction by stock markets.

For example, when home mortgage rates go up by, say, 2 percent, fewer households are able to qualify for loans to buy homes, and thus mortgage lending slows and new housing starts decline. Although builders do not stop building—they typically have a backlog of sold but not yet built homes—professional investors anticipate the downturn and lower future earnings and start selling the stocks of home builders and their suppliers. Said another way, they sell because they think the stocks are overpriced. So who is doing the buying if professional investors want to sell? The answer is other professional investors who think they see a bargain and individual investors who are still looking at the previous period's strong building and demand information and who missed the indicators of a downward trend.

World Situation

Stock markets and their investors do not like unpredictable world tension. When this happens, investors sit on the sidelines or convert to cash by selling stocks and mutual funds. However, U.S. stock markets have always reacted favorably to war because war means higher government spending. The economy benefits because more money flows into it, and investors tend to discount the fact that the money ultimately must be repaid.

The impact of September 11 had a negative effect on the stock markets. Only after a year did living with terrorism start to be an accepted part of daily life.

Investor Sentiment

Investors have a herd mentality. Savvy big institutional investors lead the movement, usually making money through disciplined buying when stocks are cheap and selling when they get overpriced. The little guys follow behind and get caught up in the euphoria of a rising market. Then they play host to the "I can't believe it is happening" attitude and are the last to get out of a falling market. In defense of individual investors, they also don't have the time to focus on the stock markets and the relationships between the 7,200 traded companies and the outside world. Worse, there are more than 6,500 mutual funds that own the stock of these and foreign companies.

For every buyer there is a seller on the other side of each trade. This seller may be taking her profits and moving on, or he has suffered more losses than he can tolerate and is getting out. At the start of a bull market it is usually the savvy institutional investors who are the buyers and the crushed individual investors who have had enough and are getting out. The same holds true when markets show real signs of a decline: the big guys are getting out and the little guys are still buying.

The University of Michigan and the Conference Board publish monthly consumer sentiment indexes that are watched closely by professional investors because consumers account for two-thirds of all spending in our economy. Each group polls a random sample of consumers and then quantifies the results into a single index value summarizing the opinions and attitudes of these consumers about the current and future strength of the economy.[20]

Major Market Tracking Indexes

It seems like there are almost as many specialized indexes as there are mutual funds. This is so that the mutual fund managers have an index (benchmark) or two to try to equal. Many of these specialized indexes are variants of basic indexes. For our purposes we are going to examine the basic indexes because they are the basis for the lowest-cost index mutual funds and exchange-traded funds that are widely available to 401(k) type plan participants.

Table 7.2 shows the attributes of six leading domestic stock indexes. Ultimately your investment strategy should include index funds and exchange-traded funds that track domestic stock indexes, a developed countries global stock index, and a domestic bond index.

Either to differentiate themselves or to introduce what they think is a better index, Schwab, Morgan Stanley, and others have created variants of these indexes. Dow Jones recently acquired the rights to calculate and market the Wilshire Associates Wilshire 5000, 4500, and other indexes. For comparison purposes the old method of calculating these indexes will still be available. Only time will tell whether the modified indexes will provide an equal or better measure of performance. In the meantime comparisons are difficult. For example, the Morgan Stanley MCSI 750 index is not 250 companies added to the S&P 500 index, nor is it 250 companies subtracted from the Russell 1000 index (the largest 1,000 companies in the Russell 3000 index). This same lack of comparability exists for the Schwab 1000 index. This does not mean you shouldn't buy a fund that tracks these indexes, but only that you shouldn't try to compare performance to the S&P 500 or the Russell 1000.

S&P 500

The Standard & Poor's 500 (S&P 500) index was created in 1928 and is a market value–weighted index (shares outstanding multiplied by stock price) of 500 stocks that are traded on the New York Stock Exchange (NYSE), American Stock Exchange (AMEX), and Nasdaq National Market. Historically, the weighting makes each company's influence on the index's performance directly proportional to that

TABLE 7.2   Six Leading Domestic Stock Indexes Used by Indexed Mutual Funds

Symbol:	INX	COMPX	INDU	$IVX	$IUX	$:TMW.X
Index:	Standard & Poor's 500 Index	Nasdaq Composite Index	Dow Jones Industrial Average	Russell 3000 Index	Russell 2000 Index	Wilshire 5000 Index
Representation	Broad market	Nasdaq exchange	Large cap	Broad market	Small cap	Broad market
Year Index Introduced	1928	1971	1896	1979	1979	1970
Approximate Number of Companies in Index	500	7,200+	30	3,000	2,000	5,200+
Criteria for Inclusion	S&P selection committee, chosen by market size, liquidity, and industry group	All Nasdaq domestic and non-U.S. common stocks traded on Nasdaq	Representative of U.S. industry; chosen by *Wall Street Journal* editor selection committee	Top 3,000 Nasdaq, NYSE, AMEX U.S. stocks in ranking by market cap	Bottom 2,000 securities in Russell 3000	Most actively traded stocks of companies headquartered in U.S.
Distribution by Market Cap:						
NYSE	84.6%		85.6%	79.6%	43.9%	78.0%
AMEX	3.2%		0.0%	0.4%	2.1%	0.6%
Nasdaq	12.2%	100%	14.4%	20.0%	54.0%	21.4%
Weighting	Market cap—will be changed to reflect weighted value of traded shares by Sept. 2005	Market cap	Price	Market cap—adjusted for large private holdings, corporate cross-ownership	Market cap—adjusted for large private holdings, corporate cross-ownership	Market cap—some changed in 2005 due to new Dow Jones calculation methods to adjust for nontraded stock

company's market value. Until 1980 companies usually were not removed from the S&P 500 unless they were merged or acquired and thus their stock no longer traded on the exchanges. Since then the index has been reconstituted monthly, and companies are chosen for inclusion in the index because they are the leading companies in leading industries in the U.S. economy.

Starting in September 2004 and gradually over one year, the S&P 500 index is changing the weighted mix of index companies to reflect the shares of stock that are being actively traded. This will eliminate non-traded large blocks of stock held by company insiders and their benefit plans. For example, shares of Wal-Mart (insider family holdings) and Microsoft (Gates family holdings) will make up less of the index. This will increase the percentage representation of widely held stocks like General Electric. Many experts believe this will have negligible effect on the index and how future index data relates to historic data.

More than 50 percent of the S&P 500 is, however, made up by the market capitalization of selected companies in three industry sectors: financials, information technology, and health care. Twenty-two percent of the holdings represent the top 10 companies by market capitalization. This means that the performance of a few of the largest companies has a disproportionate influence on the index that is supposed to track the 500 largest companies.

An interesting variant on the S&P 500 index is the Morgan Stanley Weighted S&P 500 fund. It uses the same blend of 500 companies, but it holds an equal portion for each stock. Because this "index" was started only in July of 1997, there is insufficient long-term comparative data to assume it is a better index than the S&P 500. However, since inception in 1997 on a cumulative basis, the Morgan Stanley Weighted S&P 500 fund (symbol VADDX) has never outperformed the S&P 500 index, and has outperformed the Vanguard 500 fund (symbol VFINX) just once. The notable exception was 2004 when the VADDX had a return of 14.13 percent, a 31 percent higher return than the VFINX return at 10.74 percent. One year's performance should not make any difference to a long-term buy-and-hold investor.

Of the 500 companies that made up the S&P 500 in 1980 only 15 remained in 1990 and only one, Intel Corporation, was still represented on the S&P 500 in 2000. The Vanguard 500 index fund, started in 1976 by John Bogle at the Vanguard Group, was the first index fund to track the S&P 500. Over the past 20 years, and eliminating mutual funds that have not survived, only 3 percent (five funds) of mutual funds with assets of more than $100 million have beaten the Vanguard 500. These have bettered it by only 0.37 percent. Of the 157 other mutual funds that have survived 20 years, the average underperformed the Vanguard 500 (the S&P 500 index) by 1.49 percent.[21]

Nasdaq (National Association of Securities Dealers Automated Quotation System)

The Nasdaq Composite is exactly that, a composite index of all the 7,200+ stocks traded on that exchange. This index was created in 1971. The weighting is like the S&P 500, shares outstanding multiplied by price. The Nasdaq is reconstituted daily. This index covers everything from the big companies actively traded on the Nasdaq like Microsoft, down to very small-capitalization stocks trading at just over $1 per share. Companies that are not actively traded are not included in the index. This index is heavily weighted toward technology stocks.

Dow Jones Industrial Average

The Dow Jones Industrial Average is made up of 30 companies that are widely held and often traded by institutional investors. (See Table 7.3.) This often-quoted index has been around since 1896. It reflects the price changes in these widely traded stocks and is thus a good benchmark of daily market direction and sensitivity. You will note from the list of 30 companies that they are all basic to the economy and a good composite indicator of daily market movement, but not necessarily overall economic trends.

Frank Russell Company Indexes

The Frank Russell Company is an old-line institutional investment firm that developed this series of indexes more than 20 years ago.

Russell 3000. The Russell 3000 measures the performance of the 3,000 most actively traded stocks of the 6,000 publicly traded U.S. stocks. These 3,000 companies represent 98 percent of the market value of all publicly

TABLE 7.3   Companies of the Dow 30 at December 31, 2004

Alcoa	General Electric	Merck
Altria (Philip Morris)	General Motors	Microsoft
American Express	Hewlett-Packard	Pfizer
American International Group (AIG)	Home Depot	Procter & Gamble
Boeing	Honeywell International	SBC Communications
Caterpillar	IBM	3M
Citigroup	Intel	United Technologies
Coca-Cola	J.P. Morgan Chase	Verizon
DuPont	Johnson & Johnson	Wal-Mart
ExxonMobil	McDonald's	Walt Disney

traded U.S. stocks. All 3,000 of these companies are market capitalization weighted and adjusted for any cross-ownership. If company A owns 20 percent of company B, then the index includes only 80 percent of company B. The base level of the Russell indexes was set at 100 in 1979. Unlike the S&P 500, this index is adjusted once each year in July based on May 31 market values. The Russell indexes are reconstituted based on an empirical set of mathematical guidelines. Stocks removed from the index during the year are not replaced.[22]

Russell 1000.   The Russell 1000 measures the performance of the largest 1,000 actively traded U.S. public stock companies that make up the Russell 3000 index. Their percentage in the index is market cap weighted similarly to the S&P 500, but with more large companies.

Russell 2000.   The Russell 2000 measures the performance of the bottom 2,000 actively traded U.S. public stock companies that make up the Russell 3000 index. These companies have market caps between $20 million and $300 million.

Wilshire 5000

This index was established in 1974 by Wilshire Associates and tracks the most commonly traded 5,200 stocks of companies that have their headquarters in the United States. This index is reconstituted monthly. It is the broadest market index most commonly quoted.

Morgan Stanley Capital International Europe, Australasia, Far East (EAFE) Index

This index tracks approximately 1,100 equity securities from stock markets in 24 developed countries, with only minor U.S. representation. The makeup is principally European and Japanese: 26 percent United Kingdom, 20 percent Japan, 10 percent France, 7 percent Switzerland, 6 percent Germany, 2 percent Sweden, 1 percent Hong Kong, and so on. It is a market-capitalization-weighted index (shares outstanding multiplied by price in dollars). This index has been calculated and published since 1969.

Lehman Aggregate Bond Index

This bond index reflects the market-weighted changes in various corporate bond indexes, plus mortgage-backed securities and U.S. government bonds. This is the broadest of the bond indexes and was created in 1976.

Other Indexes

Between Standard & Poor's, Dow Jones, Russell, Morgan Stanley, and Wilshire Associates there are more than 200 specialty and overlapping indexes. Each index competitor offers indexes that measure large-capitalization growth and value stock styles, and separate indexes to measure small-capitalization growth and value stock performance. There are separate indexes for foreign stocks based on each country's stock exchange, stock exchanges by region of the world, and growth and value by region.

Kenneth L. Fisher, a respected money manager who writes for *Forbes* magazine, made an interesting observation in his November 27, 2000, column. Fisher explained, "Recognize that all correctly constructed major equity indexes (market-capitalization-weighted) end up with almost identical 30-year returns. Investors never believe this, yet it's true whether the index is the S&P 500 (which covers U.S. large caps), the Nasdaq Composite (technology), Morgan Stanley's EAFE (for Europe, Australasia, and the Far East), or Morgan Stanley's World Index (the broadest one). And it is even true for country returns: Japan's, Britain's, France's, or anywhere that isn't tiny. They all have average annual returns for the last 30 years within 0.75 percentage points, plus or minus, of 13.8%. Like the S&P 500 at 14.1% or Nasdaq at 13.6%."[23] Why is this? Money moves to opportunities in a constant worldwide flow.

Hence, picking a long-term benchmark isn't about getting the best returns; it's about stomaching volatility. Investors hate wild gyrations. The best benchmark is one that gets you to that 35-year future return with the smoothest ride.

Accepting Ken Fisher's premise that all indexes balance out in 30 years, I have chosen a 6-year, an 11-year, and a 21-year comparison to look at volatility. Figures 7.2 and 7.3 compare the performance of the Vanguard 500 index fund (symbol VFINX) that tracks the S&P 500 index of corporations with large market valuations (stock price times shares outstanding) and the Vanguard Balanced index fund (symbol VBINX). The Vanguard Balanced index fund is 60 percent indexed stocks (Wilshire 5000 index) and 40 percent bonds (Lehman Aggregate Bond Index). This is the usual asset allocation suggested for people approaching retirement. The data is directly from the Vanguard web site, which allows many different comparisons of Vanguard and other mutual funds over many historic time intervals.

Figure 7.2 shows the comparative volatility of the two portfolios in the six-year short term, but note in Figure 7.3 how their performance converges over an 11-year span. Figure 7.4 substitutes the Wilshire 5000 index performance for the stock portion of the Vanguard Balanced fund because the fund was not created until 1992. The thing to note is that the compounding of the stock earnings during the addi-

FIGURE 7.2   Riding Out the Storm: Six-Year Sample of Index Fund Performance 1999 through 2004

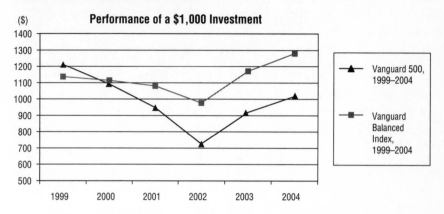

tional 10 early years provides an even better cushion for losses in the down years of 2000 through 2002. Be aware that this is historic data and may not represent future performance of the markets. Later, when we consider various asset allocations, we will look at projections of how different asset allocations perform in preretirement asset-gathering portfolios and postretirement portfolios when you are drawing out funds on which to live.

FIGURE 7.3   How Strong Is Your Stomach? 11-Year Sample of Index Fund Performance 1994 through 2004

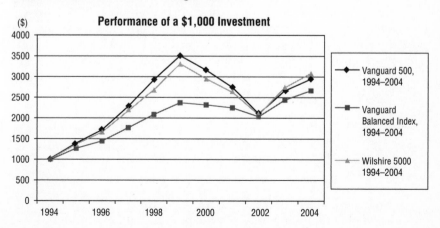

FIGURE 7.4   Over 21 Years the S&P 500 Does Add to Your Portfolio: Comparison of Index Fund Performance 1984 through 2004

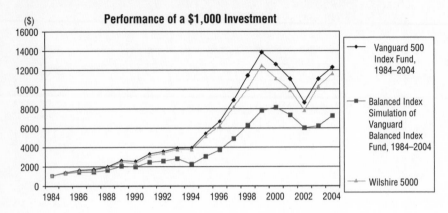

Investment Strategy

Armed with insights from successful professional investors and data from academics, we have a new understanding of what has been wrong with our approach to investing. After all, it is counterintuitive to think we can buy and hold investments while doing next to nothing and actually get a higher average annual return. But index funds will change that for you forever. Aside from no longer squandering profits by paying high management fees, buying and holding allows your money to sit there while enjoying the miracle of compound interest. History shows that money made and compounded in the good stock market years keeps us ahead of losses from the few bad years.

My goal is to limit your risk while helping you earn the highest possible return. But what level of average investment return should we expect from our portfolio? For my retirement savings examples I have used the commonly accepted 8 percent average annual return while shrinking the portfolio annually by 3 percent for inflation. However, the 8 percent average return reflects the high-fee mutual fund world we have now abandoned. Starting with the 8 percent expected average return, let's see how what we have learned can add to our return:

Base historic return	8.0%
Add: savings from not paying high management fees and higher trading costs in actively managed mutual funds	1.0%
Add: savings from not paying sales commissions or redemption fees because you no longer trade in and out of mutual funds to try to beat the market	1.0%

Add: savings from not buying last year's hot funds
that will underperform the indexes this year by more
than their fees and costs   2.0%
Add: additional gain by rebalancing your portfolio   0.4%[24]
                                                            _____
                                                            12.4%
                                                            ========

Proof:

35-year average return for the S&P 500	14.10%
20-year average return for the Vanguard 500	14.08%
27-year average return for the Vanguard 500 (started in 1976)	12.48%
10-year average return for the Vanguard Balanced index fund (started 1992)	9.60%
20-year simulated performance of balanced index fund	10.73%[25]
27-year average return for the Lehman Aggregate Bond index (started 1976)	9.38%
14-year average return for the Vanguard Small-Cap index fund (converted to an index fund in 1990)	11.02%
27-year average return for the Morgan Stanley MSCI EAFE Developed Markets index (started in 1969)	11.3%

What a Difference a Few Percentage Points Add to Retirement Income

Combining this extra average investment yield from indexed products with the compounding effect of our buy-and-hold strategy provides a whole new picture of retirement savings growth. A series of graphs will help demonstrate this. I have again used the more aggressive Vanguard 500 index fund (symbol VFINX) to approximate the S&P 500 and compared that compounded return to the Vanguard Balanced index fund (symbol VBINX), which is 60 percent stocks (Wilshire 5000) and 40 percent bonds (Lehman Aggregate Bond index). The 10-, 20-, and 27-year examples all use a portfolio that starts with $1 million and compares the annual account balances when income is drawn down at either the inflation-adjusted 4 percent of the starting balance or 5 percent of the year's outstanding balance.

Figure 7.5 compares the 10-year annual portfolio balances if retirement had begun in 1993 and the account had been invested between 1993 and 2003 in the Vanguard 500 or the Vanguard Balanced index fund. As we saw previously, the Vanguard 500 outperformed the conservative fund, but lost value in 2000, 2001, and 2002. It is important to note that even with this drop, both funding vehicles would have left us with a cushion of $500,000 in excess of the $1 million starting account balance at the end

FIGURE 7.5   Vanguard Balanced Index Fund (VBINX) versus Vanguard 500 Index Fund (VFINX): Annual Balances of $1 Million over 11 Years after 4 Percent or 5 Percent Inflation-Adjusted Annual Income Draw

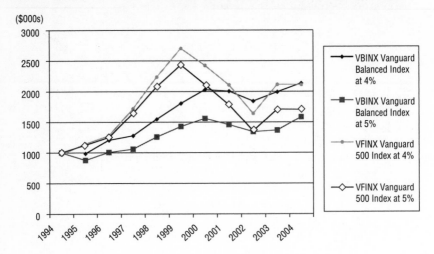

of 2002. This is because compounding in the high-yield years adds more value than is lost in the occasional bad years.

Now let's look at a 20-year example, but limit ourselves to the more conservative balanced fund. Figure 7.6 shows the 20-year performance of a balanced index retirement portfolio had retirement begun in 1984. This portfolio example also compares the same inflation-adjusted 4 percent of the starting amount or 5 percent of the outstanding annual balance as income draws. Because we are drawing out less in annual income than our average investment yield, the miracle of compounding has a big effect on portfolio growth. Compounding in this example yields account balances of more than $3 million at the end of 2003 for the more aggressive 5 percent annual income draw. This example again substitutes the Wilshire 5000 and Lehman Aggregate Bond index data up until 1992 because the Vanguard Balanced index fund was not started until 1992. Had these monies been invested at the lower 5 percent after-inflation yields (8 percent before accounting for inflation) used in the pension chapter, the account balances would have been more than 50 percent lower. More importantly, the smaller account balance would not have allowed for the use of the 5 percent income draw method, which dramatically increases your income draw while maintaining a portfolio cushion until age 100.

Had this retirement portfolio been invested in the Vanguard 500 for the 20 years prior to retirement, each $1,000 invested in 1983 and held for 20 years would have yielded $11,000. The same 20-year investment in the

FIGURE 7.6   Blended Index Fund 21-Year Comparative Performance (60 Percent Wilshire 5000 and 40 Percent Lehman Aggregate Bond Index): Annual Balances after 4 Percent Inflation-Adjusted Income Draw versus 5 Percent Oustanding Balance Income Draw

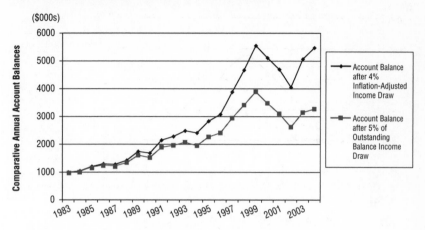

simulation of the Vanguard Balanced index fund would have yielded only $6,000.

Figure 7.7 is only a simulation using historic index values to approximate the 20-year performance of the Vanguard Balanced Index Fund, but if the future were to follow historic fund performance, a retirement portfolio with these higher returns would dramatically change the ability to safely draw retirement income. The point of the graph is to show that when you are earning more in the portfolio than you are drawing for income, each additional percentage point of higher performance allowed to compound will enable you to rethink what income you can draw while still building a comfortable cushion against a market downturn.

The bars on the bottom of Figure 7.7 show the inflation-adjusted 4 percent per year income draw per $1 million of starting portfolio value in 1984. This is the safe income level if the portfolio is yielding an average annual return of 8 percent (5 percent after inflation). This would have allowed $40,000 of income per $ million of portfolio value in the first year. The inflation-adjusted annual income grew to $53,757 in 1994 and $70,140 in 2003.

But look at the top line on Figure 7.7: the 5 percent of the outstanding balance income draw numbers. Because of strong market performance from 1984 through 1999, compounded by the higher return from low-fee index funds, the available income was significantly higher while the portfolio continued to build up a strong cushion against any future losses. Income started out 25 percent higher and reached $113,108 in 1994, 110 percent higher than the 4 percent inflation-adjusted draw, and

FIGURE 7.7   Blended Index Fund 21-Year Comparative Income Draw (60 Percent Wilshire 5000 and 40 Percent Lehman Aggregate Bond Index): 4 Percent Inflation-Adjusted Income Draw versus 5 Percent of Outstanding Balance

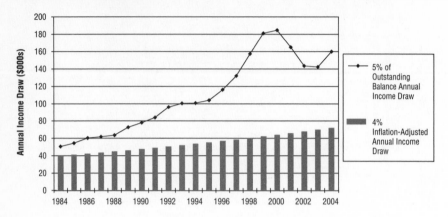

$180,644 in 2000, 158 percent higher than the prudent income level from a portfolio with an average 8 percent per year return. The lower income in 2003 (just over $140,000) was after the market and the value of the portfolio stumbled badly from 2000 through 2002.

Now What You Have Been Waiting For: Double Your Retirement Income

Why did I title the book *Double Your Retirement Income*? If you were retiring today and had applied the indexing investment strategy to the past 28 years of balanced index data, you could have not only doubled your first retirement year income draw from $40,000 to $80,000 per $1 million of retirement portfolio, but you could continue to draw down double the 4 percent inflation-adjusted portfolio income amount while having substantial growth in your retirement portfolio. This is not voodoo—it's again the combination of increasing your annual returns using the low-cost indexing strategy, combined with 28 years of compounding during retirement. Yes, you are drawing out extra money each year, but historic average index-tracking gains support these higher-income draws and offset the years the markets are down. Cumulative data shows that if you had retired in any of the 20 years from 1979 to 1999 this would have been the case. The exceptions are if you had retired in 2000 through 2002. The performance of the indexes in

2003 and 2004 have made up for those losses, but that is insufficient consolation for those who weathered that storm in their first years of retirement. If you enter retirement in a down global stock market year or if there are two bad years of stock market performance in a row, it would be a good idea to be more conservative on your income draws until the stock markets improve.

Table 7.4 shows the cumulative performance of selected general equity market indexes with each index starting in 1979 with a value of 1.00. The importance of this chart is to look at the cumulative performance of the indexes and thus their relevant index funds or exchange-traded funds. Scan down each column and note that, with the exception of years 2000 through 2002, had you saved for or entered retirement in any previous successive period the premise of continued compounded growth is supported by the numbers. These are the same growth numbers used in my examples to support the concept of an 8 percent retirement income withdrawal while your portfolio continues to grow.

Figure 7.1 showed that if you could increase your portfolio from 1 percent up to 1.5 percent per year by reducing your mutual fund costs or increasing your yield, you would increase your return by 75 percent over 35 years. This is the same relationship as increasing your return to 12 percent from 8 percent. Now add compounding to this higher yield, and the whole idea of starting to save early and not trading takes on new meaning, as you can see in Figure 7.8. Continuous compounding means your 75 percent higher yield increases to a 400 percent better portfolio yield in 35 years. Note how the lines start to really diverge in about year 15. This double whammy of higher investment returns and compounding is what adds to your nest egg during your accumulation years and overcomes the portfolio drain from drawing down double the income in your later retirement years.

The effective rate of return on your retirement portfolio has two stages:

Stage 1: During the preretirement phases, although you were earning a 12 percent average return in our examples, I subtracted 3 percent annually for inflation. In this way we could look at future account balances in today's dollars. This meant that one dollar of expected income 20 years from now would buy the same as one dollar today. This is similar to all the previous asset accumulation examples.

Stage 2: At retirement my examples adjust the income you draw in retirement for inflation each year to keep your spending power even, but allow your portfolio to grow unadjusted for inflation as in previous income draw examples. This is because we want to maintain level income and are concerned only about running out of income, not the effect of inflation on your portfolio balance.

TABLE 7.4 Historical Index Cumulative Performance 1979–2004

Year	S&P 500 (VFINX)	Russell 1000	Russell 2000	Russell 3000	Wilshire 5000	Lehman Aggregate Bond Index	Wilshire 5000 (60%) and Lehman Bond (40%) (VBINX)	MSCI Developed Countries (EAFE)	MSCI Emerging Countries (EEM)
1979	1.00	1.00	1.00	1.00	1.00	1.00	1.00	1.00	
1980	1.18	1.22	1.43	1.24	1.26	1.02	1.16	1.02	
1981	1.56	1.61	1.98	1.64	1.68	1.05	1.41	1.21	
1982	1.48	1.53	2.02	1.57	1.62	1.11	1.41	1.15	
1983	1.79	1.84	2.53	1.90	1.92	1.48	1.75	1.10	
1984	2.17	2.25	3.26	2.33	2.37	1.60	2.06	1.33	
1985	2.30	2.36	3.03	2.41	2.44	1.84	2.22	1.40	
1986	3.02	3.12	3.97	3.18	3.23	2.25	2.85	2.14	
1987	3.56	3.67	4.19	3.71	3.75	2.59	3.30	3.56	
1988	3.73	3.78	3.82	3.79	3.84	2.66	3.39	4.39	1.00
1989	4.34	4.43	4.78	4.46	4.53	2.87	3.86	5.56	1.35
1990	5.70	5.78	5.55	5.77	5.85	3.29	4.76	6.07	2.15
1991	5.51	5.54	4.47	5.47	5.49	3.58	4.75	4.57	1.85
	7.17	7.37	6.53	7.32	7.37	4.16	6.03	5.04	2.89

Year									
1992	7.71	8.03	7.74	8.02	8.03	4.47	6.53	4.34	3.15
1993	8.47	8.84	9.20	8.89	8.93	4.90	7.23	5.66	5.39
1994	8.57	8.88	9.03	8.91	8.93	4.76	7.14	6.01	4.93
1995	11.78	12.23	11.60	12.19	12.18	5.64	9.23	6.58	4.58
1996	14.47	14.98	13.51	14.85	14.76	5.84	10.54	6.87	4.76
1997	19.27	19.90	16.53	19.57	19.38	6.41	12.92	6.89	4.12
1998	24.79	25.27	16.11	24.29	23.93	6.96	15.19	8.14	2.99
1999	30.01	30.56	19.53	29.36	29.56	6.91	17.29	10.20	4.89
2000	27.29	28.18	18.94	27.17	26.34	7.71	16.96	8.65	3.34
2001	24.01	24.67	19.41	24.06	23.45	8.36	16.42	6.69	3.17
2002	18.69	19.33	15.44	18.88	18.56	9.22	15.04	5.52	2.92
2003	24.02	25.11	22.73	24.74	24.43	9.59	18.14	7.47	4.43
2004	26.60	27.97	26.90	27.70	27.52	10.02	19.82	8.78	5.42

Note: Commonly available investment products are substituted where possible. Base year starts at 1.00 and shows cumulative performance.

163

FIGURE 7.8   The Miracle of Compound Interest: $1 Left Alone to Compound at Different Rates for 35 Years—8 Percent versus 12 Percent Compounding

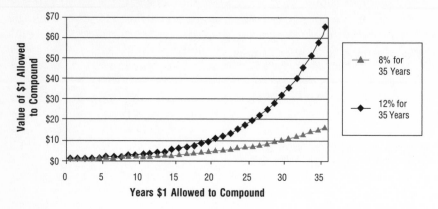

Figure 7.9 shows the comparative income draws. In this example, the annual income draw starts at $80,000 and is adjusted for actual annual inflation each year. Your immediate question should be, "Can I maintain this level of income and stay even with inflation without depleting the portfolio?" Twenty-eight years of up-and-down historic data says yes, while growing a cushion in your portfolio. It is important to note that al-

FIGURE 7.9   Double Your Retirement Income: Indexing Strategy Plus Compounding Allow Retirees to Double 4 Percent Inflation-Adjusted Annual Income, 1976–2004 ($1 Million Portfolio Invested in 60 Percent Wilshire 5000 and 40 Percent Lehman Aggregate Bond Index)

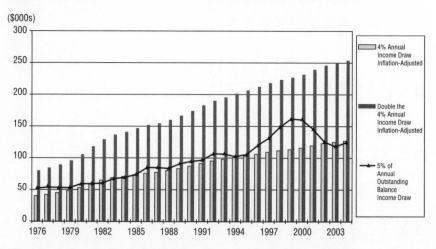

though annual retirement income in this example increased from $80,000 in today's dollars in 1976 to $250,000 in 2003, this is just keeping pace with inflation.

Figure 7.10 shows the annual portfolio balance after income draws where the monies are invested in a simulated balanced index portfolio of 60 percent Wilshire 5000 index and 40 percent Lehman Aggregate Bond index. Even if you took away the dramatic portfolio gains in the 1990s but left the drop in years 2000 through 2002, this income strategy still works with a sufficient cushion.

Figure 7.11 shows the annual performance of the simulated balanced index from 1976 through 2004. I chose 1976 to start this example because that was the first year of the Lehman Aggregate Bond index. This choice of 1976 also adds consistency with the examples using the Vanguard 500 index fund, started in 1976.

Figure 7.12 displays a side-by-side comparison of the index gains and losses from Figure 7.10 and the actual inflation (consumer price index) changes each year from 1976 through 2004. As you can see, inflation was hard to tame in the 1980s. If you had wanted your income to keep up with inflation your increase in income for 1980 would have had to be 11 percent, but only 2 percent in 1986. By matching your annual income increase to inflation, you would keep your spending power relatively the same. Consumer price inflation averaged 3.2 percent from 1982 through 2004. Even though in 9 of the 29 years shown in

FIGURE 7.10   Double Your Retirement Income: End-of-Year Retirement Portfolio Balance after Annual Income Draw, 1976–2004 ($1 Million Portfolio Invested in 60 Percent Wilshire 5000 and 40 Percent Lehman Aggregate Bond Index)

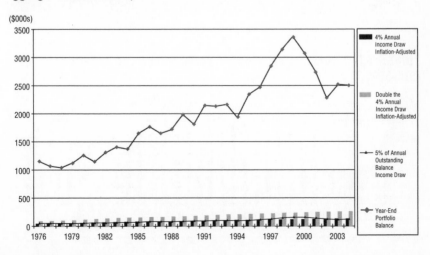

FIGURE 7.11　Simulated Balanced Index Annual Return, 1976 through 2004 (60 Percent Wilshire 5000 and 40 Percent Lehman Aggregate Bond Index)

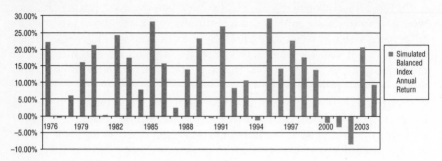

Figure 7.12 annual inflation was higher than the performance gain in the simulated index, the index performance in the other 20 years grew the retirement portfolio to 2.5 times its original value.

These graphs, although they use historic data, should be enough to convince you that squeezing out the extra percentage returns using index funds is an idea that is too good to pass up. Of course I cannot guarantee this kind of performance in the future, but I can guarantee that whatever extra return you experience will enjoy the miracle of compounding.

Picking Indexes to Track

We will now focus on the job of balancing indexes to temper the volatility of the S&P 500 while trying to perform an extra percentage point or two better than the Vanguard Balanced fund. Each stock market index tracks either an entire market (Wilshire 5000 index, Lehman Aggregate Bond index), a most actively traded cross section of the stock markets (Russell

FIGURE 7.12　Comparison of Index Performance and Inflation, 1976–2004

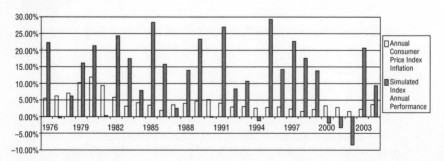

3000 index), or some size component (Russell 2000 index), style group (value or growth, small-cap, etc.), or industry segment within the universe of actively traded stocks or bonds. We are not going to consider style groups or industry segments because these require hands-on monitoring and frequent shifts to follow trends. We are going to stay with broad market indexes because we can buy products that track these indexes with long histories. These indexes contain a blend of growth and value companies in all industry segments. Most index funds and exchange-traded funds are less than 10 years old, but because of their minor deviations from the index they track we can get comfort from the index data.

There is a key principle about stock and bond markets we must understand when picking indexes: except for money lost in a down market or new money entering the markets, the rest of the trillions of dollars, yen, and euros are just moving around to follow (make) the markets in three main ways:

1. Movement between style boxes—small-capitalization stocks to mid- or large-capitalization stocks or vice versa.
2. Movement between industry groups—technology to pharmaceuticals to industrials, and so on.
3. Movement from one asset class (stocks) to another asset class (bonds).

Much of this is done offensively or defensively to follow (create) a trend. Small-cap stocks are often favored at the beginning of a bull (growth) market, while large-cap stocks are favored because of their relative safety in the latter part of a bull market. Money generally moves from the safety of bonds into stocks at the beginning (creation) of a bull market. Professionals move money out of stocks into bonds when stocks are overpriced at the top of a bull market, thus starting (creating) a bear (down) market. What happens is not the mystery; it is predicting the timing with enough confidence to follow the trends that separates winners from losers. We have stopped trying to guess trends or follow last year's hot mutual funds—thus we buy only index-tracking products.

Three Investment Time Frames Define Your Life Span

I believe there are three time frames that dictate the investment strategies of generally healthy investors and their partners:

1. Preretirement until 10 years before the portfolio will be needed to provide more than one-half of your annual income. From your retirement portfolio standpoint this is from birth until between ages 50 and 65. At the time you do your preretirement assessment at age

50 or 55 you will be able to determine when retirement looks possible and thus whether it is time to change strategies.

2. Ten years before you will retire, depending on the income and growth from your portfolio you will shift your mix of stock and bonds. This shift will be to a more conservative portfolio, but still more aggressive than many brokerage firms recommend.

3. At or shortly after actual retirement the shift will be to a more conservative investment mix. However, if you and your partner are both healthy, you must remember that you have a good chance of living 30 years in retirement. That means 30 years of 3 percent average historic inflation eating away at your retirement account balance. Thus a still conservative but slightly more aggressive approach is called for.

In Figure 7.13, for reference, are the usual pie chart asset allocation mixes for retirement accounts recommended by brokerage firms and retirement web sites.

Note the heavy emphasis on bonds in the generally recommended retirement account portfolios. Domestic bonds are safe and useful, but at a 6 percent average yield in a 3 percent inflationary world, the 3 percent net annual yield would probably eat up the average retirement portfolio before you no longer need it. Although bond funds that track the Lehman Aggregate Bond index are new, the index has had an average annual return of 9.38 percent for the past 28 years.[26] If you invest heavily in bonds, I urge caution in your choice of annual income draw because of the lower average annual investment return and the lessened effect of compounding.

I predict that the recent change in the federal income tax laws to cap the tax on dividends at 15 percent will both encourage more companies to pay dividends and bring about a movement from bonds to dividend-paying stocks that also have additional growth potential equal to or better than inflation. Back in the 1980s I created a personal portfolio of all the stocks from the Dow Jones Industrial Average that paid 3 percent in annual dividends. Over a 20-year investment period this portfolio produced capital appreciation of better than 10 percent on top of the dividend yield.

Three Retirement Savings Portfolios You Can Rely Upon

Your appetite for investment risk should be tuned to your ability to take risk and still have enough years to recover from a market downturn like 2000 through 2002. I believe adjusting your risk profile at three life stages is sufficient.

FIGURE 7.13   Conservative Asset Allocation Mixes for Retirement Accounts

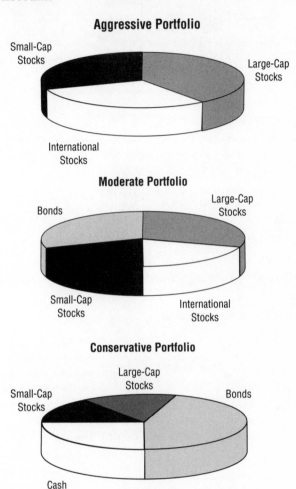

Aggressive Portfolio

Small-Cap Stocks

Large-Cap Stocks

International Stocks

Moderate Portfolio

Bonds

Large-Cap Stocks

Small-Cap Stocks

International Stocks

Conservative Portfolio

Large-Cap Stocks

Small-Cap Stocks

Bonds

Cash

Birth to 10 Years Before Retirement

This period is important because your income from work is paying the bills and your discipline is allowing you to put money away for retirement. This is also the period where you get the biggest boost from compounding the contributions and income in your portfolio. As you saw in the pension chapter, IRA accounts for working young people and new college graduates in the workforce gain tremendously from this compounding. During this period you should be in a balance of domestic and foreign stock products. As you can see in Figure 7.14, historical data

FIGURE 7.14   Performance of the Three Life-Cycle Portfolios 1984 through 2004: Comparative Growth of $1

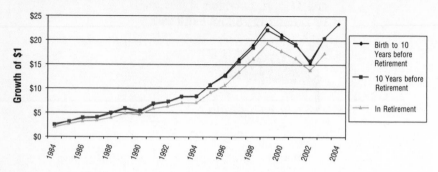

show that the three life cycle portfolios have similar returns. This more aggressive portfolio helps you get slightly better returns early in life, which improves your compounding. Suggested in Table 7.5 are proportions of either indexed mutual funds or exchange-traded funds. Later in this chapter you will find suggested ETF and mutual fund vendor alternatives, but your choices may be limited by your plan administrator.

Ten Years before Retirement

Ten years before you will begin to need your portfolio to provide half or more of your retirement income is the time to start getting conservative. This is when you want to add bonds to your portfolio to cushion volatility in the stock markets. However, shifting to 40 percent bonds during these high-contribution years may decrease the size of your retirement portfolio and limit the upside potential. (See Table 7.6.) Later you will learn about rebalancing, which will control the risk of this higher percentage of stocks.

Your Retirement Portfolio Mix

At retirement you should shift to a more conservative portfolio to limit stock market volatility and not jeopardize the source of your income

TABLE 7.5   Birth to 10 Years before Retirement: 100 Percent Domestic and Foreign Common Stocks

Broad or total market	30%
Large-cap (S&P 500 index)	25%
Small-cap (Russell 2000 index)	25%
International developed country stocks (MSCI EAFE)	20%

TABLE 7.6   Ten Years before Retirement: 80 Percent Domestic and Foreign Common Stocks and 10 Percent to 20 Percent Bonds

Broad or total market	15%
Large-cap (S&P 500 index)	20%
Large-cap blend (VBINX type)	30%
Small-cap (Russell 2000 index)	15%
International developed country stocks	20%

stream. Remember that if you are healthy, you are going to live off this money for 30 years, so this money must still grow to ward off inflation. For this reason, I suggest a balance of stocks and bonds similar to the 60 percent stocks/40 percent bonds ratio of the Vanguard Balanced index fund (VBINX) used in the examples. (See Table 7.7.)

Figure 7.15 illustrates that not all of the indexes I have suggested you follow perform the same. The Lehman Aggregate Bond index is conservative and ideal for a retirement portfolio. This index is 40 percent of the Vanguard Balanced fund (VBINX) used in previous examples. The Morgan Stanley Capital International EAFE is the developed country index, exclusive of the United States. Money is moving out of selected companies in U.S. markets into stock markets in developed foreign countries. This index should perform better in the years to come.

Staying Fully Invested—Cash Has Little Value in a Retirement Account

You have no need to keep any cash in a retirement account during your accumulation years unless you are accumulating it to reach a minimum purchase level for an index fund. After retirement, several months' worth of cash may allow you to sell your investments less frequently

TABLE 7.7   Your Retirement Portfolio: 64 Percent Domestic and Foreign Common Stocks and 36 Percent Bonds

Broad or total market	54%
International developed country stocks	10%
Bonds or percent bonds in a blended fund (could be 90% VBINX and 10% MSCI EAFE)	36%

FIGURE 7.15   Comparative Performance of Major Indexes 1979 through 2004

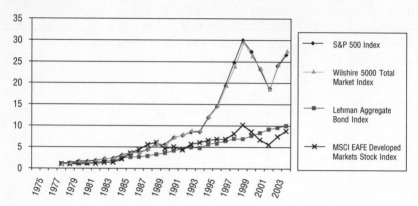

and reduce your selling costs. Stay fully invested and stick to your asset allocation.

Rebalancing Your Portfolio—Keeping What You Have Made

Proper rebalancing can add 40 basis points (0.4 percent) to your average annual portfolio return.[27] Rebalancing is the process of adjusting the mix of the investments in your portfolio back to the percentage allocations you decided are right for you. This concept has been around for a long time, but after the technology bust brought the Nasdaq down from 5,048 in March of 2000 to 1,200 in late 2002 and the other domestic stock markets fell by 40 percent in 2001 and 2002, academics with computer models have spent a great deal of time looking at the concept of rebalancing. Rebalancing can add value by controlling risk and increasing returns. The biggest resistance to rebalancing comes from us, the investors. No one willingly wants to move money from an index fund that is doing well into a fund that tracks another index that is not doing as well? Rebalancing cushions market downside, especially when there are big percentage differences in the performance of indexes. Remember the underperforming S&P in 1998 and 1999 relative to the Nasdaq? Had exuberant investors followed rebalancing theories preached then and now, they would have cushioned their portfolios from the market losses from 2000 through 2002, while still benefiting from the earlier rise in the Nasdaq. The asset class with the highest expected return, typically the Nasdaq, will drift the most from its allocated percentage.

Computer simulations have shown that the penalty you can expect to pay increases the farther out from your target return you let an asset class drift before you rebalance.[28] Using historic data for many major indexes, experts seem to agree that you should rebalance when an asset class drifts 5 percent from your target allocation. It is critical to note that this 5 percent drift can take place in a month, a quarter, or a year. Rebalancing at each 5 percent drift is the only reason you need to keep an eye on the asset allocation in your portfolio.

When drift happens, you should place new plan contributions selectively to bring about the reallocation. Acting quickly should keep you from having to sell or buy existing investments to rebalance because transaction costs can outweigh the benefits. One author suggests and supports the conclusion of only rebalancing in halfway steps[29] back to your target allocations, which should help in retirement accounts where money goes in slowly and rebalancing may take awhile. The portfolio tracking templates on my web site are designed to alert you to rebalancing and help you with the math.

Sample of Index Products

Table 7.8 is a partial listing of index mutual funds and exchange-traded funds available early in 2005. I have tried to pick the ones with the lowest management fees and small or no acquisition costs. These may differ from products available through your plan administrator. My web site, www.RetireYes.com, has a more complete and up-to-date listing.

Active Portfolio Management Can Pay for Itself, Especially in Your Taxable Account

Individuals with more than $1 million in a taxable (nonretirement) account are well-served to explore the services of a professional asset manager, especially one of the new breed who manage using so-called modified indexing. These managers often come from institutional backgrounds and have a full understanding of indexing and its advantages. Modified indexing simply means that they eliminate from the holdings of a particular index the stock of companies they do not think will perform well during a particular window in time. Unlike the S&P 500, which is partially subjective, most indexes use all the actively traded companies in a particular size, style, or other category that defines that index. By eliminating the prospective underperformers from their portfolios that mimic their chosen indexes, modified indexing practitioners hope to beat the indexes. These managers often have fees in the range of .05 percent to 1.0 percent of money under management. For this fee they tailor the asset allocation to your needs. More importantly, they harvest income tax losses over the course of the tax year to add 2 to 3 percent of additional after-tax gain to your portfolio.

Watch out, though, for active management schemes that accept as little

TABLE 7.8 Sample of Available Index-Tracking Products

Fund Name	Type: Mutual Fund (MF) or Exchange-Traded Fund (ETF)	Symbol	Management Fee	Year of Inception	Index
Large-Cap Blend					
Vanguard 500	MF	VFINX	0.18%	1976	S&P 500
Standard & Poor's Depositary Receipts	ETF	SPY	0.11%	1993	S&P 500
iShares S&P 500	ETF	IVV	0.09%	2000	S&P 500
Fidelity Spartan U.S. Equity Index Fund	MF	FUSEX	0.19%	1988	S&P 500
Fidelity Spartan 500 Index	MF	FSMKX	0.19%	1990	S&P 500
Schwab S&P 500	MF	SWPIX	0.35%	1996	S&P 500
Scudder S&P 500	MF	SCPIX	0.40%	1997	S&P 500
T. Rowe Price Index	MF	PREIX	0.35%	1990	S&P 500
Transamerica Prem. Index	MF	TPIIX	0.25%	1995	S&P 500
USAA S&P 500	MF	USSPX	0.18%	1996	S&P 500
Broad or Total Market					
Vanguard Total Stock Market VIPERS	ETF	VTI	0.15%	2001	Wilshire 5000
Fidelity Spartan Total Market	MF	FSTMX	0.26%	1997	Wilshire 5000
T. Rowe Price Total Market	MF	POMIX	0.40%	1998	Wilshire 5000
iShares Russell 3000	ETF	IWV	0.20%	2000	Russell 3000

Large-Capitalization Stock Index Products

Vanguard Large-Cap VIPERS	ETF	VV	0.12%	2004	MSCI US Prime Market 750 Index
Vanguard Large Cap Index Fund Investor Shares	MF	VLACX	0.20%	2003	MSCI US Prime Market 750 Index
Schwab 1000	MF	SNXFX	0.46%	1991	Schwab 1000
Small-Cap					
iShares Russell 2000	ETF	IWM	0.20%	2000	Russell 2000
Vanguard Small Cap Index	MF	NAESX	0.27%	1960	Russell 2000 through 2003, then MCVSI 1750
International					
iShares MSCI EAFE	ETF	EFA	0.35%	2001	MSCI EAFE
Vanguard Developed Markets Index Fund	MF	VDMIC	0.34%	2000	MSCI EAFE
Fidelity Spartan International Index Fund	MF	FSIIX	0.47%	1997	MSCI EAFE
Blend					
Vanguard Balanced Index Fund Investor Shares	MF	VBINX	0.22%	1992	Wilshire 5000, Lehman Aggregate Bond
Bonds					
Vanguard Total Bond Market Index Fund Investor Shares	MF	VBMFX	0.22%	1986	Lehman Aggregate Bond

as $25,000 or $50,000 and put you into one of several style buckets they or their brokerage firm recommends. Their management fees can range up to 3 percent, plus trading costs—eliminating any advantage other than a warm body to talk with.

What Have You Learned?

The experts and the computer models both should have convinced you that a balanced portfolio of index-tracking funds will outperform a portfolio of actively managed mutual funds because the combination of lower fees, buying and holding, plus rebalancing can raise your long-term average yield from 8 percent to 12 percent. Combine this with the miracle of compounding and you can double your retirement income. This holds true whether you have $300,000 or $3 million. But none of this will happen unless you start saving early so you can enjoy the higher returns and the compounding on whatever your balance is at retirement.

Taxable Investing

The investment principles you'll apply in your taxable investment accounts are the same used for your nontaxable pension accounts except for additional wrinkles imposed by the tax man. The reduced tax rates on dividends and capital gains do not lessen the serious negative impact of taxation on your long-term portfolio growth. For investors with less than $2 million in their taxable accounts, I suggest staying with a passive indexing type strategy and harvesting tax losses to offset gains each year. Only investors with more than $2 million can expect to command the attention of a competent active money manager who will harvest tax losses and work to maximize their annual after-tax returns. Don't forget that indexing still beats the vast majority of active managers both pre- and after-tax, no matter how many zeros you have in your account balance.

Let's look at the consequences of taxable investing from the tax man's viewpoint. Taxes are a cost just like management fees. Although tax rates have come down recently in an effort to stimulate the economy, remember that Congress may raise rates at any time, especially when the government is spending 25 percent more each year than the incoming tax revenue. If you intend to invest for the long term, don't let tax rates control how you invest. Just try to avoid large unplanned gains that can't be offset with losses.

From a portfolio investment standpoint, the tax man sees three general types of income: dividend income, long-term capital gains, and all other income. The federal government taxes dividend distributions from stocks and dividends passed through by mutual funds at 15 percent. Profits from sales of capital assets (stocks, bonds, and mutual funds) held for longer than one year are also taxed at 15 percent. Capital assets held less than one year are taxed at the ordinary income rates. The tax rate on ordinary income is a graduated tax rate from 10 percent to 35 percent. The higher your taxable income, the higher the rate.

During the Reagan era the top marginal tax rate was lowered from 70 percent to 50 percent in 1982, and dropped again in 1986 to 28 percent. Then in 1993 during the administration of George H. W. Bush it went back to 39.6 percent, only to drop during his son's first term to the now 35 percent top marginal rate. The point is that all the rates will continually bounce around.

Sixty million American taxpayers also pay an alternative minimum tax (AMT) on top of these rates. Originally the AMT was introduced to impose a 28 percent tax rate on people who otherwise were able to avoid taxes by sheltering income from taxation. The AMT is essentially a tax on the increase in your net worth—a balance sheet tax. In 2005 the first $58,000 ($45,000 for 2006) of a married couple's income is exempt from AMT and $40,250 ($33,750 for 2006) for single filers. The way AMT works is you make a separate federal tax calculation adding back items subject to the alternative minimum tax. The tax rate on these items added back in the computation ranges from 26 percent to 28 percent. A partial list of these items includes:

- Large state and local income or sales tax or property tax deductions.
- Large long-term capital gains or qualified dividends.
- Large deductions for accelerated depreciation.
- Large miscellaneous itemized deductions.
- Mineral investments generating percentage depletion and intangible drilling costs.
- An exercise of incentive stock options.
- Large amounts of tax-exempt income that are not exempt for state tax purposes.
- Certain mortgage interest, such as from a home equity loan, if the loan proceeds are not used to buy or improve your first or second home, or are used in your business.

What this means is that if you add back high state income taxes and property taxes and have a large capital gain, you will lose the effect of the lower 15 percent long-term capital gains rate and have to pay a 26 percent tax on the otherwise deductible state income tax and property taxes.

No matter how you slice it, having 15 to 35 percent plus the AMT taxed away on any portfolio gain detracts from the miracle of compound interest. It is critical that you put your taxable portfolio into an environment you or a money manager can control. Most mutual funds are enemies of the long-term taxable investor. Managers of actively managed mutual funds operate to maximize return with total disregard for taxes. With the exception of specific tax-managed funds, a mutual fund manager's job depends on getting the highest return he or she possibly can, quarter after quarter, year after year. Their average buying and selling turnover is 80 percent of their portfolio each year. They are stock pickers who sell what they think is out of favor and buy what they hope will generate gains. Each year the tax law says 98 percent of their net mutual fund trading gains must be distributed to you, usually in the last three weeks of December. From the mutual fund manager's standpoint, balancing gains against losses to minimize taxes is your problem. Worse, if you check the box to reinvest mutual fund distributions you also have to find the cash with which to pay the tax on this phantom income.

In *Common Sense on Mutual Funds* (John Wiley & Sons, 1999), John Bogle uses the resources of the Vanguard Group and others to arrive at some interesting factual conclusions on how much you give away each year in management fees and income taxes. Bogle used composite averages from 1971 through 1995 comparing actively managed mutual funds and tax-managed index funds based on statistical work done by James P. Garland of Jeffrey and Company.[1] During this period the S&P 500 index earned a compounded return of 12 percent (before taxes). Garland reported that after expenses and taxes the average actively managed mutual fund had a compounded return of 8.0 percent and tax-managed funds compounded at 10.2 percent. Using the 1999 tax rates, the taxable fund investor in actively managed mutual funds kept only 40 percent of the average pretax gain. Remember that 98 percent of mutual fund gains must be distributed to investors each year. For tax-managed mutual funds the investor kept 67 percent of each year's pretax gains. Imagine the enormous negative effect this would have on your cumulative compounded return! The difference between 8 percent versus 12 percent returns equals *Double Your Retirement Income.*

This negative income tax effect is what makes exchange-traded funds (ETFs) so important to the taxable investor. Although they look like indexed mutual funds, they operate under tax rules that don't require annual distributions. Barclays Global Investors, who bring you the popular iShares ETFs, proudly advertised that they made no taxable distributions to iShares investors in 2004. Sure, if you sold shares you had gains or losses, but if you held them and didn't need to harvest losses, you reported no taxable gain or loss. Recall from the previous chapter that ETFs have lower management fees than index mutual funds and, if purchased in lots of more than $60,000, have similar acquisition costs. These factors make exchange-traded funds the ideal low-cost, tax-managed investment for your taxable accounts. Barclays Global Investors offers 96 ETFs that track the major indexes, both domestic and foreign. Vanguard Group, Charles Schwab, and other discretionary brokers also offer ETFs.

Taxable Portfolios Less Than $2 Million

Before I chose this $2 million breakpoint between being a do-it-yourself investor and having the luxury of entrusting your money to a really good money manager, I did some polling. There are money management firms who accept accounts of less than $2 million, but usually they put your money in one of several buckets based on their firm's lifestyle and risk categories. At a 1.0 percent to 1.5 percent annual management fee they can't afford to give you much specialized attention. There will always be exceptions, but be cautious.

So, back to the principles we discussed in the previous chapter on pension investing. Except for modest rebalancing during any year, gains (or losses) occur only when you sell exchange-traded funds. This means you control when you take gains and harvest losses to offset gains from outside your portfolio or as you rebalance your taxable portfolio.

A good portfolio mix for your birth to 10 years before retirement taxable portfolio is a mixture of iShares ETFs or similar ETF indexed products. A favorite of mine going forward tracks these indexes:

Russell 1000	50%
Russell 2000	30%
MSCI EAFE	20%

You may ask why this was not discussed in the preceding chapter. It is hard enough to find any indexed products available to pension investors, let alone exchange-traded funds. Many people do not enjoy the flexibility of a fully discretionary account at Schwab, Fidelity, or Vanguard.

I have chosen to track this mix because of the way the indexes are calculated and because of my particular feelings about how and why companies perform well or poorly. The old adage is that the rich get richer. The same is said about big multinational corporations. Today well-managed big corporations usually have both the capital and the people to continue to succeed year after year. To add positive shareholder value above some cost-of-capital breakeven rate, the large institutional investors tell these companies what their annual growth rate must be. If they maintain or exceed that rate, then they continue to have the use of that investor capital with which to grow. If they fall below that rate, they get punished by the capital being removed (shares sold) or they get a stern wake-up call to improve performance, change management, or make other moves.

These big multinational companies choose both the markets they go into and the products they introduce and continue to support. Like the

S&P 500, nearly half of their revenue and operations come from outside the United States. In a time of a continuing weak dollar they are selling products that are underpriced in foreign markets relative to foreign competitors.

The largest 1,000 corporations publicly traded on U.S. stock exchanges make up the Russell 1000. Like most indexes, the representative percentages are market weighted. This means General Electric, Microsoft, Wal-Mart, Procter & Gamble, and the other biggest companies represent a disproportionately large percentage of the index and thus the investment mix.

The Russell 2000 index is made up of the next largest 2,000 corporations traded on the exchanges. These are the successful smaller companies who are using their capital and people to grow bigger. This index is also market cap weighted. This means that big smaller companies like Barclays Global Investors, UBS Financial, and Sun Trust make up a disproportionate part of this index. By choosing these two indexes I have eliminated the bottom 4,200 publicly traded companies, who although they may be successful, struggle to attract capital and must supplement it with expensive debt to grow. This means that as interest rates go up they get squeezed. If you have particular companies you are interested in, modify the mix to include them, but understand that this means you have to be involved.

I have chosen to include only the MSCI EAFE developed countries index because there is not enough of a track record to include a similar emerging country index. The same principle that the big get bigger also holds for large companies in developed countries outside the United States. With the advent of Sarbanes-Oxley and the European Union's equivalent, corporate financial reporting to shareholders and regulators has never been better and made with such complete disclosure. This is not the case for many less developed countries where poor or questionable financial reporting is the norm. Having said this, I believe some of the most spectacular gains will come in these speculative foreign markets, but only to the lucky or those investors who have a true feel for particular country-specific markets. If you have the specific knowledge, go for it but keep your finger on the pulse of the country and its economy.

I went through the same computer modeling exercises for this Russell 1000, Russell 2000, and MSCI EAFE mix starting in 1979, the year Russell index data became available courtesy of Russell/Mellon Analytics. In the early years this sample portfolio did not perform as well as the S&P 500 Vanguard 500 index (VFINX) or the combined Wilshire 5000/Lehman Aggregate Bond index sample portfolios in the previous chapter. The S&P 500 index companies made spectacular gains when you look back at 28-year, 20-year, and 10-year slices of time. The margin by which the S&P 500 outperformed this, my new index mix, shrank as we moved into the truly global economy of the 1990s and beyond. However, a hypothetical

$1 million portfolio of this modified investment mix or the prior two mentioned still grew by a factor of three while allowing the investor to take out 8 percent per year, cost of living adjusted.

Taxable Portfolios Greater Than $2 Million

When you have worked hard enough or have been lucky enough to have a taxable investment portfolio of more than $2 million, it is time to consider having someone else manage your money. In the preceding chapter you learned that the costs incurred by an active manager trading in a mutual fund or managed account probably cost the investor 1 percent per year for accounts from $2 million to $5 million. On top of this you must add the 0.5 percent or more of transaction costs when the manager buys and sells securities. This means that the manager's skills and intuition must consistently put him or her in the top 10 percent to 20 percent of all managers just to beat an indexing strategy.

So how do you find a top money manager, and what do you look for? Back in the 1970s and early 1980s I created and managed the Executive Financial Planning division of Bank of America. The job of our 50 or so CPAs and lawyers was to provide tax and financial planning advice and locate top money managers for our affluent corporate executive and entrepreneurial clients. Although we were wealth managers, at that time the bank did not manage money directly for individuals; but we had access to top money managers whom we interviewed on our clients' behalf. We compared manager performance to index benchmarks and peer groups and narrowed our list to only the best. We then presented managers who accepted new clients in the dollar range our client had to invest. Ultimately the decision was the client's—whoever the client was most comfortable with and who would best serve his or her portfolio management needs.

Many of the best and most consistent performers and the highest-paid portfolio managers manage large university endowment funds. Because of the size of these endowment portfolios and the need for an annual income stream to supplement other university revenue, they have a broader spectrum of investments that supplement their indexing-type methodologies. Some of the best portfolio managers today are those who have left endowment management companies and other large institutional investment houses and gone out on their own. Typically, however, they accept only clients with $20 million or more to invest.

Finding a top manager is a lot of work. Ask others whom they use and why, but remember that any single investor's professed annual return can be enhanced with wishful thinking. Start your search by spending a couple of hours in the investment section of a large bookstore. There are numerous books written by prominent authors/investment managers on how to select a manager. I particularly like the 44-page investment advisers chapter in David F. Swensen's book, *Pioneering Portfolio Management* (Free Press, 2002). David Swensen is the chief investment officer of Yale University's $12 billion endowment and one of the top investment managers in the country. Another good resource is Charles D. Ellis' *Winning the Loser's Game* (McGraw-Hill, 2002).

In a nutshell, what you will learn is that a manager's performance is the product of discipline. When you come up with a short list of managers to interview, performance will be on the top of your list of questions. Prior to a face-to-face meeting, good managers will send you their annual performance numbers. Based on how conservative you want to be these numbers may differ. You should be able to compare these to the performance of benchmark indexes and sample index portfolios from tables in the previous chapter of this book. Top managers should equal or exceed these index portfolio returns. Pit their performance numbers against the indexes for as many years as you can. You should be comfortable with their answers, especially in the years when they returned subpar performance.

Secondly, choose a money manager with whom you are comfortable talking, both in person and by telephone. Even though you will probably talk only quarterly, it is critical that you feel the manager is talking directly to you and focusing upon your specific questions.

Before hiring a portfolio manager, ask for an analysis of how they intend to restructure your portfolio to meet your stated goals. If you have spent any time indexing and understand its simplicity, their explanation of why they want to make changes should be interesting. Tax efficiency should also be a topic they cover. You should expect to receive a quarterly portfolio performance review from your manager, often accompanied by a general management letter describing performance.

Aperio Group—Index-Tracking Core Portfolios

Remember that 43 percent of institutional monies are index-invested. Investment professionals from this indexed discipline have started applying these principles to individual clients and usually charge lower management fees than typical active stock-picker money managers. An example is Aperio Group in Northern California (www.aperio group.com). They are seasoned index-oriented professionals with years of experience at Montgomery Securities, Salomon Brothers, and Morningstar. Although small, with only $400 million under direct management, they also structure portfolios and offer index-tracking consulting services for an additional $4 billion in institutional assets. Their approach focuses on creating individualized index-tracking portfolios tuned to a client's specific situation.

Aperio Group establishes individual separate accounts for clients that track an index or group of indexes, but their computer optimization models allow them to invest in fewer stocks than the index and with a reasonably predictable plus or minus tracking error. A typical client portfolio would hold the stocks of 300 companies out of the S&P 500. The practical advantage of this is that within industry groups the price movement of stocks of similar companies, for example Ford and General Motors, move in parallel. If Ford stock were to decline, Aperio Group can sell and take a loss in the portfolio and buy General Motors while still being true to their index orientation. This tax loss harvesting allows them to minimize taxable portfolio gains, taking advantage of the losses when they occur, and pass them through to the investor (unlike mutual funds). The result is a portfolio that looks and acts like the S&P 500 index with the added advantage of losses that can be used to make the entire portfolio, including other investments, more tax-efficient. Big trust banks often do the same thing, but typically only once a year.

A variant on this index optimization allows Aperio to model specific portfolios for clients who have a large concentration of stock in one particular industry, typically acquired through the exercise of stock options. In these cases they are able to track an index but exclude from the mix companies similar to the disproportionately large outside holding, thereby decreasing overall exposure in that industry group.

How Do I Get My Retirement Income Out?

We have spent time until now working on gathering pension and other investment assets so that with proper index investing you will actually have enough to consider retiring. Although you may not have thought about it, systematically getting monthly or quarterly income out of your portfolios to live on in retirement is an equally daunting and hazard-ridden process. Salespeople will try to convince you to buy annuities as a secure and worry-free source of lifetime income. The uninformed will tell you to sell just enough each month to generate the required cash flow. These two approaches are both expensive and will cause you to give back much of the benefits from your good investment. I will tell you why both of these methods of generating free cash flow are wrong. I will also suggest an income tax-efficient alternative that allows you to keep control of your assets and systematically draw down an income.

Life Annuities Are an Expensive Gamble

Life annuities are a contract between you and an insurance company in which you give them some or all of your investment assets—401(k) type pension assets and other taxable monies—and the insurance company agrees to pay you a certain amount of money monthly or quarterly for your life and the life of your partner. The amount the insurance company will give you is based on conservative actuarial decisions using large statistical databases about life expectancy and assumptions about secure investment returns. The actuary deciding your financial fate will never meet you and does not know if you will die early or outlive the average life expectancy for someone of your age at the time you buy the annuity. The actuary does know how many people will die early and thereby pay a high price for this type of income security. This actuary also knows that the fixed or inflation-adjusted amounts the insurance company will provide you as an income stream will never exceed the income-producing capability of the monies you gave to them. Why do you think life insurance companies have gotten to be so big?

Life annuities go against the grain of everything we have been talking about in this book. My goal has been to make you a financially savvy person when it comes to choice. You started index investing so you could increase your average investment return and save on fees and unnecessary trading costs. I hope I have shown you that 28 years of history tells us that by index investing we can increase our average investment yield from 8 percent to around 12 percent. I ran the numbers using the annuity calculators on two popular investment product web sites from respected companies and got the following results. I said I was a male, age 66, with a wife age 61, and I wanted monthly income and a 100 percent survivor benefit until the second of us was to die. I ran the numbers for a fixed monthly amount and one that was cost of living (inflation) adjusted. For each $100,000 I would give up they were willing to give me about $540 per month as fixed income and only $320 if the amount is cost of living adjusted. For each $1 million I give up, this works out to $65,000 of annual fixed income and only $38,000 of cost of living adjusted income. This yields a 6.5 percent fixed income return on my money, and only 3.8 percent of it is annually adjusted for a cost of living increase. In my mind this is not a good trade-off. This annuity approach asks you to give up $1 million forever in exchange for a fixed amount of $65,000 per year. Conservatively investing the $1 million yourself, in contrast, should allow you to take out $80,000 annually, cost of living adjusted, and at the end probably have a $2 million portfolio after growth, net of income withdrawals, if you live 25 years in retirement. This $2 million is then in your estate and can be left to your heirs or to a good charity.

Do-It-Yourself Investing in Retirement and the Tax Man

Do-it-yourself investing in retirement is fine; the problem is tax-efficient withdrawals to generate your monthly or quarterly income. To do this you must build a large Microsoft Excel schedule to track the cost basis of each purchase by tax lots. Then you must do your trading to match losses against gains to minimize your tax bill while rebalancing your portfolio to continue to be true to your indexing strategy. Large trust banks will do this for you for a fee, but they are usually equipped to do this only annually and only for large managed accounts. I suggest you try your best to accomplish this quarterly on your own. Even if your efforts are not perfect, it beats buying an annuity and will get you thinking in the right direction. My web site may soon have a tool you can adapt for this process.

There Are No Dumb Questions—
A Solution to Low-Cost, Tax-Efficient Income

Writing this book constantly raised questions to which I had to find answers. In trying to create a tax-efficient solution to the problem of getting the income out of your retirement portfolio, it struck me that if you took the tax-efficient investment optimization software I described previously as used by Aperio Group and asked it to net tax lots and generate an income, it might be able to do just that. I explained the problem to their computer guru and the answer was, "I can make it do that." Their software already matches buy and sell trades to minimize taxes as they continuously rebalance the account portfolios to stay true to the index they and their clients want to follow. From a wealth management standpoint they can even generate excess capital gains or losses to match the clients' needs. The only rub is that the process is both computer and labor intensive and thus would require charging a fee and the service would be available only to their clients. Given the industry standard, wealth management fees of 1 percent on accounts of $3 million to $5 million, the tax savings alone should pay much of that fee.

Retirement Redefined

It is not just those who have not saved enough who are rethinking retirement. Thirty-nine percent of wealthy people surveyed by Harris Interactive in mid-2003 are very concerned about outliving their money.[1] These more affluent people are hedging their bets about when they will retire and may never completely stop working in order to supplement their incomes. According to an AARP study released in September 2003, 7 in 10 preretirees report that they will either work during retirement or never retire.[2] When respondents in the study were asked to select only *one* factor in their decision to work in retirement, the primary motivator was the *need for money*.[3] This is not surprising when you remember that the average 60-plus worker who participates in a 401(k) type pension has only $146,211 of retirement plan savings,[4] enough to add only $400 per month of income on top of Social Security. Quoting averages from large groups can often be misleading, but this number is low enough to merit consideration.

Work of some sort as opposed to total retirement seems like the easy way to explain away retirement woes, but it may be a reality to face and less painful than the alternatives. Investment managers often advise people approaching retirement age to restructure their investment portfolios toward safe, low-yielding bonds. Then, almost without consideration of the portfolio's size, they tell you to reduce your lifestyle and learn to live on much, much less. Has anyone asked those unrealistic voices to live on half—let alone asked their partner? Knowing you are going to have to work to live while your retirement assets continue to grow is a threshold you have to cross before you can come to grips with how to reduce costs going forward. This is a whole new phase in your retirement planning process.

Social psychologists who study retirement say the transition into retirement requires a plan. I advocate addressing this plan at least 10 years before retirement. Given the pension contribution limits as they exist today and, most importantly, your available cash to add to savings, you should know by age 50 or 55 whether you can project enough income to retire at age 65 or 70. If you don't think you will have enough money to completely retire, keep your mind open to the likelihood of working beyond age 65 or 70. This rebalancing of your perspective is a healthy first step in looking at the future.

Work together with your spouse and consciously discard alternatives to narrow your focus, or add alternatives you had not considered. The most obvious is where you will continue to live. Have you considered moving to other communities locally or across the country where housing may be less expensive? After carefully accounting for all the costs, the money saved could be invested to add to your retirement nest egg. For some this may be an alternative. For others either of two obstacles may be in the way:

1. Where I might like to live the prospects of making a living, even via telecommuting, are minimal.
2. We have made a decision not to move, while recognizing the added financial burden and responsibility that goes with this higher-cost decision.

There may be other challenges to consider, but having this dialogue early will help you advance the decision process.

Begin by listing the things you want to do in retirement in order to gain clues about balancing your time between work and relaxation. A list of the things you *don't* want to do is important as well. Starting these lists early will give you plenty of time to rethink your ideas and test alternative work options. Starting early gives you room for experimentation. Remember, if the choice is thought through and it is something you really want to learn about and do, you still will have learned valuable lessons even if it doesn't pan out.

Is Work Your Identity?

For many workers, the job not only defines their identity, providing a handy tool for career coaches and social psychologists alike, but it also is the very core of their self-respect. For decades career coaches and social psychologists have equated people's job or profession with their identity. For many it is who they are and their source of self-respect. For others, there is a mismatch and they can't wait to change jobs. Recall the statistic cited earlier: between 1980 and 2000 the average American worker changed jobs 9.6 times. Rethinking what you want to do for a living or how you apply your skills can help you find the right job or career that will make working in retirement a new and rewarding challenge.

One in four preretirees in the AARP study said that in retirement they expect to work in an entirely different field than their current work. Interestingly, one in five of the preretirees in the study said they are still cultivating their interests, and say they don't know yet what line of work that will be.[5] Of the working retirees in the study, half said the work they are doing is entirely or fairly different from what they did previously.[6] The study concluded that the types of jobs currently being done by retirees today will be similar to jobs available to retirees in the future. The shortcoming of this study is that it did not look at the correlation between the skills, if any, that people were using preretirement with tasks being performed in their postretirement job or vocation. Tables 9.1 and 9.2 list specific jobs held by people currently in retirement summarized from the AARP study.[7]

At 24 percent, professionals are the largest group who continued employment in their field. For the purposes of this study AARP defines a professional as anyone with a postgraduate credential and state-issued license other than teachers, who are considered separately in the study.[8]

Preretirement baby boomers in the AARP study expressed a strong willingness to take jobs after retirement in categories the Department

TABLE 9.1   Most Common Jobs for Working Retirees Who Are Not Self-Employed

Teaching—teacher, teaching assistant, substitute teacher, college professor, seminar instructor	13%
Office support/clerical worker—administrative assistant, secretary, receptionist, clerk	9%
Manager/supervisor/assistant manager	6%
Driver/courier (other than truck driver)	5%
Manufacturing/assembly line/factory worker	3%
Truck driver	3%
Security guard/security	3%
Sales (unspecified)	3%
Home improvement/home repair/handyman	3%
Retail sales—sales associate, unspecified work in department store	3%
Nursing—nurse, nursing assistant	3%
Work related to outdoors/recreation/sports—park ranger, coach, fitness center worker	2%

TABLE 9.2 Most Common Jobs for Self-Employed Retirees

Consulting	10%
Real estate agent/real estate appraiser	9%
Farming and ranching	6%
Private investigation	6%
Driver/courier (other than truck driver)	6%
Landscaper/groundskeeper	5%
Insurance—insurance agent, insurance investigator	5%

of Labor expects to have high growth potential.[9] The top eight on this list are:

1. Customer service representative
2. Teaching assistant
3. Teacher
4. Computer support specialist
5. Retail salesperson
6. Landscaper or groundskeeper
7. Cashier
8. Secretary or receptionist

Note that the first four career change options listed all involve teaching. People who man the phones as customer service representatives or computer support specialists have a special place in my heart. They are able to listen to you describe a problem you don't understand or an outcome you can't achieve, and are able to envision, articulate, and walk you through a solution. Some of these jobs will move offshore to English-speaking India, but many more will be created here. People who turn to teaching-related jobs as a second career are leveraging knowledge gained with maturity.

Challenger, Gray & Christmas, an outplacement firm that tracks job trends, gives a good view of job creation leading up to the year 2010. They see job growth in positions that cater to the aging population, particularly in nursing and health services, plus service jobs that provide information technology consulting and financial planning to this population segment. (See Figure 9.1.)

Skills Assessment: A Simple Way to Match Skills and Jobs

There are numerous tests you can take to have other people tell you what your answers say you might like to do careerwise. From experience, I can tell you that these tests work, but take a lot of time. Although in the end

FIGURE 9.1   Projected Job Openings, 2000 to 2010

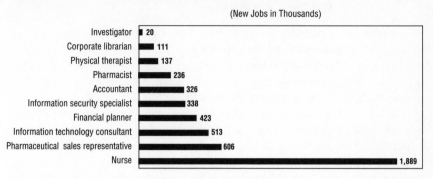

(New Jobs in Thousands)

Investigator	20
Corporate librarian	111
Physical therapist	137
Pharmacist	236
Accountant	326
Information security specialist	338
Financial planner	423
Information technology consultant	513
Pharmaceutical sales representative	606
Nurse	1,889

Source: Projection by Challenger, Gray & Christmas, as reported in the *New York Times.*

they usually don't tell you much you did not already know about your-self and your interests, they may give you insights about your interests that you do not focus on. We look at these tests and some books at the end of this chapter.

Good conversationalists often lead off with a two-part question: First they ask, what do you do for a living? When they do not see you light up and seem to want to talk about your job, they follow up with part two, what do you like to do when you are not working? The first thing out of your mouth is usually the hobby that consumes much of your free time and even more of your think time. This passion is something you often explore in far more detail than your paid career. I listen to people discussing these passions with real conviction and often de-scribing them as an escape. When thinking about a second career, do not discount your considerable skill and passion for gardening, fly-fishing, woodworking, tinkering, or writing as the basis for both a rewarding career and fulfillment of a subdued lifelong ambition. After all, you have been getting up many mornings and willingly doing this without compensation and loving it.

An example that comes to mind is Fred. Fred spent 20-plus years as a fireman and part-time fly-fishing guide. Fred, like many readers, has two great strengths: he loves people and sharing stories, and he is a great and patient teacher. Toward the end of his firefighting career Fred's job al-lowed him to sign up for extra shifts, thereby compressing his work year into eight months. This left Fred four months free to guide and teach oth-ers more about something he loves—fly-fishing. Now retired from the fire department, Fred is able to extend his guide season to five months. Fred is not getting rich guiding, but he has figured out how to capitalize on what he loves to do and more than cover his expenses for almost half of the year. On top of his pension, this gives him a good cushion. Time-wise, there is a strong parallel here for teachers and others who have seasonal jobs. As a matter of fact, one of Fred's fellow guides was a teacher.

This example does not apply to everyone, especially people who have not earned a firefighter's or teacher's pension and still need to get every last employer matching dollar into their 401(k) type plan. For these people I advocate the practical path of building up or improving and testing a skill set while still on someone else's payroll. Most employers encourage this and pay the tuition for the classes.

Recognize that specific existing jobs and earned recognition open up opportunities to make a transition into second careers that may not be available to otherwise qualified people without prior industry experience. Credentialed professionals in medicine, law, public accounting, and architecture come to mind immediately. Less obvious but equally insulated career paths are in fields like literary agents, editors, and freelance technical writers. These second-career consultants command good billing rates because they bring with them years of practical industry experience. Their experience and perfected skills are sought out by the less informed for a fee. The point of this is to focus on how you can leverage your experience to a segment of the market anxious to learn themselves or take advantage of the skills you already have.

Even if you think you are on a track to retire at about age 65, it would not be a bad idea to assess your skills and begin thinking about what you might do in retirement if you decide to work either because you might need the income or because you want to remain active by volunteering. We assume for most of this chapter you want to hedge your bet and start thinking in your 50s how to leverage your current skills to maximize your retirement earning potential so you can have more free time and be in control of your schedule.

Perfect Your Elevator Pitch

Writing this book was an educational process of learning to tighten my focus, ultimately into several sentences that succinctly conveyed the compelling highlights of my message—my elevator pitch. Imagine you are on the 30th floor of a high-rise and someone asks you what you would like to do, or, in my case, "What is your book about?" and "Why should I buy it?" Although I have had to do this many times in my business career, the process is different each time.

In my case it started with an outline of the information I wanted to organize in a way that would convince readers to take actions that were in their best interest. Soon I needed to shorten my list of topics to only the most important and the ones that, if acted upon, offered the most benefit to my readers. As the research and writing process came to a close I was presented with the challenge of boiling down more than 250 pages into 10 pages that would capture the attention of literary agents and later book publishers. This was aided by a class that forced me to concentrate on writing a cover letter summarizing my book proposal that would go to prospective agents. This tight focus led to a massive rewrite of the book because I had better defined my path to hopefully reach a successful outcome—presenting material that a publisher thought would change enough lives to be worth publishing. Ultimately I had to boil all this down into a several-sentence elevator pitch to self-promote my book.

Double Your Retirement Income reveals savings and investment strategies that the financial services industry would like to keep secret. Applying these little-known but tested strategies will allow you to significantly add to your retirement nest egg and double your income in retirement. If retirement doesn't look possible financially at age 50, my book walks you through the steps to retool your skills and possibly your career to enjoy a meaningful part-work/part-leisure later life.

There is a direct parallel between my sometimes painful process and your search for a second career. You need to boil your career decision process down into several sentences that convey your enthusiasm and qualifications sufficiently to get other people to want to ask questions to learn more about your career path. This form of oral communication is the most powerful marketing tool you have. Translating your skills into a job or career that offers you the highest probability of getting noticed in an environment where you will be comfortable and that enhances your self-esteem should be your focused goal.

This is where you get out a pad and pencil and start to build lists. Divide a page in thirds with vertical lines. In the left-hand column list your skills, starting with the pure intellectual skills like accounting, writing, or designing. Leave space between the items on your list to add related skills. In a middle column, opposite each skill in the left-hand column, list ways in which those skills get translated into a result that is physical or visual, like designing and then planting a garden, researching a topic and writing a story, or working thorough the process of how to repair something and then repairing it so it actually works. These are ways in which you create something in your mind and either execute it yourself or explain it to someone else who makes it happen. This differentiation is important because you may already know you can design it and have someone else execute it, but later in life you may be the one actually producing results from the ideas. Continuing the middle column, list things you are good at where you follow someone else's plan, whether this is building a wall or a room, or making a dress or a dish from a special recipe for dinner.

Now, move to the right-hand column. Next to each of the ways in the middle column where you translated intellect into a product or service, list particular jobs you are aware of where people use these skills. Don't omit specific jobs because you say to yourself, "I could never learn to do that." Do eliminate jobs that can never work for you because of a physical or other limitation. This is a list you will use to research occupations and investigate getting additional education or practical experience. Leave extra space in this column for jobs you don't yet know about. For example, teaching without a credential can include K–12 private and public schools, adult education classes, community colleges, vocational schools, and training for both the government and in private companies here and abroad.

An example of this three-column tool is shown in Table 9.3. It will help you zero in on ways to leverage your skills into various jobs.

TABLE 9.3   Sample Skills Assessment Table

Intellectual Process	Resulting Product or Service	Related Jobs
▪ Accounting	▪ Build a budget or estimate the cost of doing something	▪ Accountant, bookkeeper, cost analyst
▪ Analysis of a process	▪ Analyze and document a work flow process to improve a product or function	▪ Process engineer, consultant, manufacturing supervisor
▪ Writing	▪ Write a letter to the editor and get it published	▪ Columnist, writer, editor, copy editor
▪ Improvement of a flawed product design	▪ Create design drawings to improve the product design	▪ Product design consultant
▪ Research	▪ Research a topic and assemble your findings in a short story	▪ Librarian, corporate librarian, researcher
▪ Computer modeling	▪ Write down the flow chart so someone else or you can build the model or write the computer code	▪ Computer software technician ▪ Computer support specialist ▪ Help desk specialist
▪ Teaching	▪ Create a lesson plan to teach a small group of people (friends)	▪ Teacher, teacher's aide ▪ Help desk specialist
▪ Instructing others	▪ Write a syllabus and instruct others how to do something	▪ Teacher, teacher's aide ▪ Product support specialist ▪ Vocational school teacher

TABLE 9.3   *(Continued)*

Intellectual Process	Resulting Product or Service	Related Jobs
▪ Bilingual or multilingual writing and speaking skills	▪ Translate or interpret ▪ Foster cross-cultural insights	▪ Translator or interpreter ▪ Cross-cultural product marketing specialist ▪ Foreign tour guide ▪ Language instructor ▪ Bilingual aide in government, corporations, or health care
▪ Cooking a favorite or new dish from scratch	▪ Write down the recipe and reproduce the dish	▪ Chef, cookbook author, caterer
▪ Decorating a ceramic plate for glazing	▪ Write down the how-to steps and reproduce the item	▪ Designer, do-it-yourself ceramic workshop instructor/owner
▪ Designing a dress	▪ Create a pattern and make the dress	▪ Designer, dressmaker ▪ Alteration specialist
▪ Designing a wooden table	▪ Create patterns, cut wood, and assemble the table	▪ High school woodshop instructor, furniture maker
▪ Defining a flawed product image	▪ Explain why the image of a specific product faltered	▪ Consultant, ad firm idea person
▪ Proper plant selection for garden design and conditions	▪ Landscape design ▪ Plant placement and selection	▪ Landscape designer ▪ Plant consultant ▪ Nursery sales associate

Ask friends to comment on your skills and jobs matrix. You will be surprised, because their comments may expand your horizons or clarify how to leverage your skills. All observations are positive if you keep an open mind.

What Would You Really Like to Do?

Let's continue the theme that you and your skills are your best earning asset. This does not mean, however, that you need to continue to apply your skills in the same field of work. What you need to ask yourself is, "How can I leverage my skills by applying them to another field or by improving them with additional education or training?" Women, more than men, are willing to take advantage of workplace training to improve their skills or add new skills.[10]

A companion question is, "Is there something I can turn into a part-time avocation long before retirement to give it a try?" Your answer to this question could allow you to follow a passion and turn it into a new occupation or business. Who knows, if you are successful this could speed your transition into the new field and set aside any thought of retirement. You can use the list in Table 9.4 to get started.

TABLE 9.4 Examples of Translating Skills and Interests into a Second Career

Fields or Activities of Interest	Resulting Jobs
▪ Designing and planting gardens	▪ Garden and landscape consultant
▪ Repairing types of broken things	▪ Handyman—mobile or in a shop
▪ Writing for a local nonprofit or community newspaper	▪ Columnist, copy editor, editor, author
▪ Teaching part-time in a high school adult education program or community college	▪ Lecturer, professor, teaching assistant
▪ Volunteering at child day-care center	▪ Start your own or work for a child day-care center
▪ Volunteering at an after-school tutoring program for K through 12 students	▪ Teacher, teaching assistant
▪ Volunteering at a local hospital or senior health-care facility	▪ Nurse's aide, go back to nursing school, elder-care worker
▪ Becoming the treasurer or bookkeeper for a nonprofit	▪ Bookkeeper, accountant, back to school to take business courses
▪ Volunteering to prepare income tax returns in a community center	▪ Tax preparer, study to become IRS enrolled agent, back to school and take exam to get CPA certificate
▪ Cooking on a volunteer basis at a shelter to see if cooking for groups is fun	▪ Chef, prep chef, specialty chef, school cafeteria cook
▪ Getting your real estate sales or real estate appraisal license	▪ Real estate sales or appraisal
▪ Buying a house and fixing it up for resale or rental	▪ Real estate remodel and sales or start a rental portfolio
▪ Repairing and teaching computers to new users	▪ IT consultant, self-employed as new computer tech and teacher

Successful Small Businesses Require Business Skills

A bitter pill to recognize up front is that with any small business comes a required set of office and management skills. All of a sudden you become accountable for the bookkeeping and the cost and time estimating. Learning these skills during your preretirement trial period can help you adjust to the realities of running your own business. Principal among these skills are:

- Bookkeeping and budgeting.
- Materials cost: estimating the cost of something before you start and then staying on budget as you complete it.
- Labor cost: estimating how long something will take to do and then coming in on budget. Your hourly rate will be determined by the market, so efficiency translates to profit.
- Creating a marketing plan to sell yourself or your products and testing the plan, even if only with friends who will be honest with you.

These skills and many other specific skills will be necessary for you to succeed in any business you start. They are easily acquired in classes at a local junior college. Because these skills make up a cumulative bank of knowledge, with one course or self-training building upon the other, they should be started early in your career-rebuilding process.

Computer skills are basic to all businesses, and proficiency in these skills is expected. American business runs on personal computers (PCs), and PC tools are dominated by Microsoft. Industry standard is Microsoft Office, a suite of integrated tools for word processing (Word), spreadsheets (Excel), simple databases (Access), presentations (PowerPoint and Visio), and project management (Project). Although I have been computer proficient since the 1960s and have grown with the successive generations of these products, I marvel today at how closely integrated the Microsoft Office tool set has become to produce a result. Authors provide a publisher with an electronic (computer-readable) document, edited with all the text, tables, graphs, and photographs integrated and ready for the press. Much the same rules apply to hard-copy presentations of consulting proposals and teaching lesson plans or presentations. One very nice thing about the Microsoft Office tools is the online support and downloadable updates from Microsoft and, because of their popularity, the excellent third-party books that support each product.

The other element of running your own business is tracking costs and profitability. At some point you outgrow the usual accordion file for invoices and bills and must turn to the computer. The best product to do accounting is QuickBooks from Intuit. A chart of accounts and financial statements can easily be set up to run a consulting or any small business. I have also seen businesses with sales of $5 million and larger using

QuickBooks without any problems. Although QuickBooks can drive accountants crazy because individual transactions can be changed long after they are complete, the advantage is that your outside accountant can have access to the books via the Internet.

Five People Working Three Jobs Equals Both Free Time and Employer Protection

Job sharing is a concept successfully applied in the dental and other professions. The concept is simple. Two or three qualified dentists or hygienists, often mothers or dads, who need flexible schedules, share an office that they staff with at least one dentist and hygienist full-time five days a week. This allows for flexible schedules and, when need be, work substitution. This same concept can be applied to most office functions and many functions within factories and service businesses. This would be a tremendous advantage for small companies in covering key jobs during planned and unplanned time off.

Job sharing will take on new meaning when people with similar skills realize they can band together to offer themselves and employers or clients the freedom of a constantly available workforce. This could work equally well for a handyman service, computer consultants, or on-call dressmaking service. Contacts are screened and jobs are assigned to the person(s) who are available and have the right skills. Having a service staffed in this way means being available 24/7, and with enough partners while some are working others can be marketing or just spreading the word. This type of flexibility and availability should get immediate notice.

Economists are predicting that by 2010, and certainly by 2020, there will be a shortage of qualified skilled workers in the United States. At the same time there will be an eager pool of skilled "retirees" who want to work, but maybe not full-time. However, current advertising by corporations like McDonald's and Wal-Mart showing happy seniors in minimum-wage jobs is not encouraging. Until now corporate America has looked upon this retirement age labor pool as something to exploit with not only minimum-wage jobs, but no health care or continuing retirement benefits.

The generation that came of age during the rebellious 1960s and 1970s is not expecting to continue working into their so-called retirement years, and can be expected to object vociferously to the hand they have been dealt. Whether or not they were politically active 40 years ago, the lack of an adequate skilled workforce will allow them to band together and demand that corporations provide health and other benefits, especially to part-time workers. This concept may seem radical, but corporations in need of skilled labor have the capability to modify, if not reverse, their benefits thinking overnight.

Corporate America needs to begin preretirement seminars at age 50 to identify workers who, for whatever reason, want to continue to work after age 65. Yes, this highlights the problem that these employees have underfunded retirement plans, but better to work through this reality at age 50 when workers have time to plan for the future than confront them with it at age 65. The good that can come out of this proactive approach will far outweigh the bad so long as the corporation follows through with additional skill training and other programs to jointly benefit both the company and the workers. Ultimately this will require a partnership of sorts between corporate employers and educational institutions to create curriculums directed toward goal-oriented adults. These exist today, but they are mostly experimental or are geared toward nonvocational skills and are not focused on improving worker skills for the twenty-first century.

Be Realistic about Barriers to Your New Career

Barriers to your potential new career come in three potent categories: financial, physical, and educational. Understanding these barriers and being honest about how they apply to you are key to not making false steps and losing time in finding the right solution for you. The common thread to all three barriers is that someone else writes the rules and you must follow. This applies to credit grantors (the people who put up the money to start a business), the public perception that if you are old you are no longer physically fit, and, thirdly, professional certification groups that stipulate minimal levels of formal education to receive a license or certificate to work in a field.

Financial Barriers

Financial barriers are the most complicated to starting a small business. Knowing that 8 in 10 small businesses fail, banks and other lenders don't want to lend to an untested business, and if they do lend they want you to personally guarantee any loan. Because they would rather have title to your house than to a failed business, most banks will steer you toward a home equity loan to get capital to start a business. Many small businesses don't really die, they just become classified as the "living dead." This means the owners stop taking money out in the form of salaries and instead often have to put money in to keep the business going. The hard lesson to be learned is to let it die, and next time do better homework.

The prudent alternative is to start very small with out-of-pocket capital and prove whatever it is you want to start works and can make money on an ongoing basis. Only after a year or more of continuous profits should you consider injecting additional meaningful capital into the business. The one year of profits requirement probably means you have tested this concept on a part-time basis before you change jobs to pursue your new business and before you put significant risk money into the business.

After you have proven the business model and have made consistent profits, don't overlook the idea of bringing in a money partner with deep pockets. Successful small businesses all have the same problem—not enough capital to grow. Giving up a big piece of the equity ownership of your business to a partner who understands the business and is willing to inject the capital is usually a wise decision. Even if your financial partner does not work in the business, he or she brings advice and experience. Another positive trade-off of involving an investor/partner is that he or she usually requires periodic financial reporting and sound business planning to monitor your progress. Although time-consuming, these documents will force you to focus on success. Working together, you can grow the business to the point where you balance production or output and sales while maximizing profitability. At that point may additional sources of capital will be available.

Physical Barriers

Remember, you are no longer 25, so stop and ask yourself if the physical hard work required by this business you would like to start is something your body can take on a continuous basis. Fixing things around the house on weekends or replacing plants in the spring is very different from having to do construction or gardening five days a week. On the same note, taking up golf after age 50 can be equally as punishing on your back and knees.

Educational Barriers

Educational barriers to making a transition from one job into another are the easiest to overcome unless you are unrealistic. Chapter 5 on college financial aid taught you that by presenting yourself properly and asking for aid, you will most likely get it. This means that for courses in nursing, computer sciences, and education, three areas where the government predicts big shortages in the future, aid is available to pay for the education, but not sufficient to quit a job and live off the aid. In addition, there are community colleges where you can take accredited classes toward everything from accounting, real estate, real estate appraisal, and computer training to landscaping. The time and commitment involved in these classes are again the reason for starting early. Experiment early so misdirections help you tighten your focus on what it is you want to do.

I recently had the opportunity to talk with Marc Freedman and his associate, attorney Deborah M. Dalfen, of Civic Ventures, a San Francisco–based nonprofit. Marc started Civic Ventures in 1998 and co-founded the Experience Corp. Experience Corp. is a national organization that provides seniors the opportunity to be volunteer teachers, tutors, health care workers, and other vocations where their experience is a meaningful addition to the life of a student or elder. Our common interest is in the reeducation or continuing education of active agers[11] who will need to work into retirement. Marc believes many active agers will go back to college for a second time to fulfill a passion in their second career. College curriculums will need to be tuned to this influx of experience-laden adults who will bring to the classroom considerable practical knowledge—often more than the instructor possesses.

Perils of Consulting

Unless you are selling a product to the public where your success is measured by the sound of a cash register and happy customers who love to tell friends about you and your product(s), consider how you are going to market what you intend to do. Marketing is a problem for consultants. While you are working on an assignment there is no time to market yourself. Marketing happens only when the current job assignment is completed; you are unemployed and have the time to talk up your skills. This is where professional or trade organizations become a helpful way to mix with others—fellow consultants. If you have a unique subspecialty to which others will make referrals, then these organizations can be very productive. Otherwise, try to involve yourself with organizations populated by people who can become fee-paying clients.

An alternative is organizations like Robert Half Management Resources (www.rhmr.com). They and other groups specialize in matching consultants and part-time skilled workers with client assignments. They find the job assignments, place you, and mark up your fees to compensate them for their efforts. These and organizations like them are large and professional and have many clients who rely on them for quality temporary or part-time staffing. Your task is to do what you do well, satisfy the client, and submit a time sheet to get paid. After you develop a reputation with the organization as someone who can be counted on to perform, you can become more in control of your own schedule and what assignments you take and which ones you don't take.

Smaller local consulting middlemen and -women play an important role in local and regional markets. Such an organization in California is M^2 Inc. Consultants and other free agents sign up through the M^2 web site (www.msquared.com) and are prequalified. After registering, the consultant is able to access a password-protected part of the M^2 web site and look at and apply to new job postings. As with other similar consulting networks, M^2 offers one- to three-month and longer assignments managing projects and performing technical work in the areas of financial services, health care, government, computer hardware and software companies, and other industries.

Marion McGovern, one of the founding partners of M^2, has co-authored a book (with Dennis Russell) worth reading if you are considering any form of consulting: *A New Brand of Expertise: How Independent*

Consultants, Free Agents, and Interim Managers Are Transforming the World of Work (Butterworth-Heinemann Publishers, 2001).

Keep It Simple

Unless you are trying to do something cutting-edge, keep your new business venture simple. For tax purposes, report your business income and expenses on Schedule C (Profit or Loss from Business) of your personal Form 1040 income tax return. You enjoy almost the same benefits as incorporating while having many fewer headaches and almost no setup expenses. Only after the business is successful should you start to think about corporate or partnership forms of doing business.

Small businesses without payrolls do not need to worry about withholding taxes and such. You just draw money out of your checking account to pay yourself and the bills. Even the checking account should be simple. Set up another checking account in your own name, plus the business name you are "doing business as" (d/b/a). Opening a checking account in only the business name implies you are incorporated. To the bank this means you will need to have articles of incorporation and all the corporate trappings, which would cost $1,000 to $3,000, plus payment of estimated income taxes in advance. Do, however, remember that as a self-employed person you must pay the employer portion of the Social Security and Medicare tax. This doubles to 15.3 percent the 7.65 percent rate (2005) that you pay as an employee.

To be a designer or provide a service where you buy at wholesale and resell in states that have sales and use tax, you must get a resale license to do business. To get a resale license (permit) you must prepay some amount of sales tax to the city or county in which your business will be located. Some states with a sales or use tax require you to also get a resale license and pay an estimated tax in their state in order to buy for resale without paying sales tax on your purchases in their state. This is important because retailers who sell to the trade must reconcile taxable sales and nontaxable sales. Upon audit, if they cannot produce a copy of your resale license, then they must pay the sales tax. You must account quarterly for what you have resold and the sales tax you have collected, and then remit that sales tax to the taxing authority.

If you have decided on a new and unique name, it is worth the effort to see if someone else has already registered to use that name. This is usually done by going to the state's web site to research and file to operate under a fictitious name. If the business name is simple, try to register the same name as an Internet address. This can be done for less than $25 per year through Network Solutions or any number of companies. If the ".com" version of the name is taken, register for the ".net" or other naming convention.

Engagement Letters

All too often new consultants and freelance contractors are so happy to get work that they forget to define the ground rules with their client. An engagement letter, signed by both parties, is a good way to clarify everyone's responsibilities. Prepare a friendly letter that says the consultant/freelancer will perform these detailed functions and complete the job on or about a certain date. State the fee the customer will pay and when it will be paid. Make sure to specify that expenses will be reimbursed if that is the case. Present this letter to the client for signature. Keep a copy because eventually you will have a client that you need to remind of the business arrangement to collect your fees and/or expenses.

Before You Leap, Check Your Parachute's Health Insurance

The decision to become self-employed or to retire at any age raises the big safety net issue of health insurance. Make sure you can replace employer-provided group health insurance with an individual policy that meets your needs before you leap. Generally, if you were part of a group health plan protecting more than 25 people, your employer's insurance company had to provide coverage for you no matter how severe your health problems. Once you are on your own, health insurance providers look at you individually and can find any number of reasons to refuse you coverage. Group health insurance coverage may be available to you through professional organizations and group affiliations. Bottom line, know not only that you can get coverage, but also what it is going to cost and how long the coverage will last before you make a move. If you can't get individual coverage, this may be a deciding factor in choosing ongoing employment where health insurance is part of your employment package.

Employers who do provide health insurance coverage for retirees have begun limiting their financial risk by capping the amount they will pay per employee for coverage. At least half of this nation's major employers have imposed caps. Once health-care costs reach the cap, the increases are passed on to retirees. A recent study by the Kaiser Family Foundation and Hewitt Associates presents a number of examples where the total of co-payment above the cap plus Medicare Part B premiums approaches or equals 25 percent of the retiree's monthly pension or 401(k)-generated income.[12] Of employers with 200 or more employees, only 38 percent offer retirees health coverage of any kind. For companies with fewer than 200 employees the percentage providing coverage to retirees shrinks to 10 percent.[13] Most of these plans supplement basic Medicare, particularly the prescription drug coverage. How this coverage will ultimately be affected by the 2003 Medicare Reform Act is unclear.

Surviving the First Year in "Retirement"

Long before retirement, have a plan in place so you will know what you are going to do and how you are going to get it done. If your plan and your amended lifestyle are thought out and tested, this will be a seamless transition that started before your retirement date. Unless you know you have the money to burn, avoid taking an extended period of time off to catch up on things around the house or take a long vacation. Instead, fit these into your work plans as part of extended leisure time and don't think of them as a break between one stage of your life and the next stage.

Before you decide whether your new vocation or self-employment opportunity is solid enough to allow you to go out on your own, look at the practical side of replacing employee benefits. If your current employer offers good health insurance, disability insurance, and generous 401(k) employer matching, seriously consider staying on and milking these benefits for as long as possible. As we saw in the pension chapter, you can't beat the investment rate of return you get from good employer matching in a 401(k) or other type of plan.

The rest of the practical side of this transition into retirement redefined is knowing what your budget is and setting ground rules. Budgeting is important because this will determine how much income you need to have coming in. If you intend to consult or freelance in some way, this will define how many hours you must work at a given billing rate to cover your expenses and taxes. Do research to determine what competitive billing rates are in your area. And remember, it is not just the billing rate. Your gross pay is hours worked and fees collected. The same goes for other types of self-employment and selling products you make for resale. The question is, can you sell enough to pay the costs of your business and draw enough income from the business to live on? This all requires going back to the budgeting templates in Chapter 2 to make it work or see what the shortfall is.

Setting Ground Rules

Setting ground rules for your actions in retirement gets the most press because the topic lends itself to individual stories easily compressed into a short newspaper or magazine article. Easy to write about, but much harder to translate into your own life are the usual two topics:

1. Be protective of your free time.
2. Work out the day-to-day ground rules if you have a partner.

When people learn you have free time they become poachers of any free time you put up for grabs. One of the biggest concerns people have when they retire is being forgotten and isolated. The typical reaction is to grasp at everything that comes along and overallocate your time. Whether this is going on boards or volunteering or routine friendly breakfasts that consume hours, be choosy with your time. Learn to say no. If you don't, these well-intended poachers will eat up any time you might have to kick back and contemplate what comes next. However, don't discount volunteering that keeps you visible if it expands your work possibilities or gives you the opportunity to learn new skills.

Working out the ground rules for day-to-day life is more personal and may require a sit-down discussion with a spouse/partner. All of a sudden, no matter how long it has been anticipated, you are around much more and may be working from home. This change in routine is disruptive, and steps to ease the transition should be anticipated:

1. Negotiate a personal space where you can work or relax that is not in the middle of the most popular room in the house. Be sensitive to how your partner wants this to look.
2. Establish rules so as not to impose upon the other person or their routine.
3. Pay the extra money and get separate telephone lines, e-mail addresses, and computers. This will relieve both open and underlying tensions.
4. Rethink and discuss the rules on who is going to do what now that there may be more free time to share home maintenance, shopping, and cooking.

Other Tests to Help You Understand What You Might Want to Be When You Change Jobs

None of the formal tests to help you match your skills with career interests are geared specifically to moving into a new career in retirement. The key tests were included as part of a battery of personality and job-related tests I took in advance of a weeklong group media presentation skills program several years ago. We were a group of 20 senior executives from a variety of companies around the United States. We each saw our actual results while the group as a whole saw only anonymous skills in a range that included established norms for other similar groups.

The Campbell Interest and Skill Survey can be taken online and shows you how you compare to happily employed people in a variety of occupations. The more than 300 questions take a long time to complete. The results rank you on a six-point scale over a wide variety of careers and tell you careers to pursue and avoid. Online the test is available at www.pearsonassessments.com/tests/ciss.htm for a $17.95 fee.

The Meyer-Briggs Type Indicator Career Report finds the 50 most popular and 25 least popular careers for your personality type. Although the test measures your personality traits over a 30-point scale, our group found that personality type categorizations don't translate into job suggestions or prospective happiness in that job. This test is available online at www.discoveryourpersonality.com for $55.

If you take any of the tests, don't stop there. Perhaps one of the best resources about careers was started in 1970, when Richard Nelson Bolles first wrote *What Color Is Your Parachute?* Bolles takes a more practical approach that has stood the test of time and spawned a 34-year-old publishing business. In addition to the two books cited next he has a web site with career tests and a lot of practical information and articles (www.jobhuntersbible.com).

What Color Is Your Parachute? 2005: A Practical Manual for Job-Hunters and Career-Changers, by Richard Nelson Bolles and Mark Emery Bolles, Ten Speed Press, 2004.

Mapping Your Career: The Book That Can Help You Find the Job You Want, and Create the Career You Are Meant For, by Richard Nelson Bolles et al., Crisp Publications, 2001.

Tests or no tests, the key is to start thinking about what you are going to do in retirement long before that day comes.

Volunteerism

I mentioned volunteerism as a good way to spend time working in an organization or vocation of your choice while gaining or perfecting valuable job skills. Marc Freedman suggests this in *Prime Time: How Baby Boomers Will Revolutionize Retirement and Transform America* (Public Affairs, 1999), but in that book Marc had not yet started focusing on the necessity for many people to continue to work for market wages to pay the bills in their part-work/part-leisure later years. Marc is a pioneer in continuing education for seniors, both academic and vocational. Selected corporations have worked with Marc's organization and others to provide pilot programs to ease the transition from work years into retirement. These have been large corporate employers with traditional defined benefit pension programs and some other benefits for their retirees. At least today these employers are in the minority. Not until some years from now, and only when faced with the glaring need for scarce skilled workers, will corporations as a whole provide other than nominal retraining for existing workers to keep them on the payroll long into their retirement-age years.

For those who want to research volunteerism, here are web sites for the major national volunteer organizations.

http://civicventures.org

www.pointsoflight.org

www.experiencecorps.org

www.elderhostel.org/ein/intro.asp

www.cns.gov

www.habitat.org

www.score.org

Tips to Remember As You Develop Your Strategy: Your Semiannual Checkups

This chapter contains information to review and checklists to complete in your semiannual checkup (September) and your annual checkup at income tax time in February and March. The checklists apply equally to both checkups. Not all of this information will apply to you, but going down the checklists will force you to consider topics and actions you may have forgotten to consider or do. These checklists and topics follow the chapter order in the book.

Chapter 2—Budgeting: Finding New Money to Save for Retirement

Chapter 2 urged you to develop a budget to better monitor your spending habits. Any changes in lifestyle expenses or unforeseen events mean taking a fresh look at your budget. This is also the time to investigate new savings opportunities.

Scan Your Budget for Changes and Adjustments

❑   Did you refinance your house and change your monthly payment amount?

❑   Did you make purchases, like a car, boat, or health club membership, that require monthly payments?

❑ Have your credit card payment habits changed? Do you need to factor in a monthly payment or work on a plan to pay off an outstanding balance?

❑ Do you have any different insurance with larger or smaller payments or a different payment plan?

❑ Have any of your habits changed any of your expenses? These can include commuting or other job expenses like lunch.

❑ Have you adjusted your budget to account for any other increased expenses or withholding deductions for benefit programs at work? Equally as important for budgeting, did any change in your income get reflected in your budget?

Refine Your Budget and Look for New Money to Commit to Savings

❑ Go back and take a fresh look at the budget you prepared. If you downloaded the template from the web site this will be easy. Save a copy of the template and give it a current date in the file name so you can keep a copy of the old budget and review your progress on successive budgets. If you did a paper budget, consider downloading the template. The template will not be hard to use and you will then have it saved on your computer.

❑ Pay particular attention to controlling your fixed expenses, especially if you are a two-income household.

❑ If available, sign up for flexible spending account(s) at work. These are big money savers on medical, commuting, and child care expenses you incur anyway.

❑ If your employer's payroll service allows it, start an automatic savings plan, even if it is only for the minimal $25, $50, or $100 per pay period. Some Internet home banking services also allow you to set up automatic deductions just after each payday.

❑ If a new car is in your thoughts, remember the great long-term impact of buying a nearly new car instead of a brand-new car. New or used, go back and read the advice in Chapter 2 so you don't overpay both for the vehicle and on the finance charges.

❑ Spend $10 and subscribe to *Consumer Reports* magazine. The advantage of the online subscription is that you have access to all the past product reviews. It is probably the most valuable research tool available for getting the right product at the right price.

Chapter 3—Two-Income Households: Affording a Home and Retirement While Avoiding Bankruptcy

Being a two-income family gives you extra savings opportunities you should not willingly pass up. Having two employers may give you two sets of benefit plans from which to pick and choose. These are important considerations, especially if you are thinking of going to a single income.

Two-Income Checklist

❑   If contemplating or committed to becoming a one-income household, go back to the budget templates to assess the impact and where to cut costs.

❑   If you and your spouse/partner are both working, make sure you participate in both pension and savings plans and choose the best benefit package between the employers. Before switching health or life insurance from one plan to the other, make sure you qualify and can switch back if need be. Open enrollment periods, usually November, may differ between employers.

❑   Request your free credit reports from each of the three credit reporting agencies to check for negative activity in your credit files.

Chapter 4—Buying a Home

Perhaps you already have a home. If not, it is time to find more money to save and go back and research the various loan alternatives and housing programs talked about in Chapter 4. If you intend to buy or move, go back and reread Chapter 4.

Homeowner Checklist

❑   Clean up your credit report six months before you need to apply for a loan.

❑   Review your replacement-cost homeowner's insurance.

❑   Tune your type of mortgage to how long you intend to stay in the house. If interest rates are still favorable, test the value of refinancing.

Chapter 5—Paying for College with Other People's Money

Even if your student is not yet in high school, do a preliminary expected family contribution (EFC) computation to see where you stand. In Chapter 5 you learned to be realistic about the cost of college early in the game and the EFC calculation that determines how much the government's computation says you are capable of contributing each year toward your child's education. Remember, college funding costs are likely to go up faster than your income, so this preliminary computation will probably remain good. Be honest with yourself and your student about what you can afford, but first go through the EFC computation and planning tips— you may be pleasantly surprised.

College Planning Checklist

❏   Don't take out a second mortgage to pay college costs. Interest on a second mortgage is not deductible for the alternative minimum tax (AMT), which is not cost of living adjusted and applies to more and more taxpayers each year. Go for as much free grant aid as possible, and make up the difference with low-interest-rate student loans. But remember the money you save has to go into your pension plans or other savings—don't spend it.

❏   Based on your child's test scores and grades, research on your own or spend time (money) with an outside college admissions adviser to develop a list of both public and private colleges your student might attend. Remember the types of schools and the strategy: sure things, probable acceptances, and the ones where acceptance is a reach, but a possibility. This will help you focus on financial needs, which may change your list.

❏   Determine the enrollment yield for each college of interest. This is the ratio of acceptance letters sent out by the school compared to the number of students who enroll. A table to do this is on my web site and lists approximately 500 colleges. The data can also be sorted by the availability of grant aid.

❏   Remember the basic college aid formula: The college's cost of attendance (COA) minus your effective family contribution equals the maximum government grant aid. (This does not limit private college grant aid.) The COA minus grant aid is the maximum you can borrow in the form of student loans.

❏   Remember, your student's assets affect the EFC at the rate of 35 cents on the dollar, whereas yours detract from your eligibility only a maximum of 5.6 cents on the dollar. Consider shifting assets out of the child's name to improve your EFC. Test this before shifting assets. Don't shift assets from you to your children solely to take advantage of the child's lesser tax bracket. Tax laws and financial aid formulas are at odds.

❑ Consider using any monies in a child's trusts, other than 529 type savings plans, to pay for expenses *before* the taxable year when the child starts their senior year in high school and for college start-up expenses like computers and cars. The trade-off is that if you are looking at only public universities and state budgets remain tight, your only access to college aid may be low-interest-rate loans.

❑ Always file the FAFSA form. Remember that student aid goes to those who ask for it. First go for grant aid (free money), then for loans in the order shown. The lowest interest rate with the longest repayment schedule will optimize your cash flow and ability to set money aside for retirement. Remember, if cash is abundant later you can always pay off the both your student's loans and the loans in your name.

Order of Preference in Using Student Aid

- Grant-aid monies based on EFC.
- Grant-aid monies based on appeal.
- Subsidized Stafford loans.
- Unsubsidized Stafford loans.
- PLUS loans.
- Loans offered by the college.
- Sallie Mae loans.

❑ Enlist the aid of someone at the college who wants your student to attend and can add another voice:

- If you have a good student, call upon the admissions officer for help, not the financial aid officer.
- If you have a good athlete, call the athletic director. This is important in NCAA Division III, which has many private colleges.
- If you have a good musician, call the music department.

❑ By the time your student starts senior year in college, the prior year's financial data has been used to apply for this year's financial aid. Shifting assets to pay off student loans anytime after the senior year begins does not affect the financial aid computation unless the student is immediately going on to graduate school. However, if the low-interest-rate student loan payments are not a burden, consider keeping the loans outstanding. Again, the amount you save annually needs to be committed to your retirement accounts.

❑ If you have the option of taking a bonus during your first student's sophomore year in high school rather than the junior year, do it. The idea is to reduce your income and accelerate expenses during that student's junior and senior years in high school, and freshman, sophomore, and junior years in college. Refer back to Chapter 5; testing your EFC and doing tax planning can pay off. If a college student is ready to start college during this period, the EFC outcome gets better.

Chapter 6—Your Pension Plan = Your Retirement Lifeline

We have already established how important it is to contribute at least to the point you maximize employer matching in your 401(k) type pension plan. If you are at this point, try to find additional money to increase your contribution. This checklist applies mostly to people contemplating a job change.

Job Change and Pension Checklist

❏ Before you jump from one employer to another, check the timing of when employer contributions vest in your current 401(k) type plan. Loss of these monies could outweigh the modest salary increase, but maybe not the expanded opportunity offered by the new employer.

❏ If you terminate or are terminated, you have 60 days to move your 401(k) plan to a rollover IRA or add it to a new employer's 401(k). Moving it from your old employer to a rollover IRA allows you to start or improve on your index-tracking investment strategy and get out of any concentration in old employer stock.

❏ If rolling over your old 401(k) type plan into an IRA, choose a mutual fund or investment house that offers no-commission, low-fee index-tracking mutual funds and exchange-traded funds.

❏ Although not a subject in this book, if you are planning a job change and have outstanding stock options they usually need to be exercised before you resign or are terminated. The human resources department at work can help you roll through these options and convert the gain to cash.

❏ If you are offered early retirement, evaluate the alternatives— especially if the early retirement inducement package goes away if you stay and are then subject to a layoff. List your options by category in columns A, B, C, and so on. Try to explain to a friend the options and your choice to make sure you are not overlooking something.

Chapter 7—The Winning Investment Strategy for the Twenty-First Century

This is the chapter each of you should already be following because the advice is universally in your best interest. If you are not a convert to indexing, go back, read the chapter, and ask yourself why not. I successfully do indexing in IRA accounts with as little as $10,000. What you may have forgotten to do is rebalance. This should be done by adjusting the allocation instructions given to your plan administrator. If you have IRA accounts, rebalance with one-half your annual contribution, wait six months, and then rebalance with the other half.

Rebalance Your Pension Accounts

❑ Review your percentage holdings to agree with your written strategy. The best way to assure yourself that what you are doing is right is to go to a web site that allows you to compare your funds' performance against the indexes they track. The best sites use Commodity Systems Inc. (CSI) graphing. These are home pages for www.msn.com, www.yahoo.com, www.prodigy.com, or CSI's own site at www.csidata.com.

❑ Adjust your percentage holdings to agree with your written strategy. Rather than selling anything and incurring costs, adjust future contributions to index-tracking funds or exchange-traded funds (ETFs) to correct percentages.

❑ If you are an Excel or a Lotus user, create a schedule to track your performance. Although tracking information is available every trading day, it is best to use end-of-calendar-quarter and end-of-year data because these will give you the best comparisons.

❑ Volunteer for the employee committee that monitors your pension administrator. This will allow you to better understand your options and costs. Your employer, not you, still bears the fiduciary liability for making sure the plan is properly administered in the best interests of the employees.

Chapter 8—Taxable Investing

Harvest Tax Losses When Rebalancing

Taxable investing offers the additional opportunity to harvest tax losses to offset gains and thereby reduce your annual income tax bill. This is best done each time you rebalance your portfolio and makes rebalancing into a cost savings opportunity worth doing rather than just a necessary chore.

❑ Near year-end, if you have not rebalanced your taxable portfolio recently, take this opportunity to both rebalance and harvest any losses to offset taxable gains from index funds. Unless you traded, there may be no gains on your ETF holdings, but there will be on index funds.

❑ Evaluate any additional long-term capital gains and consider taking any losses to offset them.

❑ If you have capital loss carryforwards, consider taking capital gains to put to use the loss carryforwards.

Chapter 9—Retirement Redefined

It is always the right time to start thinking about a rewarding career to investigate or fulfill a lifelong passion, especially if it pays well and eventually adds freedom to your part-work/part-leisure later years.

Retirement Reality Checklist

❑ Build a skills and jobs matrix or dust off and refine a previous one. Ask yourself if you have a firmer idea of what alternative job you might like to pursue.

❑ Request a catalog from the local junior or community college and look for classes that interest you and that fit your work schedule.

❑ Investigate vocational and other training programs offered by the local high school.

❑ Go online and investigate volunteer programs that will allow you to test your interests in a hands-on way. Several of these programs are listed at the end of Chapter 9 and updated on my web site at www.RetireYes.com.

❑ Ask the human resources department at work what kind of financial aid your employer offers for continuing education. This may open up the option of more expensive private classes and training programs.

Semiannual Checklist

This is an additional checklist to be used in both September and March.

Income Tax Items to Check before Calendar Year-End

❑ Did your income change since the last time you or your accountant tested your federal and state income tax withholding?

■ If your income went up, you may be underwithheld and will owe taxes and maybe a penalty in April.

- If your income went down or you had a big refund last year, you may want to adjust your withholding to match your tax liability. How to adjust your withholding is explained in Chapter 2. Have the money now rather than waiting for a tax refund in May or June.

❏ If you itemize your deductions on your income tax return, are there additional items you intend to donate to charity before year-end?

❏ If you participate in an IRC Section 125 flexible spending medical reimbursement plan at work, have you used up your annual balance and filed for reimbursement? If you have used up your balance but did not contribute up to the $1,000 maximum, consider doing so. Refer back to Chapter 2; you can save an amount equivalent to your federal income tax bracket: 15 percent, 25 percent, 28 percent, 33 percent, or 35 percent.

❏ If you participate in an IRC Section 125 flexible spending plan for dependent care, have you used up your balance toward day care for children or dependent adults? Your pretax contribution of $3,000 for one dependent or $6,000 for two dependents can save you 15 percent, 25 percent, 28 percent, 33 percent, or 35 percent in federal income tax.

❏ If you participate in an IRC Section 125 flexible spending plan for commuter expenses, you can be contributing pretax $100 per month toward public transportation or $190 per month toward parking. Again, big savings.

❏ Have you contributed the maximum possible to your 401(k) type pension plan? If not, can you adjust your withholding to increase your amount at least to maximize the employer matching contribution?

❏ Review taxable securities accounts to harvest tax losses and rebalance to agreed ratios. You can claim tax losses of $3,000 in excess of gains.

❏ If you have capital loss carryforwards (prior-year losses), these can be used up to offset gains, plus $3,000 of total losses in excess of gains in any year.

❏ Review any stock options to exercise and sell for tax reasons, because of your feeling about the price of the stock, to lessen concentration in employer stock, or due to approaching expiration dates.

Other Items Not to Overlook before Calendar Year-End

❏   Health insurance open enrollment comes around in November or December. Do you have any reason to change insurance programs or add dental?

❏   A 401(k) type pension plan allows you to sign up or make changes in November or December. Signing up is a must, even if you contribute only a small amount. If already signed up, take a look at your budget and try to increase your contribution up to the maximum. That is $14,000 if you are under age 50, and $18,000 if you are age 50 or over.

❏   November or December is when you sign up for flexible spending for medical, dependent care, and commuter expenses.

❏   If you are taking classes and your employer has a tuition reimbursement program, have you used up the annual maximum? If not, check to see if you can prepay any of next year's tuition.

❏   If your employer matches charitable contributions, are there any you intend to make before year-end that qualify for the match? Do not forget the school contribution drive late in the fall.

❏   Federal law passed in 2003 allows you a free look at your credit reports from each of the three major credit reporting agencies once a year. Request credit reports online from www.transunion.com, www.experian.com, and www.equifax.com and review them for errors. Credit grantors are now required by law to inform you if they report a ding in your credit to the credit agencies.

❏   If you have college-bound students, remember to file the FAFSA form as soon after year-end as possible. Wait for your W-2 form from your employer(s) before you file. You can, however, go back and amend the FAFSA form after you complete your final tax returns. Some colleges have a FAFSA form cutoff date as early as the first week in February. See Chapter 4.

Chapter 1 *Facing Reality: What's It Going to Take to Be Able to Retire?*

1. *EBRI/ICI Participant-Directed Retirement Plan Data Collection Project for Year-End 2002*, Appendix, page 3, by Sarah Holden, ICI, and Jack VanDerhei, Temple University and EBRI Fellow, September 2003.
2. *How Has the Shift to 401(k)s Affected the Retirement Age?* by Alicia H. Munnell, Kevin E. Cahill, and Natalia A. Jivan, Issue Brief 13, Center for Retirement Research at Boston College, September 2003.
3. Combined contributory pension participation number courtesy of the Stark Institute, the trade association for 401(k) administrators, as reported in the *Wall Street Journal*, December 17, 2003, page D1.
4. "The Tax Cut Con," by Paul Krugman, *New York Times Magazine*, September 14, 2003, page 62.
5. *How Are We Growing?*, by Dr. Irwin Kellner, Economic Report, Hofstra University, September/October 2003.
6. *The Great Unraveling: Losing Our Way in the New Century*, by Paul Krugman, New York: W.W. Norton, 2003.
7. *How Has the Shift to 401(k)s Affected the Retirement Age?*
8. Combined contributory pension participation number courtesy of the Stark Institute, the trade association for 401(k) administrators, as reported in the *Wall Street Journal*, December 17, 2003, page D1.
9. "Job Changers: Chill on Your 401(k)," by Jane J. Kim, *Wall Street Journal*, November 13, 2003, page D2.
10. Ibid.
11. Ibid.
12. Per Watson Wyatt study reported in "Save an Arm and a Leg," *Fortune*, October 27, 2003, page 208.
13. Per Kaiser Family Foundation reported in "Save an Arm and a Leg," *Fortune*, October 27, 2003, page 208.
14. Alice Mundell, Boston College.
15. *Retiree Health Benefits: Savings Needed to Fund Health Care in Retirement*, by Paul Fronstin and Dallas Salisbury, Employee Benefit Research Institute (ERBI) ERBI Issue Brief 254, February 2003, page 13.

16. Bridgeworks LLC, as reported in the *Wall Street Journal*, November 11, 2003, page B10.
17. *Baby Boomers' Retirement Prospects: An Overview*, Congressional Budget Office, November 2003, page 5.
18. As reported in "The $44 Trillion Abyss," by Anna Bernasek, *Fortune*, November 24, 2003, page 114. The authors of the Treasury Department study were Kent Smetters and Jagadeesh Gokhale.
19. Ibid. The authors of the Treasury Department study were Kent Smetters and Jagadeesh Gokhale.
20. "The $44 Trillion Abyss," page 116.
21. U.S. Census Bureau, 2002 data from the American Community Survey.
22. "Family," Public Agenda Online, www.publicagenda.org/issues /overview.cfm?issue_type=family.
23. *Trends in College Pricing 2003*, The College Board, 2003, page 3.
24. "Professor's Irrational Route to 'Genius' Grant, Matthew Rabin Studies Procrastination at UC Berkeley," by Kathleen Pender, *San Francisco Chronicle*, June 16, 2000.
25. "Procrastination on Long-Term Projects," Ted O'Donoghue, department of economics, Cornell University, and Matthew Rabin, department of economics, University of California, Berkeley, February 24, 2003, an unpublished paper available at www.people.cornell.edu /pages/edo1/long.PDF.
26. The Motley Fool web site (www.fool.com). Various versions of this say Einstein called compound interest the eighth wonder of the world, the greatest mathematical discovery of all time, the greatest invention, and so on.
27. $464,000 is the total after 35 years from $6,000 of savings in each of the first two years of vehicle ownership from the lower used vehicle price and the reduced new car devaluation. Add $3,000 of employer match equals $9,000 invested at 5 percent after inflation. Investments are made in each of the first two years of a four-year vehicle ownership before selling and starting over again.
28. *How Has the Shift to 401(k)s Affected the Retirement Age?*
29. Ibid.
30. National Compensation Survey, U.S. Department of Labor, March 2003.
31. *2003 Trends and Experience in 401(k) Plans*, Hewitt Associates, September 2003.
32. *Trends in Student Aid*, The College Board, September 2003, page 4.
33. *2003 Trends and Experience in 401(k) Plans*.
34. *Winning the Loser's Game: Timeless Strategies for Successful Investing*, by Charles D. Ellis, New York: McGraw-Hill, 2002, page 4. The 1998 edition has a similar percentage. Ellis's original 1975 article had an 85 percent number.

35. *Staying Ahead of the Curve 2003: The AARP Working in Retirement Study*, by S. Kathi Brown, Strategic Issues Research, AARP, page 5.
36. I want to thank Judy Barber, a family counselor who specialized in money problems in marriage, for a wonderful afternoon of her thoughts on this process.

Chapter 2 *Budgeting: Finding New Money to Save for Retirement*

1. Confirmed by Richard Galanti, Costco corporate spokesperson in telephone interview with this author, November 12, 2003.
2. "The Only Company Wal-Mart Fears," by John Helyar, *Fortune*, November 24, 2003, page 158.
3. Ibid., page 160.

Chapter 3 *Two-Income Households: Affording a Home and Retirement While Avoiding Bankruptcy*

1. "No Quick Fix for Silicon Valley—Study Predicts Jobs Won't Return to Boom-Era Levels for Years," by John Shinal, *San Francisco Chronicle*, September 23, 2003.
2. *The Two-Income Trap: Why Middle-Class Mothers and Fathers are Going Broke*, by Elizabeth Warren and Amelia Warren Tyagi, New York: Basic Books, 2003. Book jacket text.
3. Ibid.
4. Ibid., page 18.
5. Ibid., page 20.
6. "Surprise Jumps in Credit Rates Bring Scrutiny," by Jennifer Bayot, *New York Times*, May 29, 2003.
7. Courtesy of Fair Isaac and its web site.

Chapter 4 *Buying a Home*

1. "In Most of the Nation, a House Is a Home and Not a Real Estate Bonanza," by David Leonhardt and Economy.com, *New York Times*, August 6, 2003.
2. "What's Next for Real Estate," by Jon Birger, *Money*, March 2004, page 91.
3. California Association of Realtors and DataQuick, as reported in *San Francisco* Magazine, November 2003, page 62.
4. U.S. Department of Commerce, as reported in "Homeownership Builds to Record," *Wall Street Journal*, October 29, 2003, page A2.
5. CHFA Loans "CHAFA" Mortgage Loan, at www.fha-home-loans .com/chafa_fha_loan.htm.

Chapter 5 *Paying for College with Other People's Money*

1. *Peterson's Four-Year Colleges 2005*, Thomson Peterson's, page 45.
2. *Trends in College Pricing*, The College Board, September 2004, page 3.
3. *Trends in Student Aid*, The College Board, September 2004, page 4.
4. Ibid., pages 3 and 16.
5. *College Financial Aid: College Financial Planning at Any Income*, by Rick Darvis, 2003, discussion group comment.
6. Ibid.
7. Ibid.
8. *Trends in Student Aid*, page 4.
9. *College Financial Aid*, page 65.
10. *The EFC Formula, 2004–2005*, U.S. Department of Education, Notes to Worksheet B.
11. Ibid., Table A6, page 19.
12. Ibid., Table A4, page 18.
13. *College Financial Aid*, page 106.
14. *The EFC Formula, 2004–2005*, Notes to Worksheet B.
15. Ibid., Notes to Worksheet B.
16. Ibid., Notes to Worksheet C.
17. Ibid., Formula A, page 2.
18. Ibid., Formula A, page 2.
19. *College Financial Aid*, page 43.
20. Internal Revenue Regulations §1.152-1.
21. IRC §25A(d).
22. IRC §151(d).
23. *Trends in Student Aid*, page 4.
24. IRC §25A.
25. IRC §25A.
26. IRC §25A(d).
27. *College Financial Aid*, page 43.
28. *Trends in Student Aid*, page 4.
29. "Fees Jump on College-Savings Plans," by Jane J. Kim, *Wall Street Journal*, October 1, 2003, page D2.
30. Revenue Procedures 2001-59 and 2002-70.

Chapter 6 *Your Pension Plan = Your Retirement Lifeline*

1. "Appendix: Additional Figures for the EBRI/ICI Participant-Directed Retirement Plan Data Collection Project for Year-End 2002," by Sarah Holden, ICI, and Jack VanDerhei, Temple University and ERBI Fellow, September 2003 EBRI Issue Brief, page 9.

2. "Is Working Longer the Answer for an Aging Workforce?" by Gary Burtless and Joseph F. Quinn, 2002, Issue in Brief II, Center for Retirement Research at Boston College.

3. "Beneath the Smiles, a Churning Anxiety," by Louis Uchitelle, *New York Times*, Money & Business, November 2, 2003.

4. *How Has the Shift to 401(k)s Affected the Retirement Age?* by Alicia H. Munnell, Kevin E. Cahill, and Natalia A. Jivan, Issue Brief 13, Center for Retirement Research at Boston College, September 2003.

5. "Pension Gaps Drag Down Earnings," by Larry Dignans, *Fortune*, April 22, 2003; "A Lump-Sum Threat to the Financial Health of Pension Funds," *New York Times*, August 14, 2003.

6. "Congress to Weigh Easing U.P.S. Role on Pension Funding," by Mary Williams Walsh, *New York Times*, September 16,2003.

7. *2003 Trends and Experiences in 401(k) Plans*, Hewitt Associates, September 2003.

8. *The 401(k) Bill of Rights*, TheStreet.com, October 13, 2003.

9. *2003 Trends and Experiences in 401(k) Plans*.

10. Ibid.

11. Courtesy of the American Society of Actuaries web site.

12. *National Vital Statistics Report*, Vol. 51, No. 3, Table B, United States Bureau of Census, December 19, 2002.

13. Hewitt Associates study reported in the *Wall Street Journal*, "Job Changers: Chill on Your 401(k)," November 13, 2003, page D2.

14. IRC §219(g)(2)(A)(ii).

15. IRC §219(g)(3)(B).

16. IRC §408(q).

17. IRC §219(c).

18. IRC §219(g)(7).

19. "Pending Bankruptcy Legislation Would Protect IRAs," by Laura Bruce, Bankrate.com, August 29, 2001.

20. IRC §408A(d)(2).

21. Reg §1.408A-3.

22. IRC §401(a)(17); IRC §415(b)(3).

23. IRC §415(b)(3).

24. IRC §404(q).

25. IRC §404(a)(7)(A)(i).

26. IRC §404(a)(4); IRC §415.

27. IRC §404 and IRC §416.

28. "Appendix: Additional Figures for the EBRI/ICI Participant-Directed Retirement Plan Data Collection Project for Year-End 2002," by Sarah Holden, ICI, and Jack VanDerhei, Temple University and ERBI Fellow, September 2003 EBRI Issue Brief, page 1.

29. Ibid., page 3.

30. Ibid., page 19.

31. Ibid., page 19.

32. Ibid., page 8.
33. Ibid., page 15.
34. Ibid., page 15.

Chapter 7   *The Winning Investment Strategy for the Twenty-First Century*

1. Quote from *A Random Walk Down Wall Street*, by Burton Malkiel, New York: W.W. Norton, 1999.
2. Jason Zweig, Money.com, August 2001.
3. "Tracking S&P 500 Index Funds," by Alex Frino and David R. Gallagher, *Journal of Portfolio Management*, Vol. 28, No. 1, Fall 2001, page 45.
4. Recent Financial Engines survey reported in www.BenefitNews.com, December 12, 2003.
5. *2003 Trends and Experiences in 401(k) Plans*, Hewitt Associates, September 2003.
6. *Winning the Loser's Game: Timeless Strategies for Successful Investing*, by Charles D. Ellis, New York: McGraw-Hill, 2002, page 4. The 1998 edition has a similar percentage. Ellis's 1975 article had an 85 percent number.
7. "An Index Fundamentalist Goes Back to the Drawing Board," by John C. Bogle, *Journal of Portfolio Management*, Vol. 28, No. 3, Spring 2002. Also available from the Vanguard Group web site, www.vanguard.com/bogle_site/sp20020430.html.
8. Statistic provided courtesy of Aperio Group.
9. My Schwab commission on the purchase of 1,000 shares of iShares 3000 (IWV) was $29.95. The IWV management fee is $.009 and the Vanguard 500 fee is $.018. After one year the account balances were the same using the Vanguard 500 rate of return to limit the comparison to costs.
10. "The Mysterious World of Mutual Fund Costs," by Jonathan Fuerbringer, *New York Times*, November 9, 2003.
11. Ibid.
12. Principal Group's web site, fees Class A and Class B shares.
13. Cost and fee disclosure from the Charles Schwab & Company web site.
14. William Sharpe, "Mutual Fund Performance," *Journal of Business*, January 1966.
15. Mutual fund performance databases are inherently inaccurate because they eliminate funds that do not survive from the statistics. This survivorship bias then makes the surviving mutual funds appear to have performed better than the universe of funds that actually existed at the time. During the five-year period from 1992 to 1998 survivorship bias increased the reported performance of large-cap mutual funds by 1 percent, from 17.9 percent to 18.9 percent. At the end of the same period small-cap funds were overstated by 2.2 percent, rising from 10.4 per-

cent to 12.6 percent at the end of the period as funds were removed from the statistics. As calculated by David F. Swensen, *Pioneering Portfolio Management*, New York: Free Press, 2000.

16. "Stock Funds Just Don't Measure Up," by Jonathan Clements, *Wall Street Journal*, October 5, 1999.
17. "The Loser's Game," a 1975 article in *Financial Analysts Journal*, by Charles D. Ellis, has led to refining this fact in four editions of his book *Winning the Loser's Game*, 1997–2002.
18. *Winning the Loser's Game*, page 28.
19. *2003 Trends and Experiences in 401(k) Plans*.
20. www.stls.frb.org/publications/re/2003/b/pages/confidence.html. A description of the consumer confidence indexes is on the St. Louis Federal Reserve Bank's web site.
21. "How Well Have Taxable Investors Been Served in the 1980s and 1990s?" by Robert D. Arnott, Andrew L. Berkin, and Jia Ye, *Journal of Portfolio Management*, Exhibit 3, Vol. 26, No. 4, Summer 2000, page 86. See note 15 re survivorship bias.
22. From the Frank Russell Company web site, www.russell.com/us /indexes/us/3000.asp.
23. Kenneth L. Fisher, "America versus the World," *Forbes*, November 27, 2000.
24. "The Benefits of Rebalancing," by Gerald W. Buetow Jr., Ronald Sellers, Donald Trotler, Elaine Hunt, and Willie A. Whipple Jr., *Journal of Portfolio Management*, Vol. 28, No. 2, Winter 2002, page 26.
25. Simulation used the Vanguard 500 index fund (VFINX) for 60 percent and for 40 percent used the Lehman Aggregate Bond index until 1992 when the Vanguard Balanced index fund (VBINX) was created.
26. Computed based upon information provided by Lehman Brothers.
27. "Benefits of Rebalancing," page 26.
28. "Rebalancing," by Seth J. Masters, *Journal of Portfolio Management*, Spring 2002, pages 52–57.
29. Ibid., page 56.

Chapter 8 *Taxable Investing*

1. John C. Bogle, *Common Sense on Mutual Funds*, New York: John Wiley & Sons, 1999, page 284.

Chapter 9 *Retirement Redefined*

1. "Wealthy People Grow Pessimistic about Finances," by Lynn Cowan, reporting on a Phoenix/Harris Interactive Wealth Survey, *Wall Street Journal*, August 13, 2003, page B3B.
2. *Staying Ahead of the Curve 2003: The AARP Working in Retirement Study*, S. Kathi Brown, Strategic Issues Research, AARP, page 5.

3. *Staying Ahead of the Curve 2003*, page 6.
4. "Appendix: Additional Figures for the EBRI/ICI Participant-Directed Retirement Plan Data Collection Project for Year-End 2002," by Sarah Holden, ICI, and Jack VanDerhei, Temple University and ERBI Fellow, September 2003 EBRI Issue Brief, page 9.
5. *Staying Ahead of the Curve 2003*, page 7.
6. Ibid., page 8.
7. Ibid., page 50.
8. Definition courtesy of S. Kathi Brown, Strategic Issues Research, AARP, Washington, D.C., and the editor of the AARP Working in Retirement Study.
9. U.S. Department of Labor, Bureau of Labor Statistics, *Occupational Outlook Handbook, 2002–2003 Edition* (Online Edition). Also Arlene Dohm, "Gauging the Labor Force Effects of Retiring Baby Boomers," *Monthly Labor Review*, July 2000, pages 17–25.
10. *Staying Ahead of the Curve 2003*, page 24.
11. "Active agers" is a phrase coined by Dr. Bob Rosenberg and Guy Lampard in their book *Giving from Your Heart: A Guide to Volunteering*, iUniverse, 2005.
12. "Employers' Caps Raise Retirees' Health-Care Costs," by Ellen E. Schultz and Theo Francis, *Wall Street Journal*, November 25, 2003, page B1.
13. Kaiser/HRET Survey of Employer-Sponsored Health Benefits, 2003. Kaiser Family Foundation, at www.kff.org.

INDEX